Troubled Pleasures

Troubled Pleasures

Writings on Politics, Gender and Hedonism

KATE SOPER

VERSO

London · New York

First published by Verso 1990
© Kate Soper 1990
All rights reserved

Verso
UK: 6 Meard Street, London W1F 0EG
USA: 388 Atlantic Ave, Brooklyn, NY 11217

Verso is the imprint of New Left Books

British Library Cataloguing in Publication Data

Soper, Kate
Troubled pleasures : writings on politics, gender and
hedonism.
1. Pleasure – Philosophical perspectives
I. Title
171.4

ISBN 0-86091-313-9
ISBN 0-86091-536-0 pbk

US Library of Congress Cataloging-in-Publication Data

Soper, Kate.
Troubled pleasures : writings on politics, gender, and hedonism /
Kate Soper.
p.   cm.
Includes bibliographical references and index.
ISBN 0-86091-313-9. — ISBN 0-86091-536-0 (pbk.)
1. Social values.   2. Hedonism.   3. Feminist criticism.
I. Title.
HM216.S587   1990
303.3'72—dc20

Typeset in Baskerville by Leaper & Gard Ltd, Bristol
Printed in the United States

Contents

Acknowledgements

Sources of previously published chapters are as follows:

'Rethinking Ourselves', first published in *Prospectus for a Habitable Planet*, ed. E.P. Thompson and D. Smith, Penguin Books 1985.

'A Difference of Needs', from *New Left Review* 152, July–August 1985.

'The Socialist Humanism of E.P. Thompson', a revised version of an article first published in *E.P. Thompson: Critical Debates*, ed. K. McClelland and H. Kaye, Polity Press 1990.

'Marxism and Morality', from *New Left Review* 163, May–June 1987.

'Patchwork Dragon Power?', originally published in *END Journal*, October–November 1986, and reprinted in *Marxism Today*, October 1986.

'The Qualities of Simone de Beauvoir', from *New Left Review* 156, March–April 1986.

'Feminism as Critique', from *New Left Review* 176, July–August 1989.

'Feminism, Humanism, Postmodernism', from *Radical Philosophy* 55, Spring 1990.

Permission to reprint them here is gratefully acknowledged.

Introduction

It was an act of stealth
And troubled pleasure

My title is a phrase from Wordsworth's *Prelude*, where he recounts stealing a boat for a night row on Windermere. But I make use of it here to express rather more than the troubling of pleasure by the quality of its conditions. I invoke it in part as a summation of my reactions to the extraordinary events of the period during which I was assembling the material for this book. When I began the Berlin Wall had just been breached. Like almost everyone else I responded to this collapse of the major symbol of East–West confrontation with enormous pleasure – and perhaps with some special zest given that my political energies had been so largely absorbed since the beginning of the decade in campaigning, through my involvement in European Nuclear Disarmament, for an end to the Cold War. The pleasure was all the greater because of the magnitude of the reversal it represented in relation to all expectations of a few years previously. At the beginning of 1984 the first Cruise and Pershing missiles had just been deployed in the Federal Republic. The Geneva negotiations were breaking down. Ulrike Poppe and Baerbel Bohley, and other independent peace activists in the GDR, were facing charges carrying twelve-year prison sentences. If someone had suggested at that point that before the decade was out the citizens of East Berlin would be passing freely through the Brandenburg Gate, one would have dismissed it as no less fantastical than Alice's climbing through the looking-glass.

History, then, had confounded realism, and the rarity of finding an extreme 'optimism of the will' confirmed in the actual event, made the pleasure seem all the more entrancing. But a great deal has happened since to trouble that moment of heady delight, and it is difficult not to view the victory of the Christian Democrats in the East German elections (news of which has in fact just come through as I write) as a sign of its having been definitively compromised.

On the one hand, then, there is the pleasure of the Iron Curtain having been swept aside, of open borders, of democratization, and the institution of some meaningful electoral process. On the other hand, there is the troubling of it by the free hand now given to capitalist entrepreneurialism and rampant commercial opportunism; by the emergence of disturbing forms of nationalist sentiment; by the prospect of a united Germany integrated into the NATO structure; by the anti-democratic moral the conservatives in the USSR are likely to draw from the right-wing electoral success and the strengthening of their own position which may result from it; and last but not least by the sense that the 'freedom' of the election itself had been rather seriously curtailed by the media management and manipulations of the Bonn experts in 'plural' politics, most notably Chancellor Kohl. And this is to speak only of Germany. For one might sound variations on these themes in respect of a good deal that has been happening elsewhere in Europe in the wake of the breakup of the old order.

There is no nostalgia for the old order to be read into these remarks. Its passing is an indisputable good. But the exploitation of the Golden Curtain of currency differentials now that the Iron barrier to commerce has been lifted will not be in the interests of social justice or ecological well-being. It promises to yoke the East European economies beneath the sovereignty of Western capital, and the poorest and already most exploited sectors of the community will have to bear the worst of the burden. Some of the more disastrous sources of pollution in the Eastern territories may well be checked if Western 'aid' is used to finance more sophisticated forms of industrial equipment and cleaner methods of production. But capitalism never advances anywhere without a retinue of everything which eats up material resources, wrecks the landscape and offends the senses: more motorways, more airports, more offices, more banks, more shops, more carparks. And, of course, the whole exercise is always designed with one end in mind: to enhance 'prosperity', in other words to get as many people as possible to consume as much as possible with as much disregard as possible for its effects upon the global ecosystem.

Equally troubling to contemplate is the fragility of the opportunity for 'third-way' renewal in Eastern Europe, and the prospect of it now having been irredeemably lost. I am thinking here, primarily, of the ways in which 'actually existing socialism' spoilt the chances for socialism. (One cannot help wondering, for example, how different things might be today in East Germany had Honecker not expelled all the reformists from the Communist Party at the beginning of 1989.) But I am also thinking of the extent to which the grass-roots initiatives – whose various more countercultural, eco-pacifist and market-sceptical groupings played such a crucial role in the recent revolution in Eastern Europe – are being deprived by the all too familiar machinations of professional power politics of any serious influence on the future direction of events. The degree to which this is happening differs between countries and the survival power of the 'alternative' politics associated with such groups is as yet unclear. Czechoslovakia is today led by a Charta 77 activist who in 1987 told the *END Journal*:

From the little I know, I have the feeling that in so far as they call attention to the underlying problems of present-day civilization, the green movements seem, here and there, to have brought to the surface issues which have been neglected or down-played by the major traditional parties. These issues concern the meaning of life, such as whether there is any sense in the constant drive for increased production when it is to the detriment of future generations. I must say that this entire trend, as well as these movements' proclaimed non-ideological stance and their advocacy of non-violence are things very close to my heart.[1]

It is a pleasure to contemplate these words, and to know that Havel has acted in accord with them in his military policy, even if he has also said and done a number of things since which might trouble the pleasure. And when multiparty elections take place in the Soviet Union, and these are now in prospect, they may also, in the light of a recent poll of potential support for a putative 'Green Party', not prove entirely negative from the point of view of those issues concerning 'the meaning of life' which Havel refers us to. Overall, however, one cannot help feeling that the advocates of such issues are going to find themselves as marginalized in the Eastern half of the continent as they have hitherto proved to be in the Western.

Moreover, and perhaps most dishearteningly, it is a very troubled pleasure to see East–West tension easing only as North–South relations become more fraught. The USSR is no longer the 'evil empire', the USA no longer the 'imperialist aggressor'. But as this rhetoric has been seen off, other abysses of ideological difference have opened up – such as between Islamic and Western culture – across which the charges of 'barbarism' are being hurled with increasing frenzy. We know, too, that the condition of cementing better East–West relations is the expansion of forms of economic activity in the Northern hemisphere which will do rather little to correct the material factors which underlie the North–South divide, and will help to fuel its ideological resentments.

This sense, then, that as every political horizon clears new storm clouds gather, is the most general understanding I bring to the notion of 'troubled pleasure'. I have illustrated it here by reference to events which took place after the larger part of the essays in this book were written. But it is through the idea, all the same, that I would plead the pertinence even of the earlier political discussion included here (none of which in fact predates

1985, even though the *annus mirabilis* of 1989 has given a slightly dated air to any political commentary which precedes it, by however short a period). For one of the major sources of anxiety at the present – and in many ways gratifying – turn of events in Europe is their seemingly negative implications for any of the dramatic alterations of outlook and practice which will be needed if we are to allow ourselves the pleasures that can come with real democracy, social justice and ecological responsibility; and it is a continual refrain of these writings that our future flourishing depends on a hedonist conversion along these lines.

At several points, moreover, these arguments engage with aspects of modern consumption which allow me to place a more particular construction on the notion of 'troubled pleasure'. Indeed, if I have so far been elaborating on my choice of the phrase in terms of the general metaphor it provides for our responses to historical 'progress', it would seem quite literally descriptive of the kinds of conflict of need experienced by many of those enjoying the benefits bestowed by advanced industrial society. Of course, many of life's pleasures have always involved aspects of pain and anxiety – some of them accountable to our biological nature, others to deep-rooted and seemingly very prevalent human sentiments. Thus ageing, illness and mortality cast their shadow over conviviality and parenthood, faithful love has its tensions as well as its releases, the headiness of passion disrupts the calmly generous spirit of equanimity. By and large, however, we can accept these more irremovable distraints on pleasure precisely because we are aware of how far they are integral to its very possibility: it is just as problematic to think of ourselves as immortal or devoid of emotional possessiveness as it is to confront the 'obstacles' of death or sexual jealousy. But we are beginning now, in addition, to have to contend with a compromise of pleasure which is altogether more contingent and specific to modernity. Today, many of our simplest, most universal, and hitherto less tension-ridden needs – for food, travel, recreation, enjoyment of nature – have become experienced as problematic, either because we provide for them in ways which we know to be ecologically damaging and hence in the long term self-destructive; or because we know that the sophisticated satisfactions we have come to rely upon coexist with deprivation elsewhere of the most minimal means of life, and cannot be supplied to the human community at large (or even indefinitely to some affluent sector within it); or because (as in the case of our relationship to nature) we sense a loss or corruption of the object of pleasure itself.

To recognize these 'complications' to modern pleasure is certainly to want to contest much that is currently on offer for consumption (and this includes some indisputably attractive and exciting sources of gratification). It is also to call in question modernity's general definition of pleasure – individualistic, materialistic, nonchalant regarding the future and narcissistic – even while acknowledging its power. But these are not challenges which can be made without laying oneself open to the charge of puritanism and self-righteousness. Asking others to be 'troubled' by their pleasures, which any responsible political movement must now do, is itself troubling, and a source of potential embarrassments and rancour even among the politically like-minded, let alone across divisions of wealth and class. If a certain element of puritanism in these writings causes offence I would hope that it be understood in the light of these remarks. I, too, would prefer my pleasures unadulterated and do not want them dampened by earnest reminders of their 'difficulty'. But in more positive vein, I would also insist that what is at stake here is not so much an ascetic rejection of pleasure as the development of new forms of sensuality: in scrutinizing rather than veiling the element of 'trouble' in our modern pleasures, by associating pleasure itself with less economically fixated and materially burdensome passions and obsessions, can we contribute to the evolution of less destructive and exploitative, but for that reason all the more seductive, forms of enjoyment?

It is with reference to this combination of moral seriousness and qualified utopianism that I would want to situate my own argument in relation to contemporary intellectual debates. The idea of 'troubled pleasure' does not ring with metaphysical certainty and faith in human amelioration; and through it I cast doubt on some of the standard Marxist and socialist projections. The future does not hold out the promise of indefinite abundance, conflict-free development of 'rich individuality', moral harmony, the withering away of the state, and the definitive overcoming of all forms of alienation. Nor is the process of historical transformation to be simplified down to a matter of class struggle in which we can point to the proletariat as the obvious and ultimately victorious agent of emancipation. In this sense, 'troubled pleasure' registers my sympathy with a certain vein of postmodernist scepticism which would have us disturb some previous forms of theoretical confidence: confidence in the idea of historical meaning and progress; in Marxist analysis and prescription; in humanist accounts of subjectivity and agency. But my emphasis is precisely on disturbing rather than shattering these sources of confidence, and alongside the troublesome doubts I would also record some abiding convictions. For reasons I discuss in the essays in my opening section I remain convinced of the need to break with the capitalist mode of production and to institute forms of economic practice guaranteeing a more equal distribution of wealth and a fairer and sustainable use of resources. In such pieces as 'Socialist Humanism', '*Constructa ergo sum?*' and 'Marxism and Morality' I defend a conception of subjectivity and moral and political agency which rather draws on phenomenology and existentialist argument than defers to postmodernist deconstruction. In the writings on gender in the final section I speak to commitments which, critical as they are in certain respects of de Beauvoir's existentialist position, again have more affinity with that general wing of feminist argument than with the 'maternal' and 'difference' feminisms which have developed under the impact of structuralist and poststructuralist critiques.

In my thinking around all these areas, moreover, I remain committed to a philosophical realism which rejects the 'aestheticism' associated with structuralist and poststructuralist critiques: the disposition, as it has been described, 'to see "art" or "language" or "discourse" or "text" as constituting the primary realm

of human experience'.[2] To be cognizant of the conceptual
dependency of social realities and of the role played by language
in their shaping is one thing. To assume that language provides
an analogue for all forms of sociality or that reality is exhausted
in the effects of discourse and 'textuality' is quite another. Such
global pretensions for 'language' can only be made by so
stretching the meaning of the term that the critical claims of the
'linguistic turn' in theory are paradoxically sacrificed to an
uninformative positivism which defines as 'real' only that which
is discursively constructed. To retain the critical insights of
discourse theory is to respect the specificity of language. But to
do this is to recognize its particular qualities and limits. It is to
recognize that the world is comprised of different kinds of
practice, of which linguistic communication is only one even if it
is true (a truism indeed) that discourse and conceptualization are
integral to these practices and nothing can be said or written
about them independently of some form of linguistic code. The
fact – to invoke Wittgenstein's analogy from construction [3] – that
builders cannot build without a knowledge of the language of
building materials does not mean that slabs and blocks have the
ontological properties of words, or that what they construct is a
house of discourse. Language – including its very considerable
powers to order the universe of which it speaks, to play upon the
ambiguities of its 'being', to reverberate in all our responses to
this universe – is only possible because of the existence of a realm
of being which is both non-linguistic *and* always intrusively in
play as a determinant upon what is or can be said. To reverse
this relationship, to treat the world as the construct of language
(or, in a more accurate description of the discourse perspective:
to argue that there is nothing experienceable which is not
linguistically constructed) is to create a Kantian divide between a
'phenomenal' realm of the discursive/textual, and a 'noumenal'
realm of the unsayable and – from the point of view of everything
which matters in life – ineffective materiality. Equally unsatisfactory, though more sensitive to the difficulties of this divide, is
Foucault's attempt to straddle it by presenting 'materiality' (the
'body') as both the construct of discourse and the victimized site

of its impact. For the body is neither simply the effect of discourse nor simply a point of 'brute' resistance to it, but a centre of experience which is actively involved in the construction of discourse itself. Flesh and blood cannot, for example, be left on the far side of what is sexually significant as if sexuality were simply a matter of 'things said'. Instinct and feeling, both physical and emotional, everywhere intrude to influence what is said – just as the things which come to be said intrude back upon feeling. It is a question, in short, of preserving a certain dialectic between the material and the linguistic, the verbal and the nonverbal: a complex dialectic which it is difficult to specify since it is true, as poststructuralist critique has rendered clearer to us, that the relationship here is not simply one of representation between word and thing.

If we ask, for example, in what does sexuality consist in so far as it is *not* discursively constructed, we cannot point in answer to some simple, universal 'material' dimension of being. We are also aware, I think, that in so far as sexuality *is* constituted in discourse, this discursive dimension does not refer us directly to something other than itself in the sense of representing sexual experience in its fundamental and replete 'materiality'. I can share with discourse theory the insight that the role of discourse in the construction of existence does not operate as a semiotic level at which another 'truer' and more 'material' level finds expression, but what I cannot accept is that discourse is exhaustive of reality, or that there are no relations of necessary dependence between what is sayable at any time and the ways the world happens to be materially organized.

Through this notion of 'material organization' I refer to the world both as it is given to us in 'nature' (the properties of organic and inorganic matter) and as it is structured for us socially at any point – a form of 'givenness' in which there can be no doubt of the centrality of the economic mode of production and its class relations in conditioning what is said and done. But in recognizing this, I am not subscribing to any analysis which pits the 'determination' of the economy, class structure, etc. against the supposed arbitrariness of the 'linguistic turn'. For while in one sense it is true that by severing the reference to a non-linguistic 'determining' reality (of economic circumstance, etc.) discourse theory plunges us into an uncontrolled – and arbitrary – relativism for which the aspiration to truth ceases to be even a regulative idea, in another sense, precisely because it refuses any social or psychological explanation for the discourses which happen to prevail, it reintroduces a determinism at the level of language itself. And as I argue in '*Constructa ergo sum?*', in doing so postmodernist argument, even in its critique of Marxism, reproduces in its treatment of subjectivity the same errors which afflict the anti-humanist interpretation of historical materialism. Material circumstances (economic and social institutions and relations) can no more be analysed as structures wholly determining the nature of the human subjects upon whom they are dependent for their creation and persistence, than can language and discourse be consistently viewed as constructing a subjectivity which had no hand in their making. Once again, it is a question of adopting a dialectical perspective which allows us to be the creators of the conditions whose creatures we also to a significant degree become, and these conditions are reducible neither to language, discourse and text nor to an infrastructure of 'real' relations conceived as wholly autonomous of (hence in a position wholly to determine) their modes of representation.

In arguing along these lines I acknowledge that I am open to the charge that I have accommodated to philosophical currents whose logic is ultimately subversive of the position I am defending. I would resist the charge on the grounds that the dialectical approach is a mode of thinking which precisely refuses to be drawn into that form of logical reductionism. It is true, however, that my stance is a qualified stance, and as such liable to distortion and always prey to readings which will discover it to be theoretically vacillating if not directly inconsistent. I expect some such accusations to be laid against these writings from both the Marxist and the postmodernist camps. But I also sense that it is important to bring together insights drawn from both sides of that divide even at the cost of being exposed to accusations of equivocation; and I suspect that I am not alone in sensing that need. As far as Marxism is concerned, in fact, I would say that any serious Marxist-influenced analysis of our times has long recognized the need to qualify the classic nineteenth-century visions of the socialist future and the means of arriving thereat, and in this sense subscribes to postmodernist critiques of classical Marxism, while refusing for that reason to settle for nihilist or escapist modes of political response. The fact that we have been made wise to a certain glibness in the solutions offered in the traditional left-wing canon to the problems of economic inequality, national and racial tension, sexuality, morality and hedonism is not for this more self-critical Marxist approach a cause to give up on the very form of socialist rationality or to abandon any remedial efforts whatsoever. Equally, it seems to me, there are rather few who espouse the postmodernist position and are able to practise the modes of political dissociation that are the logical implication of some of their critiques. There is too much bodily pain and mental suffering already, and too much of it being heaped up for future generations, for anyone of average sensibility to find a genuine escape in the pleasurable flux of the actual (which is to say in a mode of living entirely freed of all forms of troubled conscience). Conversely, there is still too much promise held out in the resources now at our command, both spiritual and material, to make the nihilist response seem anything but rather spurious (an excuse for inaction or a voguish bravado rather than a thought out philosophy of indifference to all values). A more authentic reaction is that of the 'troubled pleasure' perspective – a reaction, in other words, which is sensitive to the difficulties which dog all efforts at improvement without giving up on the task itself, and without confusing the critique of various forms of rationality, objectivity and power, with the triumph of irrationalism, relativism and impotence.

It is a perspective, moreover, which I would argue can be viewed as all the more progressive and utopian for bringing some newer forms of scepticism and irony to bear on the old ideas of progress and utopia. For as I argue in 'Marxism and Morality', there was always something, if we are honest, a little disquieting about the idea of harmonious plenitude held out to us in the unquestioning optimism of earlier socialist conceptions. We are no longer, I think, in quest of a world in which we are freed of all tension, abrasion and difference, but rather of a world in which our pleasures can be edged with these sources of disharmony without plunging us into the most loathsome types of violence, greed, animosity and self-destruction. Indeed, I would go so far as to say that a utopianism of our times is one that needs to trouble some of the blander images of pleasure and in doing so associate an anti-capitalist and egalitarian politics with more complex affective and moral understandings that we are offered in either *News from Nowhere* or *The Critique of the Gotha Programme*.

There are two areas in particular – both of them potentially sources of considerable pleasure – where I sense the lack of sophisticated and compelling 'ideal images' of future directionality: art and sexuality. As concerns the former, there has been, I think, too little 'utopian' questioning of how far the advancement of more harmonious social and personal relations is compatible with the preservation of a dynamic artistic culture given the extent to which art derives its strength from its critical and tragic dimensions. It is no accident that almost all utopian fictions and projections are at their weakest in their treatment of art, tending to absorb it into various artisan functions or anodyne modes of carnival and public ritual. At the same time, I appreciate the spirit which moves Raymond Williams to remark: 'But is not the end of hope the very root of tragedy?',[4] and agree that in this sense it is a strengthening and invigorating move to shift from a tragic to a utopian mode. But as Williams also suggests, this shift cannot be made in a way that enlivens our struggles against present conditions, if it is made in too purely a voluntaristic manner, which is to say without proper sensitivity to our uncertainties about what we want, and the ways these uncertainties relate to current experience (and the pains occasioned by breaking with its modes of need and desire):

> It is easy to gather a kind of energy from the rapid disintegration of an old, destructive and frustrating order. But these negative energies

can be quickly checked by a sobering second stage, in which what we want to become, rather than what we do not now want to be, remains a so largely unanswered question. To the significant degree that our reasons for not answering or trying to answer this question are connected with the now painful divisions and contradictions – as painful to shift as to experience – it seems inevitable that a tragic stress must still be made, but in that form which follows the whole action and which is thus again profoundly dynamic.[5]

In the case of sexuality, we seem to be offered a rather clear example of the problems attaching to any simple shift to the utopian mode. Rightly we aspire to remove the social sources of sexual oppression and to establish less divisive gender relations. But given the cultural influence of the present upon the formation of desire, the question inevitably seems to arise as to how far we can imaginatively transform the modes of sexuality of some ideal future while remaining erotically enticed by the vision. Our erotic feelings and romantic sentiments are so integral to the pleasures we currently derive from love and friendship, and so much a part of our identity, that we can be very loath to contemplate their mutation, however appreciative we are of the political and ideological necessity of instituting the social changes which will lead to such alteration. In this sense, I would say that feminist argument and the new modes of awareness it has introduced constitute a further area of 'troubled pleasure'. On the one hand, we are beckoned by the promise of a quite dramatic revolution in relations between the sexes which could bring an end to all the old divisions of labour and status, and allow us forms of communion and sharing undreamt of by previous generations. On the other hand, we are troubled, I think, by a failure of imaginative grip on such a future: we are not quite sure what it will entail for our forms of sexual desire and whether we will be capable of the kinds of self-change it will require. To date, I would say, feminist discourse has not properly addressed this dilemma of its own 'utopia'. For though we are offered a number of pointers – to the 're-' or 'de-gendered' society, to the 'polysexual' society, to the society of 'bodies and pleasures' – these do indeed remain rather gestural ideas and by no means uncomplicatedly attractive ones either.

I do not claim that the writings on feminist issues included here do any better in this respect, though they are certainly informed by a sense that there has often been something too simple and overly self-congratulatory in feminist approaches to these troublesome issues. The responses of separatist and 'difference' feminisms seem to me to be particularly open to this charge in so far as they invite us to fix on certain supposedly 'womanly' forms of experience and disposition and to seek a solution to the problems of 'otherness' in its reclamation: in the celebration of a distinctively 'feminine' ethics, cognition and sensuality. The problem with these responses is not simply that they tend (despite disclaimers to the contrary) to reinforce an essentialism of gender attributes which is very questionable, but that by viewing all forms of experience and understanding through the grid of gender opposition (and there are, in fact, many ways of thinking, feeling and acting which are not particularly sexually differentiated) they polarize the sexes in a manner which is artificial and divisive. The paradox of this approach to gender is that it reasserts what the 'feminist' in me precisely wants to deny, and finds so inimical in the conventional 'masculinist' perception: the idea that there is no dimension of being which overspills sexuality, and that my identity as a person is exhausted in my existence as a woman.

It is from this perspective that I can applaud de Beauvoir's instinct to preserve the 'woman–person' doublet; both to sustain and refuse the 'otherness' of her femininity. In similar spirit, I appreciate Kristeva's percipient discussion of the 'masculine' Symbolic as both the impossible and indispensable register of 'femininity', even though I am less persuaded that any mediation here can be sought in the 'maternal' semiotic. And it is in terms of a comparable experience of 'bi-location' in regard to the Joycean 'symbolic' – of sensing oneself to be both a belonger within and an exile from its cultural perception – that I elaborate in 'Stephen Heroine' on the quality of my feminine 'identification' with the masculine protagonists of *Ulysses*, most noticeably with Dedalus (Joyce) himself.

Though in the broadest sense 'Stephen Heroine' might count as literary criticism, I would prefer to describe it as an auto-biographical rumination on the 'troubles' of my feminist reading of one of the books which has given me most pleasure. The piece is intended to reflect only my personal engagement with Joyce's fiction and has no pretensions to scholarship. Its approach is more subjective than is quite proper to academic writing, and I recognize that in this respect it stands somewhat apart from the other essays collected here.

This difference of style and approach is even more obvious in the final piece of writing I have included, since this is itself fictional – an extract from a recently completed novel. *Excess* is a 'green' allegory, which charts the very deeply troubled pleasures of its tycoon 'hero' Eric Sicton. It is loosely based on the little-known Greek myth of Erysichthon which forms the subject of a poem by Callimachus, and to which I refer in passing in my review of Michael Ignatieff's *The Needs of Strangers*. I expand on the myth and contextualize the extract in a separate prefatory note, and would here add only some remarks about its relationship to the other content in the book. First, I would not have included it here were it not that it forms part of a fictional treatment of themes very central to the other writings here, though it is a treatment of the 'troubles' of modern pleasure which brings a starker and more repellent light to bear on these. *Excess* is about the nemesis inherent in the hubris of current attitudes to nature, and the compulsions of its central character provide an emblem of the self-spiting quality of modern consumption and of the conceptions of need and pleasure which drive it. It therefore reflects considerations about human need, about both their philosophical conceptualization and the role to be accorded to them in our thinking about politics, which have been a main preoccupation of my theoretical writings. But this brings me, finally, to a more formal reason for including some fiction, which is precisely that it does represent another style of writing and in doing so also reflects a certain ambivalence in my own attitude to theory, and a growing sense I have had of late that I do not want to be tied down to that as the only vehicle of expression.

It is not easy to state the reasons for this ambivalence since although they may relate in part to fairly standard objections to theory (that it is abstract and general, does not engage with individual psychology and experience, lacks drama, is too dispassionate, etc.) I am aware that similar things may be said of a good deal of non-realist fiction, which nonetheless offers to the reader insights and pleasures which are not those of theory. (One may need, in any case, to qualify this description of theory itself, which is not without its particular kinds of narratives and often focusses on highly specific ideas and forms of experience.) For me, I think the difficulties with theory have more to do with its quest for explicitness. Good theory always aspires to set forth everything it apprehends with the maximum precision possible. This is the source of its explanatory power and of the particular intellectual pleasure (which I would argue is also in its way a form of aesthetic satisfaction) which it can offer. But these gains are necessarily at the expense of a more intimated, but for that very reason sometimes more revealing, apprehension provided by a more oblique approach. Because it is more distanced from the didactic and explanatory modes, literature can bring an illumination to bear which is the more powerful for being less underscored. And although I do not agree with those critics of theory who regard it as insensitive to the vaguer and more nuanced quality of things, I think it is true that literature is often better able to grasp these precisely because it does not set itself the task of rendering them explicit.

There is a further reason for my ambivalence, however, which has less to do with the limitations inherent to theory and more to do with my resistance to a current theory industry which is tending to spoil the pleasures of both literature and theory, and to create a nervy and competitive climate in the academy (at least as concerns the study of the humanities) which is not conducive to genuine scholarship. Students and teachers are increasingly caught up in a dynamic of poststructuralist critique and methodology which is distancing them from the core materials of their work and creating such a powerful orthodoxy that it is very difficult to swim against the current. The reading of 'primary' texts (both literary and theoretical) is subordinated to the acquisition of a battery of critical skills and poststructuralist wisdoms whose effects can be quite disabling – depriving students of the confidence to approach texts in any intuitive manner, and denying them the enjoyment of a more presuppositionless reading of them. Their teachers meanwhile are generating increasingly parasitical forms of metatheory and are themselves subject to a tyrannical pressure not only to have absorbed all the latest products of the theory industry, but if possible to have got the better of them: to be in a position to have the cleverest last say on them, or even better the most pointedly ironical last laugh.

But to make these points, which are not original and have been much better expressed by others, is still of course to be caught up in the game, and in the end there must always be something self-defeating about expressing an ambivalence about theory within the thoretical mode. Better simply to try one's hand at something else. But in this move, too, I make no claims to originality, but rather associate myself with a number of primarily academic writers who have felt the same urge – and acted upon it with varying degrees of success. What is perhaps more unusual, however, is that one's publishers allow one to put together both fictional and non-fictional modes in the same book, and I am grateful to Verso for this tolerance.

There are a number of other thanks owing. Various people have commented on the review articles included here. I am grateful in particular to Perry Anderson, Robin Blackburn and Norman Geras for their help and generosity in this respect; and I am indebted in a general sense to the *New Left Review* for the space and encouragement it has given to my writing. I would also like to acknowledge here the stimulus provided by my friends and colleagues in END and to thank in particular Edward Thompson, Dorothy Thompson, Mary Kaldor, Paul Anderson, Mark Thompson, John Williams, Dan Smith and Louis Mackay for what they have contributed to the development of my own thinking through their writings and personal and collective discussions. Among the many other friends and associates who have helped and encouraged me in the writing of this book, and have contributed in various ways and at various stages to its making as editors, critics and sources of inspiration, I must thank: John Mepham, Keith McClelland, Hilary Wainwright, Roy Bhaskar, Cora Kaplan, Jonathan Ree, Jean Grimshaw, Martin Jacques, my students and fellow philosophers at the Polytechnic of North London and the *Radical Philosophy* collective. I am also grateful for the support shown me by Leonie Soper, Jude Ryle and Madeleine Ryle. My greatest debt is to Martin Ryle, who has influenced so many of my ideas, and who has fulfilled with his usual magnanimity the task I always impose on him of both criticizing and applauding everything I write. This book is dedicated to him with thanks.

Kate Soper
Rodmell, February 1990

Notes

1. Interview with Václav Havel, *END Journal*, March 1987, p. 14.

2. This concept and its definition are to be found in Allan Megill, *Prophets of Extremity: Nietzsche, Heidegger, Foucault, Derrida*, Berkeley 1985, pp. 2–3, and are cited by Bryan D. Palmer in the course of his recent critique of the 'descent into discourse'; see *Descent into Discourse*, Philadelphia 1990, p. 7.

3. L. Wittgenstein, *Philosophical Investigations*, London and New York 1953, pt I, section 1–3.

4. R. Williams, 'Afterword to *Modern Tragedy*', in *The Politics of Modernism*, London 1989, p. 102.

5. *Ibid*, pp. 104–5.

PART ONE

Towards a New Hedonism

1

Rethinking Ourselves

I have hesitated to include this piece, let alone to open with it. How much water has gone under the bridge since it was written (in 1985), and how dated it now seems in many respects. This is due in part to its journalistic quality, which means that its references belong too much to the moment of its writing to sound now with the same immediacy. SDI, Libya, the Falklands war, it is not that these no longer retain their import nor persist with us in varying ways, but that our focus on them has shifted: they no longer stand out for us with the same prominence, but from today's retrospection are already situated within the other historical eventuation of their period.

But the dated feel of the piece is above all due to the dramatic transformation during the dying months of the decade of the context itself of all other historical events. I am speaking here, of course, of the convulsion in Eastern Europe, and of the promise it holds out of a definitive closing of the postwar Cold War epoch.

This means that much of my argument here, particularly that of the opening sections, is, fortunately, obsolete in its recommendations. It is addressed to the untying of a knot of superpower confrontation in Europe which has already come loose politically and economically and which will hopefully do so also in its military strands in the not too distant future. Perhaps, therefore, I should have cut out this argument or jettisoned the piece altogether?

On reflection, however, I decided that there were several reasons to include it, and in an unrevised form. In the first place, there is a purely archival reason. I offer it as a record of what I, as a peace movement

23

activist and officer of END, was feeling and thinking at the mid-point of the decade. I do not claim it as particularly representative, though I know that there were many with whom I was working at the time who subscribed to its general sentiment. It is, however, essentially a personal witness, and hopefully has its place, along with numerous others of the same kind, as part of an archive of peace-movement preoccupations on the eve of the turning point of 'glasnost' and 'perestroika'.

But a second, and perhaps more persuasive, reason to include it is that I believe a good part of its argument, especially that addressing the North–South division and the military consequences of economic national-ism, still to be very relevant to our times despite the shift in East–West relations. Indeed given the business vultures in the West which have greeted the collapse of the old regimes in Eastern Europe, the rechan-nelling of aid away from the Third World countries into the Soviet bloc,[1] and the commitment of the new societies within the region to the more affluent forms of consumption associated with the market economy, such arguments may be viewed as having a broader pertinence today than when I first set them down. One must not deny the very considerable dis-crepancies in levels of consumption (and – inversely – in levels of pollution) between the established capitalist societies of the West, and the currently marketizing societies of the East.[2] These are likely to persist for a good while to come (and make the hunger in the East for Western-style living standards difficult to condemn from a position of relative affluence in the West). But it has to be accepted that the more conventionally 'successful' the economies of Eastern Europe manage to be, the more likely they are to exacerbate the destructive trends I have associated with Western industrial culture: exploitation of the poorer nations, ecological exhaustion and potentially explosive competition for dwindling resources; and the more applicable also to both halves of Europe will be the points I make in this connection about the necessity of a revaluation of lifestyles and the development of a new 'eroticism of consumption'.

And finally, I would say that as the production and trade of arms continues apace, and as we are waking up now to the idea that the Cold War may be ending only to give way to the equally, if not more, alarming prospect of a North–South ideological confrontation backed by weaponry of mass destruction, then my concluding remarks on militarism would seem to be not only not obsolete but not even beginning to be obsolescent.

Back in 1983, when President Reagan first announced his 'vision of hope for the future', we took it to be the optical illusion of an ageing man. To envisage the machinery of Star Wars actually placed in space was tantamount to seeing real shapes in clouds: 'dragonish' clouds maybe, in which we might discern signs of 'black vesper's pageants',* but still, only symbolically as it were. It had to be a mockery of what could happen in reality.

The contradictory aspiration to render militarism obsolete by recourse to militarism remains – as it always will do – fantastical. Yet the 'vision' itself has not dissolved away but rather gains in distinctness even as we watch and wait. Not only in the USA, but here in Britain, too – and the pattern is being repeated elsewhere in Western Europe – it daily acquires more substance. Business as usual has already come to mean Star Wars business. Clandestine research agreements, haggles over funding and the scope of American surveillance, secret contract negotiations: these are now almost routine aspects of scientific and technological activity. Political discussion has immediately followed suit; prompt to familiarize itself with the SDI idiom, it has adjusted with alarming rapidity to this monstrous new arrangement. Reagan's delirious whim, in being indulged, has also been made sanitary and reprocessed as rationality, thanks to its comforting association with ordinary people and their ordinary goings on in the commonrooms of Heriot–Watt or the canteens of Plessey and British Aerospace. 'What am I working on? – Fibre optics, well, yes, part of the SDI programme – want another coffee?'

Let us call this the military manufacture of reality – a process which, did it not work by undermining our powers of disbelief,

*Sometimes we see a cloud that's dragonish;
A vapour sometime like a bear or lion,
A tower'd citadel, a pendant rock,
A forked mountain, or blue promontory
With trees upon't, that nod unto the world
And mock our eyes with air: thou hast seen these signs;
They are black vesper's pageants.

Shakespeare, *Antony and Cleopatra*

ought to astonish us greatly. For consider: a US administration is preparing to sink each year a sum equivalent to the New Zealand GNP in a project as bizarre in its philosophy as it is technically unworkable. The ultimate idea behind it, so it would appear, is to permit all US aggression to remain immune to its own effects – in other words, to render hatred inviolate; the means to this end is an unearthly apparatus whose complexity bumps up against the limits of scientific conceptualization.

Consider further, that all this is already being implemented in the name of our defence by the combined powers of the NATO alliance, and not only with the – no doubt predictable – connivance of the present British government, but with no very fearsome roars as yet from the Opposition. As I write, there has been one debate on SDI in the House of Commons (the record of the House of Lords has been rather better) – and this debate took place only *after* the signing of the Memorandum of Understanding, only *after* Lt-Gen. Abrahamson, the Star Wars chief, had come and gone, British SDI participation a more or less guaranteed eventuality. In the end, however, parliamentary opposition is seldom more noisy than it needs to be. Perhaps we have to infer from all this that Star Wars is going ahead with the compliance of the vast majority of British citizens?

But if this is so, then we should realize what we are up to. For to encourage this folly either by deed or word, or simply by failure to protest (which in these matters amounts to tacit consent), is to assist a nightmare to come true. Defensive mirrors in space are not the phantoms of a troubled conscience they might once have seemed; they are not simply the metaphors of an astral looking-glass world from whose disquieting dream we shall shortly awaken. If we stand idly by, they will most certainly be installed. And the Soviet mirrors will most likely be erected in their image, and glint evilly back at them – until sooner or later, one or other of their imperial architects, in fury at the reflection of its own unblinking gaze, will put through a fistful of ballistic missiles, and the whole extraordinary edifice will shatter in fragments over a burning world.

Yet there is a silver lining of sorts to be found even in this clouded vision, and it lies in the very swiftness with which its crazed imagining has been converted into concrete materiality. For if the so-called 'military–industrial' complex, and its many advocates and lackeys, can wreak such major changes upon reality so suddenly, then may there not be reversals equally dramatic and equally rapid in our toleration of the alterations it effects?

It is true that this would involve the kind of quantum leap in attitude for which there would seem to be no precedents in history. Yet the emergency we now confront is also without historical precedent and there can be no certain prediction that it will not summon forth an equally exceptional struggle to surmount it. Indeed, the vast and growing peace movement is a very evident sign of its beginning to do so. What is undeniable, however, is the necessity of a deeper and much more widespread concern for the present crisis than has yet been felt, and the emergence of much greater public faith in the possibility of nuclear disarmament.

If this is to come about then a very prevalent complacency about the arms race must be disturbed. People will have to stop thinking of it as a kind of permanent bad weather to which they have no choice but to adapt. They will have to review their own adjustment to it and to the onus it now places on each succeeding generation, on individuals who are expected in their passage to adulthood to accustom themselves not only to the fact of individual mortality but to a prospect outside the range of previous human experience: the possible violent death in their lifetime of their species and all its works. They must question their society's acceptance of this prospect as if it were a henceforth inescapable feature of the human condition, and work to restore a sense of outrage that all life should be lived under this shadow. By whatever means available to them, they must try to restore faith in the powers of humanity to turn round and come out from its nuclear cul-de-sac.

For the arms race is not an inevitable blight of nature, but a humanly contrived disablement. And as such it ought to inspire, not resignation, but fury. Why, after all, should our chances of survival and happiness be constantly sacrificed to something within our powers to alter? Supposing we were to reverse this process, reinstate the moment of 'pre-nuclear innocence' and throw off this unremitting restraint on human well-being?

We should encourage this anger and its storming and railing at our present handicap; and we should indulge in the imagining of alternatives which in part provokes it. For the more desire we generate for a demilitarized world, the more likely we shall be to enjoy it. We too, then, should begin to have visions: visions of life in a disarmed society. But if one aspect of this enterprise is 'utopian' projection, the other must be realistic scrutiny of our present acts and attitudes. It has to be recognized that peace cannot be achieved simply by protesting against various items of military hardware. We have to tackle the processes which sustain the arms race and are used to justify its continuance – and these include habits and expectations of which we may be scarcely conscious, and whose military consequences we certainly do not intend.

In the first instance, however, we should ask ourselves a quite straightforward question: why the arms race, what is its purpose? There are those (Mrs Thatcher, for example) who will tell us that the arms race must continue because we know how to make nuclear weapons. But they do not explain how this knowledge can be made responsible for their production in numbers sufficient to end all human life; nor do they explain why we are not more given to eating each other, since we know perfectly well how to do so. Let us turn, then, to what may seem a more promising line of explanation: the arms race is there because it keeps the peace. But do any of us seriously believe that the prospect of the Third World War recedes as the nuclear mega-tonnage mounts up? If we cast our minds, not over the next decade or two, but over a hundred, two hundred years, then we must surely acknowledge that this frenetic accumulation cannot continue forever, and there are really only two options facing us: extermination or an end to Cold War and the relentless amassing of arms that goes with it.

For the arms race, in fact, is neither the inevitable consequence of technical know-how, nor is it about avoiding war. What drives it is animosity – an animosity, moreover, which derives at least a part of its force from the existence of the weapons which it supposedly justifies: the fact that it is upon 'us' that the 'enemy's' weapons are targeted in part explains – and quite reasonably so – the hostility that we direct towards the 'enemy'. Yet this, of course, cannot be the whole story, for it begs the question as to what it is that allows this enmity to gain ground in the first place and to hold us all so powerfully in its sway that it could now sweep us all to our deaths in a half hour. The answer to this question is not easy. On the one hand, we want to say that it has no obvious rationale, and that there is little in the history and culture of Europe, and even less in our personal feelings towards the individuals who collectively comprise the 'enemy', that can explain or justify it. Italian bricklayers almost certainly do not want to annihilate Hungarian carpenters, British dancers bear no grudge against their Soviet counterparts, Polish nurses do not want to fry Belgian children; at one level, none of us wants to blow up any of the others at all. On the other hand, we have to face the truth that we are also members of societies that have girded themselves to take the kind of action whose consequences for each of us personally will be precisely of this character. In this sense then, we are also collectively held in thrall to a consuming hatred of the 'enemy', even as we disown any individual animosity.

That people can countenance this situation, and in the process even lend themselves with enthusiasm to an overarching nationalist or 'public' aggression, is no doubt in part explained by a desire for the sort of self-identity that membership of an 'exclusive' grouping can satisfy, and by the uplifting feelings of solidarity and camaraderie that go along with such forms of belonging. And it is precisely this desire which nationalism or religious or racial fanaticism is able to play upon – often to such terrible effect. No one needs reminding of the kind of irrationally ferocious collectivities that have been massaged into existence under these stimuli.

Appalling, however, as the results of these inflated aggressions have been in the past, they have never until now been able to draw on the sort of military hardware that is now available to them in such abundance. This means that we face today a situation in which the very survival of life on earth depends on our capacity to make a decisive shift in the affective 'field' of these passions – away from the pole of the aggressive impulses towards those of compassion. The aim must be to resist all those pressures and forms of manipulation that encourage us into a hostility that as private individuals we seldom ever really feel, while at the same time fostering all that more personal part of our being that empathizes with the 'enemy' plight, can find no reason to slaughter its individual members and recoils from the prospect of doing so. When the peace movement calls for a 'people's detente' it is precisely calling for this kind of shift of perceptions. It is saying that the Achilles heel of Cold War antagonism lies in the ability of the individual to transgress the artificial boundaries between nations and peoples that are so assiduously and so destructively sustained at governmental level, and to go talking and walking or kicking balls or making music together in the common 'human' space that lies beyond them.

The capacity for such transgressions depends in part on the extent to which people can credit themselves with possession of more complex feelings towards the 'enemy' than the simplistic jingoism of the minority is prepared to allow them. It depends, for example, on a readiness to acknowledge that overall they felt gladder about the contest on the football field in Mexico City – when England was defeated by Argentina in the 1986 World Cup – than about the battle of Goose Green, even as they appreciated, wryly, sadly, angrily or bemusedly the parallels between the two.

But what is at issue here is not simply our ability to go trespassing on the grass together beyond the state-drawn borders, but our moral duty to do so at the present time. For just as government-planned genocide has in the past been assisted on its way simply by citizen default, it is likely to be so again unless sufficient numbers of us are prepared to reach out for an alternative, to seize the initiative from government and to protest 'but the emperor has no clothes: there is no reason to arm ourselves'.[3] To switch the dramatic reference: we Europeans could do with some of the spirit of Dikaiopolis, the 'honest Joe citizen' in Aristophanes' play *The Acharnians*, who, in frustration at the repeated failure of the Athenian and Spartan governments to agree to any peace formula,[4] makes his personal treaty with the 'enemy' – and thereafter enjoys a private peace and plenty that becomes the envy of the state warmongers.

We can be encouraged, moreover, in such moves by consideration of the fact that it is now the Cold War itself, rather than any enemy as such, which poses the major threat. For in generating ever more substantial national and international frictions, it creates its own 'logic' for the hot war towards which it is tending. The East–West division may have had its origin in the oppositional economic system of capitalism and communism, and this may remain in part its justification. But in that case we should recognize how paradoxical it is that East–West trade and economic cooperation has continued however icy the political climate has become. We should recognize, that is, the extent to which Cold War rhetoric has clung to the 'two-systems' idea simply for reasons of militarism itself, and that in this process the more pronounced evils of both systems have been continuously reinforced. In a situation where each side has sought to deny that there could be anything even potentially attractive about the other's way of doing things in order to justify a persisting hostility, inequality and class division in the West have conspired with repression in the East to reproduce the worst abuses of both. An enmity whose official 'causes' could in principle be removed by changes in both systems thus militates against such changes – and in doing so, of course, sustains itself. The Cold War, in other words, depends on a constant projection on the part of the antagonists of their own major shortcomings, the social inequalities associated with capitalist market freedoms being defended as part of the necessary bulwark against Soviet totalitarianism, and the latter being justified by reference to the social divisiveness supposedly entailed by any more liberal policy. In this process the emancipatory elements of both liberal and socialist philosophies are denied, and all impulses to their achievement repeatedly repelled. As unemployment and poverty in the West condemn more and more people to circumstances of existence which either numb the will to change or else divert it into violent and self-destructive paths, the lack of proper channels of political expression in the East induces a mirroring of this nihilism in the cycle of rebellion, repression and disillusionment. In Handsworth, the youth go on the rampage. In Warsaw, authorities inform us that young people have lost their zest for life.[5]

Let us acknowledge, therefore, that the Cold War not only aggravates the worst features of both systems but also inhibits the realization of those aspects to which they respectively appeal in ideological self-defence. For the militarism and repressive apparatus of Soviet-style socialism has relied upon, and continuously reproduced, hierarchies and inequalities of power and income, just as the aggressive defence of Western 'freedom' has issued in oppressive measures of 'law and order' enforcement and seriously eroded democracy. And nowhere is this more pronounced than in matters of defence. Today, in East *and* West, decisions which will ultimately determine the destiny of the collective citizens of Europe (and indeed of the world at large) are made by oligarchies – by the Kremlin potentates there, by the NATO High Level Group here.

The persistent questioning of Cold War psychology and its sinister indoctrination is, then, the first priority, for it is the East–West ideological confrontation that poses the most immediate danger. At the same time, however, we must acknowledge the more long-term threat to global survival which lies in the North–South division and is perpetuated by the relentless economic expansionism of the First World nations. Here, too, individuals have responsibilities to the future which need to be thought through, in the first instance, by consideration of the link between affluence and war. For it is the spiralling competition for the dwindling resources essential to maintain – and advance – First World living standards that spurs on the military stockpiling that heightens the risk of nuclear confrontation. The USA accounts for around 80 per cent of world oil consumption – a room-sized tank per capita per annum. A domestic pet in the UK commands many times the purchasing power of a Sudanese peasant. These facts testify to a century and a half (at least) of aggressively imperialist consumption which is as unfair in its consequences for the Third World peoples now as it is careless of the resource needs of future generations. As part of this same destructive process, discrepancies of privilege within the First World itself have been accentuated, existing class divisions have been continuously reconfirmed, and the political sovereignty of the West European nations has been ever more jeopardized by their reliance on American capital and hence subsumption to its whim.

None of this need be, however. As Lucio Magri has argued, Western Europe possesses now, as it did not thirty years ago, the economic, technological and cultural means to assert its own political autonomy, and to help sustain another path of development for the Third World. But, as he also says, the condition of this would be the following:

> reorientation of the European economies away from the quantitative multiplication of goods for consumption and export and the wastage of natural resources that goes with it, towards another style of development: one that was sober in its consumption, exported technology rather than commodities, sought a reduction in labour-time performed, gave priority to improvements in the quality of living. Such a model of development would no longer find its centre of gravity in heavy technology and industrial concentration, but in decentralized production and communication systems. It would be based not on the expropriation of nature, but on its reconstruction and valorization.[6]

To pursue this route would not be to cast off into a world without joy. The aim is not deprivation but a different balance of gratification: to become abstemious in the consumption of material commodities, but more profligate to compensate in the so-called 'goods of the spirit'. Community, friendship, sexual love, conviviality, wild space, music, theatre, reading and conversation, fresh air and uncontaminated land and water: it is with these attractions we should be cultivating desire and pandering to the senses, rather than with images of improving shares, the flight to the Bahamas and the second car. We should aspire to a new eroticism of consumption, an altered aesthetic of needs: one which makes the senses recoil from commodities which waste the land, throw up ugly environments, pollute the atmosphere, absorb large quantities of energy and leave a debris of junk in their wake.

These commodities are not without their uses, nor do we need to dispense with them altogether. The point, rather, is that they should be 'compromised'. We need to begin to pit their negative qualities against their more positive attributes, and thus little by little complicate a former more spontaneous urge to make use of them. As we watch the Nissan or Range Rover disappearing into a TV sunset at the desert's edge, or gliding noiselessly through leafy English lanes, we should recall that what these vehicles much more typically do is trap us in the din and stench of urban traffic jams, bring cuts in much less wasteful public transport (especially through leafy lanes), and depend on non-renewable oil supplies continuing to flow in from highly militarized and volatile areas of the globe.

To commit ourselves to alternative 'sober consumption' policies on standard facilities such as road transport, air freight, domestic appliances, and the like, would be to open the way to a lifestyle very different from that of the industrialized nations at present. But it would be nowhere like as primitive, arduous or tedious as dismissive modernist critics of all green projections of this kind like to imagine. It is very important, in fact, as a first step to achieving what are, given our present crisis, realist rather than utopian programmes, that we resist the caricatured versions with which a myopic and self-righteous pragmatism seeks to discredit these conceptions. We are not here mired in romantic nostalgia, nor bent on returning to medieval squalor, ill health and hard labour. We are suggesting ways of avoiding descent into previously unimagined barbarism and degradation, ending with the extinction of human civilization altogether.

Admittedly, such a programme directly challenges the norms

of 'growth' and 'efficiency' which have provided the governing logic of all capitalist economic activity. It also challenges conceptions about work and technology which are common to both capitalist and socialist thinking, and which have long dictated our attitudes to time expenditure. Dominated as our culture is by the idea that all time is better saved than spent, it knows no other way to define the 'efficiency' of its economy except in terms of its labour-saving capacities, and no other way to gauge its technical progress than in terms of its economic 'efficiency'. While the capitalist nations regard any improvement in the time–product ratio as a means to keep down wage bills, thus enhancing profits, the socialist regimes are no less keen on it because of what it permits in the way of promoting the 'capitalist' lifestyle, upon whose provision they believe their legitimation largely depends. The overall result, in both instances, is recourse to technologies aimed at short-term growth rather than long-term reproduction, and designed not so much to diversify or improve the quality of work, but to curtail its duration.

Of course, labour-saving technologies can in principle help us to spend time in happier ways. In practice, however, the commitment to growth traps us in a Hobson's choice between wasting free time and denying it. If we are not to 'squander' it in the form of a ghettoized and ever more relatively deprived sector of the unemployed, then we must disallow it: we must put the people back to work. If the people are put back to work on useful products satisfying social needs, preferably paid for out of cancelled arms programmes, then this latter policy is vastly to be preferred. But we should not con ourselves into thinking it an indefinitely rational mode of procedure, given the level of our current technical abilities and the ecological constraints we are now under. More rational by far would be a policy geared to provision of a decent but not extravagant standard of living, based on part-time employment for everyone. This would be consistent not only with enjoyment of genuine leisure but with some quite drastic and arguably very beneficial changes in the conduct of domestic life, the upbringing of children and human relationships. Domestic and nurturing tasks could be shared between both sexes, allowing both a richer experience and more mutual understanding. Domestic work itself could become less constraining and tedious because there would be time and energy to provide ourselves with things and services we currently have no choice but to buy or hire. There would be time to spend on each other, to think and talk, teach and learn, make and create, and simply to be idle. Such a pattern of consumption could transform the quality of city life while giving far more people access to the pleasures of the countryside. Above all, it would be consistent with long-term peace and security.

So far are we from realizing any such alternative at the present time that we are inclined to dismiss the whole idea as fanciful. And yet against it must be set the increasingly surreal feel of those consumer paradises in which a prevailing economic rationality invites us to cocoon the imagination. Coming away from a meeting about this book, I was struck by a page in my newspaper, a page in itself quite typical and unremarkable. (Though the events to which it refers were quickly themselves – again typically perhaps – to seem quite dated.) A good third of it is devoted to an insurance-company advertisement depicting three individuals engrossed in thought. They are pondering the use to which they would put some extra cash were it by chance to come their way. The young housewife yearns for a complete new kitchen, the holiday of a lifetime and her own sailing dinghy; the rising manager dreams of his new car, house extension and speed-boat; the elderly man of his retirement cottage, holiday flat in Spain and motor cruiser. 'Like everyone else you have a dream you'd like to come true in the not too distant future ...', patters on the accompanying copy, as within a few column inches of it US warships are challenging Colonel Gaddafi across the 'death line' in the Gulf of Sirte, threatening a skirmish in the Middle East – even, who knows, a brush with a lurking Soviet submarine, a nuclear exchange?

One could go on: the imagined investors perusing their 'capital bonus' figures are in visual range not only of reported eyeball contact between Libyan and US fighter pilots; should they glance upwards they will be staring into the eyes of a heavily armed National Resistance army guerrilla in Uganda – a country where loft conversions and motor cruisers are not plentiful, and where there has been little of permanence save the steady import of arms and export of coffee. If, pausing for a moment in their calculation of their 'total illustrated maturity value', they cast an eye across the page, they will read of the very premature death of Franscina Legoeete at the hands of the South African police – and also of their government's refusal to impose sanctions on the guilty regime (partly through fear, perhaps, of the impact on British savings investments?).

Enough of this. These prudent citizens are not real people, but put-up jobs screening us from our less one-dimensional selves. Real people do not look or think like these dummies. They wince at the daily narrative of torture, death and waste. They live in fear of nuclear destruction, are appalled at the sight of starving Third World peasants, and send generous donations to Oxfam. Many of them, all too aware of the fragility of their everyday existence, join the peace movement and become very active within it. And yet real people are also terribly caught up in the concerns and aspirations of consumer shams, even as they seek to distance themselves from the identity which they are offered by them.

This is the dilemma of First World existence: that none of us can escape this other 'utilitarian–consumerist' face or see ourselves as wholly freed of guilt; yet none of us, either, know how to extract ourselves as individuals from the cycle of oppression. Indeed, not only are we so far steeped in this that we doubt whether there *is* a way out; we also, though perhaps less consciously, are fearful that in any change of our ways we might forfeit our identity as well. Yet together with this fear, there also goes deep dissatisfaction and a yearning for something else. We question the worth of life, and wonder whether we are any nearer to happiness than our forebears. We express regret at the loss of a clearly felt but elusive sense of community, and experience the invasion in its place of a sinister brittleness. So that alongside, and even implicit in the hesitations and the feelings of impotence, there would seem to be a longing for a different order of human society – and for the emergence of precisely that solidarity and common sense of purpose which could enable us to overcome our individual powerlessness to achieve it.

It will be objected, however, that so long as the military blocs persist, so long as individuals are deprived of political expression in the East, and Western societies remain so economically divisive, then any appeal to a 'we' of Europe or of the First World to improve the condition of the Third must remain rhetorical. In one sense, this is true: there is certainly, at the moment, no national or international constituency in Europe to which such a 'we' might in all good conscience be applied. And yet in one important sense there is a 'we' – the 'we' that cuts across these other divisions to unite those millions of citizens of the First World countries who feel themselves committed to nuclear disarmament and the building of long-term peace.

The historical significance of the international peace movement in laying the grounds for the emergence of this collectivity should not be underestimated. Given the crucial importance of its work, it is quite scandalous how little encouragement it receives through official political and media channels. Desperately in need of constructive support of that kind, what it daily contends with instead is a barrage of argument designed to convince all those who might otherwise come out more fully in support of it, of the impossibility of any major changes of direction.

It is immensely discouraging to press for such changes and to argue for them on moral grounds in a culture where at every turn one is rebuffed by politicians defending the greater wisdom of pragmatism, economists reminding one of the limited strategic options permitted by the movement of finance capital, or intellectuals wrily deconstructing one's humanist foibles. Moral argument and appeal, these mentors all insist, is either futile or counterproductive. Where it is not ignored, it takes effect only in the form of a resentment which reinforces resistance to its pressure. Since people never change their ways except under the prod of economic necessity, it is pointless for politicians to appeal to any better instinct than immediate financial self-interest.

Much sager, then, for them to deal with the electorate like a pack of Pavlovian dogs who only respond with the confirming X if administered a suitable consumerist stimulus.

At the same time, of course, the politicians themselves adopt the same reflex posture towards their own activities and choices, regarding these as permanently under the dictate of economic forces (the 'balance of payment deficit', 'petrodollar movements', 'sterling rates', etc.) as unassailable in status as the law of gravity. All policy, they never tire of telling us, is a matter of 'manoeuvring' within the narrow constraints imposed by a series of supposedly quite irremovable pressures.

It is this discourse and its realpolitik reminder of the possible effect of an anti-NATO vote on tariff concessions which was used so successfully to sway the Spanish people in the run-up to the 1986 referendum. It is the same language which has been used to persuade the Italians of the need for Comiso (and cuts in public spending), the Dutch of the need for Cruise (and cuts in public spending), the British of the need for Cruise and Trident, and nuclear power, and the Channel tunnel ... (and cuts in public spending).

The economic institutions which now mediate practically all international (and much of our interpersonal) exchange are undeniably very powerful and very material forces. But it would be wrong to present them as absolutely beyond all human control, for they exist, in fact, only in virtue of those elements – human will, action, energy, consent, indifference – which together amount to the exercise of such control. The law of gravity will continue to enforce its rule with or without our intervention or our leave. Market forces, NATO, the arms lobby, the Warsaw Pact, Comecon and IMF will not.

An important condition, then, of emancipation from the destructive tendencies of our culture is freedom from a way of thinking which denies the role of people in creating social processes and institutions. It is a way of thinking manifest in many walks of like: the academic preaches it in erudite discourses on the 'death of the subject'; the Cabinet Minister repeats it in voicing fears lest the rise in oil prices will mean more

deaths from hypothermia; the citizen who chucks aside the Star
Wars leaflet with a derisory snort at the futile struggles of the
peace movement is merely acting out its gloomy lesson.

It is an insidious teaching – and in that it induces impotence
by convincing us of it, it tends to be self-fulfilling. Yet its picture
is none the less distorted. The massive response to the Live Aid
and Band Aid appeals indicates that the citizens of the First
World are not quite as blinkered or incapable of initiative as the
anti-moralists would like us to believe. In sacrificing some part of
their savings for the sake of the lives of others whom they will
never see, they have shown themselves uneasy with their 'peace'
or at any rate distressed by some of its consequences. It remains
to be seen how this unease will develop. Certainly, salving
conscience with a monetary donation will not be enough. If there
is genuine concern to establish a safer and juster world, then
people must now put their political voice and energy where they
have begun to put their money. They must demand principled
political representation of the moral alternatives to which they
wish to be committed. Conversely, the onus is on the major
European socialist parties to put the 'Pavlovian' theory of the
electorate to the test by provision of a strongly argued moral
alternative for which it could cast its vote.

In the meantime, the peace movement must continue to insist
that what is here called the 'moral' option is also the only one
that can be credited with realism in a nuclear world. The sheer
destructive capacity of modern arsenals – which guarantee that
the 'whole' explodes should any 'part' have recourse to nuclear
weapons – has rendered anachronistic the conception of the
nation state as an autonomous unit with the 'right' to compete
with other nations for markets and resources, if necessary
protecting the 'vital' interests it thereby establishes by military
means. Were, indeed, every nation to adhere to American logic
on this 'right' (if the Libyans didn't want the Sixth Fleet in the
Gulf of Sirte, they should have asserted their 'right' to it,
according to a Pentagon spokesman at the time of Libyan–US
clash in April 1986) then the result, as the US administration well
knows, would be disaster for everyone. In the last analysis, if the

human race is to survive its 'nuclear epoch', it will have to adjust to the political perspective which the technical capacities of its armaments have forced upon it: it must come to accept the world in its entirety as a single body of which the separate national units are the various limbs and organs. Henceforth no one 'member' can go it alone without risking dismembering the whole upon which it itself depends for its survival.

To challenge the longstanding idea of the nation state as the ultimate political grouping is to open up a new conception of the political identity and status of the individual. It is to insist that the interests which individuals have as members of a common species are at odds with the 'nationalistic' interests fostered by the state, and can find no adequate representation in the latter. Individuals, for their part, must seek, as part of this same conception, to replace patriotic and nationalist loyalties by a 'species responsibility' – by a consciousness of the organicity of the planet and of the duties that each person has towards it as part of a collective human subject. For though as individuals we can only engage at any time in particular actions in particular geographical regions, it is these specific and local doings in the aggregate that decide the history and fate of our species taken as a whole. In this sense, as Rudolf Bahro has suggested, human beings are subjects of their history, not only individually but also as a species, and it is only if we refuse to look at the matter in this larger perspective that we can continue to insist that social forces and institutions are autonomous of individuals and unamenable to their control. As he puts it:

> Everything which looms as a danger to human beings [the social ensemble], everything which threatens them or it, is either their own alienated power or is obeying their alienated command. The central control rooms may be lords over death, but they are not lords of the process which put them in this position.[7]

But recognition of a 'species-responsibility' along these lines must itself be grounded in appreciation of the physical and psychological ties uniting all members of the human race and rendering them a species in common. For paradoxical though it may seem, it is through a heightened awareness of those qualities we deem 'personal' that we are best able to arrive at a sense of ourselves as members of a larger transnational collectivity. In other words, the assumption of 'global subjectivity' goes together with a shift in values in which those characteristics we share with others in being human are given a much more positive estimation than hitherto, while those we share specifically as British (or American, or Russian or Chinese ...) are viewed more circumspectly. In this process, as feminist peace campaigning has always rightly insisted, it is crucial that we begin to give their proper due to those 'private' domestic activities which have hitherto always been subordinated to the 'larger' concerns of a 'public' domain — where war, polity and the pursuit of wealth supposedly make trifles of these 'womanly' pursuits. The human race will not survive unless it wakes up to the fact that giving birth, caring for our offspring, and all forms of nursing and ministering to each other, both physically and emotionally, are far more vital to the ultimate well-being and protection of our species than anything we do in the way of military defence.

To give priority in this way to unmediated person-to-person emotional ties and physical dependences is to begin to dismantle that enmity which flourishes on the idea that an entire population can be designated the bloodless and bodiless 'other' of an equally incorporeal, abstracted 'self'. To give ourselves (and our enemies) bodies and minds again, which bleed and caress and love and feel afraid, is immediately to invest ourselves with an important source of power against the degenerative spiral of militarism. For every twist in that spiral is accomplished only with the aid of personnel, both military and civilian, who are prepared and able to refuse identification with the victims of planned aggression.

Militarism works through inculcating a resistance to empathy which is self-reproducing and self-confirming. It is this failure of compassion which encourages the 'nuke 'em' philosophy, makes possible the tolerance of preparations for annihilation, and lies behind the impassive contemplation of the use of

42

nuclear arsenals. In working to check militarism the peace movement is therefore struggling against repression and apathy, and attempting to stop the rot of something even more danger-ous than lethargy: the crowing 'Gotcha!' Falklands mentality which cannot for a minute permit itself to identify, not with the 'getter' but the 'got'.

Very few of us are actually able to be so wholly insensitive to the sufferings of others. Yet we should recognize none the less that time is running out, and that militarism kills not only in war and in the massive Third World casualties of the global arms race, but also by a progressive deadening of our emotional responsiveness and energy. Built into the 'exterminist' process, as part of its cancerous advance, there is a mutilation of the affective and moral being, an enfeebling of the will to live and general blunting of our sensibility to the pain and loss of fellow human beings. If we are finally snuffed out by our own doing, it will be this lapse of will and feeling that ultimately will be to blame. The alternative is to fan the flame of human forbearance and mag-nanimity: to summon up the resolution to survive – and flourish. For there is still much 'capability and god-like reason' left in us, and we should turn it now, not to vengeful deeds, but to those acts of peace which need so urgently to be done. The nuclear shields with which the arms race is currently threatening to eclipse the future are certainly intricate devices, and the product of complex forces. Yet there is nothing we have humanly engineered which is not vulnerable in the end to our refusal to allow it to continue. Against the Goliath of the 'technical fix' we must now pit the David resources of the human spirit.

Notes

1. The USA is currently redirecting funds from Third World programmes towards Eastern Europe, and Italy recently requested of the OECD that its aid to those economies should count as Third World funding.

2. For further elaboration of these points, see my contribution with Martin Ryle on 'Ecology and the New Detente' in M. Kaldor, G. Holden and R. Falk (eds) *The New Detente*, London 1989, pp. 287–306.

3. The image is invoked by the Hungarian writer Andras Hegedus in an article printed in *END Journal*, Summer 1986.

4. The play is written and set during the Peloponnesian war between the city states of Athens and Sparta, which began in 432 BC and lasted nearly thirty years, to the detriment of all parties.

5. The overall conclusion of an official survey of youth attitudes in Poland, reported in the *Guardian* 10 March 1986, is that hardly anyone under thirty-five cares anything for People's Poland, and that most suffer from a notable 'lack of vigour'.

6. Lucio Magri, 'The Peace Movement and Europe', in *Exterminism and Cold War*, London 1982, p. 132.

7. Rudolf Bahro, *Building the Green Movement*, London 1986, p. 144.

2

Who Needs Socialism?

To raise this question in the current political climate might seem to be inviting a rude retort: practically no one, it would seem. Of course there are still the loyal few, faithful to the principle, but they are an insignificant minority. Mrs Thatcher and Václav Havel would seem conjoined at least in this: socialism is no longer viable. Perhaps, then, it is naive to come back to the question, as I propose to? Certainly as one whose political energies in the 1980s were much given over to supporting those elements in Eastern Europe which now that they have gained a political voice would have us disown the vocabulary of 'socialism', I sense the difficulty if not the naivety of my question quite acutely.[1] I am troubled by speaking to the concept in the midst of a democratic revolution conducted so largely in the name of socialism's demise: troubled by the sense of clinging against the grain of my political commitments to an idea which now so widely – and with so much justice – is perceived as their betrayal. To pursue the issue of 'socialism' and of the 'need' for it – is this not at best to show oneself fixated with an obsolete agenda, at worst to persist with an argument and language now irredeemably tainted by its totalitarian 'realization'?

The academic philosopher in me advises against this glibness: that it still does, after all, depend on what is meant by 'socialism' and what is meant by 'need'. There is some good sense in this, and I propose to follow its admonition. Inevitably this will lead my argument into some fairly abstract considerations though without it ever, I hope, losing sight of the present political context. My overall purpose in this is to unsettle the confidence of the two contrary responses invited by the question 'who needs socialism?'. For while to socialism's opponents the answer may seem obvious, to its loyal friends the question itself must remain a trifle absurd. But neither of these reactions, I think, does justice to the political ferment of our times.

I shall begin with a preamble around the notion of the 'politics of need' – an idea upon which, I suggest, we can put two differing constructions. On the one hand, we may focus on disparities in consumption at national and global levels: on the massive deprivation of the poorest peoples of the world relative to those living in advanced industrial societies, and on the less starkly contrasting but nonetheless still striking differences of living standard within the affluent nations themselves. In this approach needs are conceived primarily in terms of biological exigencies – our basic human requirements for food, health, shelter and the like – and the key political issue is how to make good absolute deficiencies or relative disparities at this level. If there are political controversies in this area, they are seldom about the existence or nature of the needs themselves, but why they have arisen, who is responsible, and what social and economic programmes might best correct them.

In another conception, however, which hitherto has been less central to political theory and practice, the idea of a 'politics of needs' refers us not to basic need satisfaction but to the question of what is needed as a condition of human flourishing and happiness. I shall call this the question of 'true' need, though I do so with some misgivings lest I be thought to be defining the 'truth' of our needs in relation to some essential human nature. 'True' needs are not what all human beings need in order to be truly happy. I use the term not to suggest that needs can be finally fixed, but to indicate the value concept through which we raise questions about the relationship between happiness and existing lifestyles and patterns of consumption. Indeed, it is as if our needs are politicized in this 'true' need sense at precisely the point at which we refuse to see them in the fixity of a particular historical mode of gratification. And in claiming that a 'politics of need' in this construction has hitherto been kept off the mainstream political agenda, I am claiming that there has been hardly any questioning by government and opposition parties of the relationship between happiness and existing norms of consumption. The issues of contention have almost always revolved around the distribution of wealth, not about the worth of the goods which money can buy. They have been about shares in the good life, not its definition. The same has largely been true across the divide of the Cold War. For despite the communist onslaught on capitalist 'consumer decadence', both economic blocs have sustained very similar conceptions of what constitutes 'improved living standards' and how to measure advances towards them. There has been, then, throughout the Cold War period a left–right, communist–capitalist complicity around the issue of human needs and the quality of the 'good life', and there are strong indications that this will be carried over and reflected in the more pluralist party political systems currently being established in Central and Eastern Europe.

This is not to deny the extent to which this complicity is now being challenged, and a more 'ends-questioning' rather than 'means-contending' politics coming into play. But the key factor in this challenge is a growing ecological awareness of the contradiction between the pursuit of prosperity as currently conceived and the survival of the planet: an awareness which has elbowed itself forward almost in spite of the old party and ideological divides, and which has only very recently found any official political representation.

This challenge, which is a 'true' need politics in the sense that it addresses itself to the question of what is conducive to human flourishing rather than to economic improvement, is very welcome and is being quite clearly registered now in both halves of Europe. It also allows us to make the link back to the 'politics of need' in the first of our senses. For there can be little doubt, I think, that without some serious questioning by the more affluent peoples of the globe of how far their existing patterns of consumption contribute to their personal fulfilment, little will be achieved in the way of promoting a more equitable distribution of material satisfactions. In other words, it is only when a significant percentage of those currently pursuing the pleasures of industrial civilization begin to see it as in their own interest to enjoy themselves rather differently, that they are likely to lend themselves to measures which better provide for the basic needs of those less fortunate.

Such measures, however, will be socialist at least in the sense that they will conflict with the logic of the untrammelled market. They will involve, if not the abandonment of any form of market provision, forms of planning and redistribution of wealth of a kind which run counter to the goals of the capitalist economy and undermine its global stranglehold. If this is correct, then the questions about 'true' need which are now moving into the centre stage of politics as a consequence of ecological concern have some important implications for our initial question: the question of how far one can speak of a continuing need for, or interest in, socialism among the peoples of the industrialized nations.[2] It is to this question I now turn.

The first thing to make clear is that in considering the support for socialism in Europe today, I intend by 'socialism' neither the Stalinian version which has prevailed till recently in the Eastern bloc, nor the programme of the European 'Socialist' Parties and our own Labour Party. I mean by socialism a politics which aspires to an egalitarian and democratic order and views the dismantling of capitalism as the essential condition of its re-alization. Let me make clear, secondly, that I accept that there is a great deal of evidence suggesting a dramatic decline in support for socialism as so construed.

There is the evidence, first, of the ballot box: the evidence in this country of a decade of Tory power and of the trimming to the right which has seemed essential to the Labour Party recovery. There is the evidence, second, of a more general shift in intellectual climate: the sea-change of 'postmodernist' decon-struction which has contrived to present socialism as both a new form of domination and an out-of-date humanism, both totali-tarian in what it would impose on human subjects and quaintly

48

nineteenth century in believing there are such subjects – and on both scores unwanted and anachronistic. So powerful has been this convulsion within the academy and traditional left circles that it is only the more insensitive Marxist who will remain indifferent to its disruption. As for the other Marxists, the *Marxism Today* Marxists, they have responded to the new times by going rather quiet about smashing capitalism and urging instead the more peaceful 'consumer Communist' route to revolution.

Lastly, and to return to where we began, there is the evidence of what is happening in Central and Eastern Europe, where the extent of the support for perestroika would seem to indicate, if not a wholesale capitulation to the market philosophy, a significant collapse of resistance to its principles. The situation, of course, is very much in flux, and the evidence partial and open to differing interpretations. Socialists in the West who have always argued that the 'actual existing socialism' of the Soviet bloc had all too little to do with any 'authentic socialism' will not, if they are to prove consistent, view the move away from Breschnevian orthodoxy as in itself indicating a break with socialist principles. On the contrary, they will want to discriminate between elements in the reform programme which hold out the promise of establishing a more genuinely socialist order based on a democratic but non-capitalist management of the economy, and elements threatening to nip this promise in the bud. And they would probably insist that before we pronounce the demise of socialism in Eastern Europe we shall need a better sense of the popular will on these matters. But even if we argue that the enthusiasm for glasnost/perestroika must be seen as primarily expressive of the desire for political pluralism and its freedom rather than as an index of opposition to any form of socialist economy, there is surely no denying that many citizens in Central and Eastern Europe have come to regard market freedom as indissolubly linked with political freedoms and indeed the condition of their realization. In this sense, we must accept that popular support for reform is evidence of a failure to discriminate between the two which itself bespeaks a relative lack of interest in the present time in pursuing a distinctively *socialist* programme of political and economic reconstruction.

Now, as said above, it is not my purpose to deny this evidence but rather to pursue some more general questions about the relations between it and the conclusions to be drawn from it, and in so doing to consider whether there are not some other kinds of 'evidence' of which we also need to take account before pronouncing any final verdict on the fortunes of socialism.

As a way into the discussion, let us first look at the arguments which standardly have been offered in explanation of the 'failure' of socialism. I suggest that broadly speaking these have been of two kinds: those which refer it to the idealism of its conceptions of human nature (which, it is said, is not capable of the self-effacement and generosity of spirit essential to a harmonious egalitarianism); and those which refer it to the superiority of capitalism in meeting the material, self-interested needs of the mass of people. We might note in passing that the openness of socialism to these antithetical types of charge is not unrelated to an equivocation in its own moral appeal. On the one hand, socialists have deplored the greed and selfishness which have kept capitalism on course and too often prevented even the most minimal sacrifices of privilege (at both individual and national level). In this sense, socialism's appeal is to an *un*selfishness: to the moral justice of fairer shares for all – and thus implicitly to a 'nature' that is 'better' than merely self-seeking. At the same time, however, it has always sought the allegiance of the working classes and dispossessed by an appeal to their self-interest: to what they can hope to gain from the overthrow of capitalism and its class politics. I am not suggesting that this equivocation is to be seen as a sign of incoherence. It follows, in fact, from the premise of egalitarianism itself and the fairly complex affective structure with which it credits human kind (a structure including both social and personal commitments, both desire for justice and an interest in individual self-fulfilment). I am suggesting only that it is an equivocation which makes it liable to contrary types of indictment: as a politics of altruism, socialism is said to be out of touch with the realities of human nature; as a politics of selfishness to have been upstaged by capitalism's greater capacity to deliver the goods.

Though both lines of criticism continue to be sounded, with the increased prosperity of the working classes in the industrial nations we have heard rather more of the second – and voiced in Britain not only from the right, but in a spirit of self-criticism or pessimism or disillusionment by socialists and one-time socialist sympathizers themselves.

One version of the argument was spelled out by E.H. Carr over a decade ago in a *New Left Review* interview:

> The organised workers have gained enormously in strength, and have not hesitated to use that strength for their own ends. Yet the one thing that has not happened is the proletariat revolution. Wherever in the capitalist world revolution has momentarily loomed on the horizon – in Germany in 1919, in France in 1968 – the workers hastened to turn their back on it. Whatever they wanted, it was not revolution. I find it difficult to reject the evidence, that in spite of all the chinks that have developed in the armour of capitalism, the mood of the workers is less, not more revolutionary today than it was sixty years ago. In the West today, the proletariat – meaning, as Marx meant by the term, the organised workers in industry – is not a revolutionary, perhaps even a counter-revolutionary, force.[3]

Carr goes on to explain this development, moreover, less in terms of the traditional fear of revolution and more in terms of the guaranteed level of consumption that capitalism offers the mass of workers – at least for the duration of their life span. 'If capitalist profits collapse,' he writes, 'so does the provision for old age of the workers. "Where your treasure is, there shall your heart be also." The workers now have in many ways a large stake in the survival of capitalism.'[4]

More recently, and more polemically, David Selbourne has pressed his arguments against the 'middle-class romantics, whose illusions about "the working class" are evidently fonder than either fact or reason'.[5] He puts it to the socialists that the new working class culture may well be militant – but militant on behalf of sexist, racist and chauvinist values. The fall in traditional support for the Labour Party and the hostility of many trade unionists to what they perceive as the 'excessive powers' of their own trade unions are, according to Selbourne, but two of the more striking symptoms of the abandonment by today's working class of any commitment to the traditional moral and social purposes of the British labour movement. Such a shift, he claims, is not glibly to be attributed to the brain-washing power of the media nor even simply to disaffection with the performance of successive Labour governments: the suggestion is that we must now recognize, as a kind of 'fact of nature', that the British worker no longer has any aspirations towards socialism. The political agenda and political culture of the 1980s are a world away from postwar reconstruction; their 'crude prejudices and ardours, which were once contained and suppressed within the labour movement, are now become a powerful element in ruling national ideology'.[6] In short, it is either wishful or condescending or both to attempt to exonerate the mass of British workers who have voted for the Thatcher government of responsibility for their choices and the needs they express, however antipathetic we may find them.

Now, I think it is clear that arguments such as these are based on an interpretation of evidence of a kind contested by a fairly standard form of Marxist riposte: that which claims that just as the 'real relations' of society cannot be read off from their 'phenomenal' forms, so it is mistaken to assimilate the 'real needs' of persons to those they profess to have, or manifest in what they actually choose to consume. According to the 'Marxist' logic, in other words, it is only if people come to understand the 'real' nature of their society and to appreciate the extent to which the needs they happen to experience are the reflection, not of their own nature, but of a false form of social existence that their 'true' needs will come to be understood and in that process actually experienced. So long, therefore, as people are confined to the straitjacket of capitalist forms of production and remain ignorant of the role that social forces play in generating and moulding what they perceive as their 'natural' needs, it will be no surprise that we cannot detect any overt need for socialist transformation.

To bring out what is at issue between these opposing lines of interpretation, I shall here distinguish between two political paradigms of the need–consumption relationship. I shall refer to these respectively as the 'liberal' and the 'Marxist' paradigm, associating the former with an 'empiricist-behaviourist' and the latter with a 'rationalist' account of evidence for need. I should emphasize that my argument is entirely schematic. My aim is to isolate and fix an essential difference of bias rather than to reflect the actual, more nuanced and complex accounts provided in Marxist and liberal theory.

The 'liberal' paradigm is rooted in the idea that individuals are, and must be allowed to be, arbiters of their own needs. Such needs are a sovereign possession to be preserved as far as possible from the imposition of any deliberate policies on consumption. Hence the allegiance of liberalism to the market economy, since whatever other faults this system may have, it has the cardinal virtue of responding to need rather than dictating consumption. Only capitalism, in short, can protect consumers against the drift towards a totalitarian manipulation of needs inherent in the planned economy.

The epistemological implication of the liberal argument is that it is wrong to claim knowledge of the needs of others except on the basis of what they themselves claim to need or reveal themselves as needing through their pattern of behaviour. Needs, in other words, can only be said to exist in virtue of some form of observable first-person expression either by word or deed: one must either profess oneself to have the need and/or do some-thing by way of gratifying it – typically by attempting to acquire the good or service which will satisfy it. In almost all cases, this means the exercise of purchasing power.

In essence, then, the liberal paradigm identifies needs with directly experienced needs, and recognizes a distinction only between those needs which are backed by effective demand and those which cannot be met for lack of income. Unrecognized needs, or needs for which there is no evidence other than in their conscious profession or the exercise of purchasing power are not acknowledged to exist within this conceptual field. The outlook can be described as 'empiricist-behaviourist' in the sense that it recognizes needs only on the basis of certain 'perceptible' facts, and indeed a rather limited range of such 'facts'.

Turning now to the 'Marxist' paradigm, we find the 'liberal' argument more or less inverted: social production (the market economy), so far from being defended as the essential mechanism for satisfying needs, is viewed as the primary influence on their formation. The experienced needs revealed in historical patterns of consumption are not the unchallengeable 'natural' possession of the 'needing' individuals but reflect the particular structure of production relations: relations which under capitalism sustain a very unequal distribution of income and hence of actual consumption. The tendency of the Marxist argument, therefore, is to deny the existence of an inherent 'natural' pattern of needs implied in the liberal argument, and to claim that the needs which people profess themselves to have or 'reveal' themselves as having in their exercise of purchasing power are formed in response to the products on offer for consumption (a product range itself conditioned by the mode of production) and reflect their personal degree of access to the wealth generated by the economy.

From this it follows, epistemologically, that there is no good ground for seeing evidence of a need only in its profession or in actual consumption. On the contrary, if consumer aspirations and the patterns of actual consumption are the manipulated effect of the market economy, then we should precisely *not* see these indices as guides to what people 'really' need but rather as evidence of the 'false' needs generated by the needs of the economy. The inclination, in short, of the Marxist framework is to reject all criteria of need of the kind invoked in the liberal argument on the grounds that the evidence of the 'actual' – 'alienated' – society of capitalism can be no guide to what people 'truly' need or would choose to do and consume under different conditions of existence.

I submit that neither of these models is acceptable, the 'liberal' because it is too narrowly empiricist, the 'Marxist' because its 'rationalism' removes it from any form of empirical control.

One way of bringing out what is wrong with the 'liberal' model is to pursue the – arguably counterfactual – implications of any rigorous application of its 'empiricist-behaviourist' test for need. If we take, for example, a straightforward biological need, for example for food, then I think it can reasonably be claimed that even though the standard tests fail to be met there can be no disputing the evidence of the need. For lack of income, or other reasons, food may not be purchased or otherwise obtained – hence the effective demand condition is unmet. Equally, the individual concerned may fail to experience hunger or profess a need for food. The anorexic persistently denies feelings of hunger, and it is well known that those who are chronically malnourished or in advanced stages of starvation lack 'appetite' and do not suffer from hunger pangs. But that both the 'positive' tests therefore fail to be met by no means implies that the attribution of the need for food to an individual who neither searches after food nor professes to want it is purely speculative. For the wasting of the body, the diseases of malnutrition, and eventual death provide us with all the evidence for ascribing the need for food which it would be rational to require.

The case of more 'psychological' needs is, I admit, less simple. But its relative complexity can give little comfort to those relying on 'empiricist-behaviourist' criteria – which are revealed to be even more inconsequential than in the case of 'biological' need. Indeed, in respect of psychological needs, it can be argued that we are almost the more justified in positing their existence the less the 'positive' empirical tests for their existence are met. The arbitrary nature of the effective demand criterion in respect of this range of needs is, I think, fairly obvious. What purchase of goods or services, for example, shall we accept as evidence of, for example, an individual's need for love? Notoriously, too, the purchasing of goods in pursuit of this range of satisfactions is counterproductive, or at least consistent with the failure to satisfy the need. Someone, we might agree, buys sex because he needs love, but we would be far more reluctant to admit that the need is satisfied in the purchase or can be said to exist in virtue of its being made. We have here, of course, no more than a specific instance of the inadequacy of behaviourism in general: unless we define needs analytically in terms of a particular set of purchases, in which case nothing informative is being said of them, then any and every possible purchase becomes a candidate for evidence of the existence of the need and the behavioural test fails of the purpose for which it is intended.

But one can argue further that the criterion of professed or directly experienced need is equally inconsequential. We do not, I suggest, have to be thoroughly committed Freudians before we question expressions of psychological need precisely on the grounds that they belie the lack they profess to speak for. It is fairly well recognized, I think, that those least able to articulate their needs may be most in need (young children are an obvious example). Psychiatrists, in fact, tend to think of their activities as largely justified by the fact that they enable the articulation of demand, and there are few in that profession, I think, who believe that denials of desire should be taken at face value, and probably even fewer who think that lack of affirmation of desire means that their patient is without wishes. After all, if we define depression, crudely, as absence of desire for, or interest in, life, then according to the 'positive' criteria, which discovers the existence of a need in the quest to satisfy it or in the definite expression of it, there would be no depressives. In fact, to the contrary, most of us would be inclined to accept that one of the main forms of evidence of depression is that you feel no interest in being interested, and that you do not want to pursue the interest in life that you actually lack – which is what is wrong with the well-meant advice about joining the local social club, etc.

Of course it is true that in the case of these 'psychological' needs there is nothing equivalent to the diseases of malnutrition and death to point to in evidence of their existence, and this is no doubt particularly true where we are concerned, as I am here, not with the pathology of mental illness but with the grounds upon which one can ascribe needs to the healthy members of society as a whole or to some significant grouping within it. All I am arguing here is that we should not concede too readily to the argument which underlies the Carr/Selbourne line of assessment of the 'need for socialism' that there is no evidence that large numbers of people in present day society have needs for anything but to continue in their current patterns of consumption.

I shall return to this issue shortly, but before doing so it is important that I also first set out what is wrong with the standard 'Marxist' type of response to the 'liberal' position. I have suggested that the problem with the 'Marxist' account is that it is under-empirical. No one is going to deny that as people change their perceptions of the world so they change the demands they make of it, but I think we cannot be satisfied with an argument in defence of a 'real' need for socialism which relies at every turn on a dismissal of any counter-evidence for the truth of the claim, and simply refers us to the fact that individuals are precluded from experiencing their genuine needs by the distortion of the circumstances in which they find themselves. (It is, moreover, a form of argument which in the end must prove self-defeating: if professed or 'phenomenal' needs are never to be taken as guides to true needs, then the authenticity of any professed aspiration for socialism must also be called in question.) Now, the evidence here does not have to be confined to the 'empiricist-behaviourist' type. Indeed, I have set out some reasons why we should be sceptical about accepting that as in any way adequate. But there does have to be *some* kind of evidence, and in the case in question, where it is a matter of ascribing political needs, there has to be evidence that the needs in question are in an important sense 'realized' and not merely 'hypothetical': that they are ascribable because of an existing structure of experience.

The point may be made clearer by distinguishing between two differing usages of the term 'need': that in which we impute 'needs' to others quite independently of what they experience or may come to experience as their own needs, and that in which we refer to what we ourselves need. It is inherent in the logic of the second usage that the needs in question are recognized as in some sense experienced by us: as at least implicit in and

57

consistent with our subjective aspirations. A doctor, for example, may ascribe a need to a patient (e.g. to cut down on salt) without having to consult the subjective feelings of the patient. If we are to speak, however, of the patient subjectively 'having' the need, it must be on the basis of his or her experiencing, alongside the desire to eat salt as before, an antipathy, or at the very least a self-interested resistance to doing so. Now, the inadequacy of the 'Marxist' paradigm lies in the fact that it treats ascribed needs (e.g. 'the need for socialism') *as if* it were legitimate to ascribe them independently of the experienced structure of needs of actual individuals themselves. But there is an incoherence in this insofar as the Marxist ascription is not that of the doctor claiming a patient's objective need *whatever* he or she happens to want or to come to feel s/he needs. On the contrary, when Marxists speak of peoples' 'real' needs they are imputing these needs subjectively to them: they are saying that these are needs which people only actually have if/when they feel them to be their own. In other words, they are not needs ascribed regardless of the present or future affectivity of the persons concerned. But this means, in fact, that there is an implicit reference to experience as that which validates the truth of the claimed need. The Marxist argument is therefore caught in a dilemma: either it must appeal to some actual evidence in experience to ground its claims as to what is truly needed; or else it must accept that its 'real' or 'true' needs are purely objectively ascribed and hence not needs in the properly required sense.

But am I not here, it might be said, flying in the face of my earlier objections to the limitations of the 'empiricist-behaviourist' criteria of need? For did I not there imply that these lay in their failure to register a range of legitimately ascribable, but unfelt, needs; and am I not here arguing that needs to be legitimately ascribed do, in fact, have to be experienced, at least in some sense? The point, of course, is *which* needs, and *in what sense*. I am arguing that 'political' needs – needs of the kind involved in any ascription of a 'need for socialism' – *do* have to be legitimated by reference to experience but that their experienced status cannot be denied simply because the needs are not confirmed by either of the 'empiricist-behaviourist' tests. My discussion has been intended to bring out two antithetical errors in the approach to needs: the error of the 'empiricist-behaviourist' account lies in its conflation of all needs with subjectively experienced needs and of the latter with subjectively avowed or acted upon needs – an error whose logic tends to the absurdity that there can be no valid ascription of objective needs (for food, to cut down on salt, etc.) The error of the 'Marxist' account lies in treating *all* needs as if they were assimilable to objective needs, when in fact 'political' needs (e.g. of the working class for socialism) – are only needs insofar as they are experienced by those who are said to have them. To put the point otherwise: if we are to allow a 'need for socialism' it cannot be on the basis of the Marxist 'doctor's' objective ('elitist', 'authoritarian', 'totalitarian' ...) assessment of the condition of the needing individuals, but only on the basis of the evidence of their own feelings. On the other hand, the evidence for such feelings is not simply of the 'positive' kind to which we are referred in the 'liberal' approach.

Leaving aside these conceptual issues now, I shall argue in what follows that we can, despite the countervailing evidence, speak of a 'need for socialism' in the requisite sense. Indeed, I shall suggest that we might even be justified in claiming this interest or need to be greater than at any time in the postwar period. The evidence I shall adduce in support of this is not evidence on the narrow 'empiricist-behaviourist' criteria. But I have already exposed the inconsequentiality of those criteria in a general sense, and I now want to show that they fail to register significant indicators of an extensive experienced resistance to capitalism.

Let me add further, that the 'need for socialism' indicated in this resistance is a 'selfish' need or one based in self-interest. I am not hoping to win assent to my claim by displaying evidence of a widespread sympathy for the deprivations of others. There may well be more concern to correct global exploitation and injustice than is recognized or reflected at the level of party politics, but my case does not depend on proving this. To put it at its simplest, I am saying that the need in question exists in virtue of what people want for themselves rather than in virtue primarily of their distress at the sufferings of others. This means that I am not taking issue with the underlying assumption of the Carr/ Selbourne line of argument that the need for socialism is intimately related to perceived self-interest, but rather with the implied definition of that self-interest as conceived in exclusively 'material-consumerist' terms. Selbourne assumes, for example, that the workers had a 'selfish' interest in socialism so long as a certain material standard of living was denied them. Once capitalism itself had corrected that deficiency, there were no longer reasons for them to regard socialism as in their interest. I want to argue against this that the fact that the exigencies of material need have been met for the working population at large does not in itself imply that it no longer has any 'selfish' motive for contesting a capitalist system.

The implication of all this is that when we are talking about a working-class 'need' for socialism we are talking about the need of a grouping whose members are for the most part (and certainly by Third World standards) not lacking in material ways. It is tempting therefore to describe the need in question as 'psychological', though I hope to show why this is misleading in some ways. But it is certainly a 'need' that has more to do with the conditions of flourishing than with the conditions of sheer survival and minimal health, and in this sense is not 'basic': it is a need which exists (if it exists) in virtue of the kind of questioning about 'true needs' which I suggested earlier had recently come into the political arena. And certainly it is an implication of my argument that if we are to witness a resurgence of explicit support for socialism it will be because needs other than those for material consumption have emerged to prominence and spurred the demand for social change.

What kind of evidence, then, is there for such needs? First, there is what one might call the 'negative' evidence, the evidence of apathy, violence, neurosis and self-destruction. Against the evidence of the ballot box we can pit the evidence of the failure to vote at all; against the evidence of the shopping-mall self-indulgence, the evidence of drug-taking, depression and anxiety; against the evidence of the satisfied commuter-consumers, the evidence of domestic and street violence, child abuse, boredom and stress; against the evidence of racism and chauvinism, the professions of loneliness, anomie, fear and disorientation.

None of these negative cultural expressions, of course, imply the existence of any widespread, explicit interest in socialism. If they can be said to express any collective message, it is rather a retreat from political solutions altogether. But they are the symptoms all the same of a deeply troubled experience even within the midst of the 'freedom' and 'plenty' of capitalist existence. If more people have been murdered on the streets of New York in the last fifteen years than died in the Vietnam war, then it suggests that even in those areas where capitalism appears to hold sway most naturally, it is breeding some very unnatural forms of anguish and distress. Even when due weight is given to the role of poverty (which even in the most prosperous centres of capitalist industry is always the consequence for many of its bountiful progress) as a causative factor in crime, violence and self-destructive action, the signs are such as to indicate that we are here dealing with more general and intangible forms of malaise than could be eradicated simply in the provision of more material prosperity, however fairly distributed.

To these negative signs, moreover, we should now add the evidence of a more direct and explicit unease to be found in the anxiety about environmental pollution and resource attrition: an unease which can be verified even on the narrowly 'empiricist-behaviourist' criteria, since it is openly professed and has already caused a quite dramatic shift of expenditure to 'eco-friendly' products. These public reactions indicate the emergence of a new form of conscience, one might almost say guilt, about the role of private consumption in generating collective problems – to the point where many people are beginning to experience a distinct conflict of needs. All sorts of pleasures and conveniences which were previously unquestioned (for air flight, car travel, instant foods, disposable goods, etc.) have now been compromised by alarms about their ecological side-effects and by the sense that they can be neither generalized to the global community at large nor even indefinitely provided for its more privileged minorities. The potential of this contradictory structure of need for escalating into a major 'consumer crisis' for the free-market economy over the next decade or so should not be underestimated even if at the moment it presents no very serious threat to the capitalist integument.

It is true that as a majority concern, the new 'green' conscience is focused almost exclusively, or at any rate primarily, on the issue of environmental damage and only very secondarily on disparities in wealth and access to resources. For this very reason some socialists distrust the development, seeing in it a potential distraction from the question of capitalist exploitation and global injustice. They dismiss the environmental concern as too parochial – a 'not-in-my-backyardism' which will do rather little to correct the economic causes of ecological destruction and may issue in dubious forms of 'eco-colonialism' or even result in an export of yet more pollution to the already much more gravely afflicted Third World 'periphery'. 'Green consumerism', moreover, is already showing signs of providing capitalism with its new 'boom' market: a development which may do something to clean up the environment but nothing to undermine the very un-eco-friendly market economy itself. It may be said, moreover, that even if we detect the beginnings of an anti-consumerist movement in current Western ecological concern, the situation is very different in Central and Eastern Europe, where the market economy is poised to take off, responding as it does to the long denied popular appetite for Western-style consumption. Knowing as these citizens do that 'socialism' delivered them up to some of the worst pollution in Europe, it is hardly surprising if it is only rather few of them who are able to temper their enthusiasm for capitalist affluence with concern about its long-term social and ecological consequences.[7] On all these grounds, then, it will be argued that the 'unease' to which I have pointed, together with its conflicting needs, can hardly be claimed as evidence of any large-scale resistance to the spread of the market philosophy but should rather be seen as in collusion with it.

It is perfectly true that, a minority of 'eco-socialists' apart, green anxiety is not currently translated into opposition to capitalism and in many cases goes together with a conscious political rejection of socialist solutions to the environmental crisis. But it is not so clear that this can indefinitely remain the case in the future. The pursuit of capitalist expansion is, after all, on a collision course with the demands of ecological sustainability, and it is difficult not to suppose that most of those who are already insisting that these demands should be met will come over time to appreciate the truth of this. The economic alternative to which they could then be expected to give their support will almost certainly not be that of Soviet-style socialism, but it will certainly be socialist in the sense that it must involve a radical break with the capitalist law of value – a restitution, in other words, of political control over the economy.

Any suggestion, therefore, that popular concern for the environment, and the new forms of thinking about consumption it has generated, be analysed as an ineffectual and irrelevant form of 'bourgeois individualism' is, for this reason, to be resisted. It would also be inconsistent of socialists who in the past have been if anything too ready to ascribe needs to people in despite of their explicit political commitments, now to insist that it is only 'bourgeois' needs and attitudes which can be read into what are quite openly avowed anxieties about the capitalist growth economy. It would be less prejudicial to say that for the first time since the birth of the socialist movement we are witnessing the emergence of a mass, trans-class 'humanistic' questioning of the values of capitalism and of its capacities to ensure the flourishing of the human species and its planet. The 'subject' or 'agent' of this embryonic revolution is, it goes without saying, not the traditional agent of the Marxist analysis. But it was Marx himself, nonetheless, who presented the proletariat as the 'universal class' of humanity, and who consistently presented the move beyond the 'mastery' of capitalism as in the interest of human society at large, even if he never imagined that the transition to socialism would be achieved except by means of overt – and probably violent – class struggle. What today, then, we may need to consider, however heretical it may seem, is that while Marx got it right about the general inhumanity and alienation of capitalism, he mislocated the sources and agents of its eventual disruption. Or rather, in that Marx envisaged the system as being more explosively contradictory than it has proved, he was justified in inferring class struggle as the 'motor' of its dissolution: insofar as his analysis led him to believe that capitalism was incapable of correcting the misery of the proletariat, or was at any rate incapable of delivering a sufficiently decent standard of living to the mass of the working population to contain and defuse the demand for revolution, he was understandably inclined to relate the demise of capitalism to the specific needs and struggles of a particular class.

But if we accept that capitalism has survived at least in part because of its ability to gratify those particular needs, then we should also accept that it has met the demand for revolution conceived as a demand of the working class for a significant improvement in its material living standard. If, therefore, capitalism remains vulnerable it is in virtue of its failure to meet other kinds of demand bespeaking other less immediately 'material' needs. Or rather these needs are 'material' enough in many cases (they include, for example, needs for clean air and water, for an unspoilt countryside, for more humanly proportioned cities, for better insulated housing ...); but they are not the 'personalist-consumerist' needs of a particular class, nor are they gratifiable through the acquisition of individual commodities. By the same token, the possession of money – effective demand – does not guarantee their satisfaction, and hence does not discriminate as it does in respect of the range of more personal consumer needs, between a 'bourgeois' class which is in a position to acquire such goods and a working class which is deprived of them.

Of course, I am not for a second wanting to deny that differences of income have a significant impact on the degree of consumer satisfaction even in respect of this range of needs. As everyone knows, the richer you are the better placed you are to remove yourself from filth, noise, congestion and pollution. But having recognized the privileges of wealth in this respect, let us also not understate the democratizing impact of environmental degradation. For just as pollution is no respecter of national boundaries, so in the end it is no respecter of class barriers. Air, soil, water, the ozone filter, these are elemental conditions of life and health which cannot be cleaned up or preserved only for the rich or dirtied and destroyed only for the poor. Or to put it otherwise, the needs for goods such as these cannot (except perhaps in some of the wilder nightmares of science fiction) be gratified privately through the sale of commodities on the market. It is for this reason that we may now need as socialists to entertain the idea of a more trans-class, consensual contestation of a free-market system which in coming up against the absolute limits of ecological resources is also beginning to deny everyone's needs. And it is in this sense that we might permit ourselves to speak of humanity itself beginning to assume the role of humanity's 'universal class'.

Second, it would be mistaken to view this more universal 'need' to transcend the market economy as politically suspect because its motives are primarily self-interested rather than altruistic. Not only would this be inconsistent with the traditional argument of socialism, which as we have seen has always appealed without moral qualms to the self-interest of the working classes in dismantling capitalism: and rightly so, for the politics which speaks only of duties and never of pleasures, only of sacrifice and never of gain, is clearly incoherent and ultimately self-defeating. But in the case in hand, the charge of selfishness is all the more inappropriate given the more consensual nature of the demands in question and the relatively non-divisive routes to their gratification. It is true that if the 'class' of car owners wants less car-ridden cities it will have to give up driving cars in urban areas – and in this sense the need for the one gratification must be at the expense of the other. But in contrast to class-divided needs, the needs in question are the needs of the same subject group, and therefore only resolvable ultimately in that subject's favour: the resolution will involve no sacrifice except of what the subject itself of the need comes to experience as less needed.

Of course, it is also true in a general way that a reduction in the consumption of resource-intensive and polluting commodities (those of a kind which deny satisfaction to less directly material-consumerist needs) will be at the expense of capitalist profits. But again, if an ecologically sustainable society is only achievable through a reduction of that kind then it, too, together with the forms of planning and checks on market enterprise required to realize it, must be seen as in the rational self-interest even of those who stand to lose most in immediate financial terms. It will be said, no doubt, in response to this, that the profit motive is always concerned with short-term gains and therefore never prudential in the sense required. Certainly it would be foolish to envisage the captains of industry arriving at some sudden and collective agreement to curb their eco-damaging activities out of fear for what their profits may now entail for the livelihood of others not yet born. But it is not quite so foolish to envisage a future in which we have democratically elected governments with a mandate to implement an 'anti-growth–reduced-work–sober-consumption' programme and such measures of economic planning as would be needed to preserve the environment and ecological resources. Should this happen, however, it can only be in virtue of the political support of many who are currently beneficiaries and executors of the capitalist system, but who have come to appreciate the long-term wisdom – and some of the shorter term attractions – of a shift to an alternative economic order.

Finally, if we recognize furthermore that it is only, as I suggested earlier, if there is a more extensive questioning of the enjoyments of affluence that there will be any significant reduction of First World demands upon the impoverished sectors of the globe, and hence a realistic chance of inaugerating less exploitative North–South relations, then 'eco-self-interest' in the metropolis should not be seen as at odds with a more equitable and just apportioning of resources but as an important condition of its possibility.

For all these reasons, then, one may argue that so far from being absurd, the question of 'who needs socialism' is actually quite an alive one, but a question which can only be construc- tively addressed by a socialism which has put behind it both the 'rationalism' which construes the need in terms of desires unrealizable in the 'false' society of capitalism, and the 'emp- iricist-behaviourist' assessment of this in narrowly material terms. The former is the move of academic Marxist utopianism and has unwanted elitist and puritanical implications. The latter is the tendency of the official Socialist and Communist Parties and has led to a defence of what must now be seen to be highly reactionary and technocratic conceptions of the 'good life'.

The Marxist 'utopian' picture, which asks us to conceive of the pleasures of socialism as the gratification only of a higher and more evolved individual is anti-hedonist and hence deprived of political realism: it seeks to win the allegiance of individuals to a future whose pleasures cannot, by definition, attract them now since their current wants are the wants of their pre-socialist existence. It is for this reason that its vision has been charged by liberal critics with disrespect for the actual needs of people, or as it is sometimes said, with failure to take account of 'human nature': to take account of what people show themselves to need in the consumption choices they make, of their 'obvious' prefer- ences for the satisfactions of monetary wealth over other enjoy- ments.

Such liberal 'realism' is itself too cavalier of actual needs, but this has unfortunately not prevented a socialist and communist politics from falling in with its narrow-minded conceptions rather than speaking to the needs experienced on other criteria. For there is no doubt that whatever utopias may be dreamed up by the theorists of Marx's communist vision, in practice the parties of the left have allowed existing modes of consumption to go relatively unchallenged and confined their hedonist appeals to promises to provide more of the same more efficiently and more equitably. There has been a deep-seated reluctance to disturb the faith in growth and technology, or to raise the issue of the appropriateness of current satisfactions from the standpoint of the fulfilment they offer, and importantly fail to provide. Nor have we heard much talk in these circles about the compatibility of continuing along present paths of economic expansion with the pursuit of a more egalitarian distribution of resources globally.

Left argument has therefore tended to divide between two different kinds of discourse about human needs, neither of them providing a very adequate basis for thinking about contemporary realities and both of them evasive of the 'politics of true need'. Either there has been an outright rejection in the name of Marxist 'scientific' anti-humanism of the whole idea of a socialist critique of consumption – a rejection which directly fuels the productivist bias of a good deal of socialist rhetoric. Or else we have been referred, in the name of Marxist 'humanism', to rather vacuous formulas contrasting our alienation now with the emergence of socialized human beings possessed of wholly restructured needs in the post-capitalist world of the future.

I have tried to show how both these positions abstract, in their differing ways, from a good deal of existing evidence for dissatisfaction with capitalist methods: evidence I have referred to as indicating a 'need for socialism'. But perhaps a less prejudicial way of putting the point would be to say that it is not so much evidence of a 'need for socialism' which is at issue, but the anachronism of the conception of socialism to which the left has tended to cling. To dwell today in the industrialized nations on the increased material productivity and the expansion of wealth which socialism can provide is to invite people to submit to the traumas of revolution on behalf of goals which capitalism has proved quite efficient in meeting, and which now, moreover, appear increasingly as obstacles to other equally, if not more wanted, goals. It would be a more courageous socialist politics, and one more likely, I believe, to win support in the long term, which dwelt less on the expansion of consumer wealth and more on the pleasures of curbing that expansion. It would have to be quite frank about the sacrifices such a programme might involve in terms of certain familiar and expected forms of consumption. But in doing so it can appeal to a submerged, somewhat confused, but fairly pervasive moral rejection of consumerism and thus draw on the strength of sentiments which establishment parties have thought it suicidal to solicit and have therefore been largely denied expression in electoral politics. But at the same time as it drew on this general sense of malaise with consumer society and allowed it more positive and oppositional forms of expression, this argument for socialism could also appeal to people directly on the basis of their negative evidence of 'need' and in so doing inspire them with the pleasures an alternative society might afford in compensation for a more restrained material consumption.

In all this, the emphasis would not be on the victimization of working people but on their own experience, their own interpretation of that experience, and their own sense of personal agency. Rather than invoking the idea of political representation of needs, such a politics would solicit the agreement of people to the existence of unfulfilled needs directly on the basis of their own feelings and look to them for the articulation of need. Such a politics would not accord expressions of need the kind of incorrigibility that serves as a theoretical justification for never questioning their social conditioning or challenging their authenticity. But it would be fully respectful of subjective accounts of distress and desire, and focus on the possible pleasures to which they were speaking. It would be a socialism both humanist and hedonist.

Notes

1. I refer here to my involvement with END. Many of the signatories and supporters of the END Appeal, to whom END extended solidarity and dialogue during the pre-Gorbachev years of harrassment, are now quite volubly denouncing 'socialism' from their new-found positions of political power. Of course, to refuse the *vocabulary* of socialism in a context in which the word is irredeemably tainted with Communist Party practice is one thing; to reject the concept, in the sense of giving up all aspirations to economic equality, planning and democracy is quite another. Even in those circles where 'socialism' is not to be spoken of, there is talk still of 'social justice', of disarmament, of ecological reparation and responsibility, and of other policy goals associated with the socialist idea in Western Europe. It remains to be seen what the level of commitment will be to such goals, which are clearly difficult to realize in conditions of an untrammelled market economy – precisely the form of

economy which many of the more radical elements who are now at the helm of state, or in reach of political power in Eastern Europe, would seem to wish to introduce.

2. I would stress that I am concerned here only with the aspirations of those in the industrialized nations, and with the rationale for a socialist politics within those societies: elsewhere, conditions, and the needs they elicit, are certainly very different and reflect more nearly the 'material' interest of the workers in overthrowing capitalism which classical Marxism always placed such emphasis upon. However, I would not subscribe to any analysis which viewed First World workers as members of the 'exploiting class' of the poorer communities in the world. To take this line is to collapse absolutely crucial discriminations of class and economic power within both the more affluent and the more impoverished global sectors.

3. E.H. Carr, 'The USSR and the West', *New Left Review* 111, Sept.–Oct. 1978, p. 33.

4. *Ibid.*, p. 34.

5. D. Selbourne, 'Searching for Labour's Soul', *New Statesman* 2 July 1982, p. 8.

6. *Ibid.*

7. For further discussion, see M. Thompson and L. Mackay (eds) *Something in the Wind: Politics after Chernobyl*, London 1988 (especially pieces by M. Thompson and by K. Soper and M.H. Ryle; cf. Soper and Ryle, 'Ecology and the New Detente', in M. Kaldor, G. Holden and R. Falk (eds) *The New Detente*, London 1989, pp. 287–306, and I. Rev, 'The Anti-ecological Nature of Centralisation', in *Ibid.*, pp. 307–22.

3

A Difference of Needs

Seldom can a work on a philosophical topic of so little obvious popular appeal have been met with such wide and prestigious media attention and such publishing success as Michael Ignatieff's *The Needs of Strangers*.[1] The acclaim is understandable: the book is highly polished, readable and original. But it is also for me rather symptomatic of our times in being moved by an urgent political concern for various forms of contemporary malaise while refusing to engage in any comparably serious way with the primary economic and social conditions responsible for their creation. There is a certain facile piety about the book which it is difficult to complain about without sensing the more homespun, old-fashioned piety of one's own demand for 'seriousness', but which I cannot but find disconcerting given the weightiness of the questions which Ignatieff would have us think about and the scant attention they have received in the existing literature on human need.

Ignatieff fixes, for example, on the 'spiritual' dimension of needing, but he eschews standard moral or religious accounts of human purpose, choosing instead to interpret this notion as posing the Aristotelian question of the 'good life': what do we need, he asks, not merely to survive but in order to flourish? In answer, he suggests we need – to begin with – such goods as love, togetherness, respect and consolation in the face of death. Intransigent, however, as our demand may be for these benefits, no political arrangement, argues Ignatieff, can hope to guarantee their provision. Hence the 'tragic gulf' between our needs and what our collective wisdom is able to supply. How far can this be crossed, he asks, linking the question to a number of others of concern to him: are there, in fact, any universal needs? When, if at all, can one speak for the needs of others? Are there needs (such as for respect) which cannot be met except at the cost of other needs (for example, to be treated equally)?

These are difficult investigations both conceptually and politically, and one is continually struck by Ignatieff's readiness to embark upon them. Yet this is not the work to look to for substantial analysis. 'Need', it is true, is a mercurial sort of concept, difficult to fix; and it is probably best approached – as Edward Thompson has suggested – as a 'junction' concept straddling various analytic disciplines.[2] But if *The Needs of Strangers* in some sense testifies to this in the ease with which it moves between the subject matters of philosophy, psychology, political economy and history of ideas, it makes no real attempt to theorize it.

It might be said in defence, of course, that a theory of need was never part of the book's intention. But the trouble is that so much is promised at the outset yet so little achieved in the way of systematic discussion that one comes away feeling strangely duped by the initial claims to organization. Such argument as there is is frequently inconsistent – and in a manner not just irritating to the pedant but upsetting to the averagely logical thinker; previously argued points are often either abandoned altogether or else pressed into quite different service from that of their original design; and one quickly comes to realize that conclusions drawn from the discussion of one chapter will provide no guide to what comes in the next. Given its brevity, in fact, *The Needs of Strangers* is surprisingly forgetful of its content and stated purposes.

It is also curiously uncertain of itself politically, combining rather standard anti-socialist sentiment with a paean to contemporary city life and deep pessimism about ecological and nuclear trends. Marx comes in for much criticism, but it is an oddly anodyne Marx – a wishful thinker of Promethean ambition who aspired, apparently, to the realization of a 'general will'. Others rebuked for their utopianism include Rousseau and Adam Smith, who together with Marx are depicted as a triad of false visionaries committed to very differing but equally implausible forms of social reconciliation. Ignatieff condemns their visions, moreover, as much for their anachronism as for their impracticality. These dreams are no longer ours, he tells us, and must be discarded in favour of a language more truly expressive of what individuals today miss – and find – in their contemporary alienation. Today it is in the medium of separation itself rather than in the cosy but unsubtle comforts of *Gemeinschaft* that Ignatieff would have us seek for a form of belonging adequate to our times. For if the first lesson he draws from his reflections[3] is of the nullity of all humanist and secular conceptions of social harmony,[4] the second is of our will to differ – and thus essential separateness – from each other.

A Solipsistic Perspective

Those who dwell upon the solitude of the individual tend often enough to a solipsism of their own perspective upon the world. One certainly detects something of this in the detached stance of *The Needs of Strangers*, its failure to communicate any sense of identification with the 'strangers' whose calamities it describes. Symptomatic in this regard is Ignatieff's apparent obliviousness to a number of questions that are seriously embarrassing to his project. He does not ask, for example, how far we should allow ourselves to concentrate upon the needs 'to flourish' of a humanity the greater part of which is in the throes of malnutrition and starvation. Nor does he ask whether we deserve to take seriously our 'needs' for respect and human belonging, or whether we can, without sanctimony, lament the failure of modernity to supply a language for them, in a world where only a small minority is prepared actively to resist the policies leading to wide-scale death and deprivation of our species. It is not, I would stress, that such questions necessarily invalidate those he does ask – but the professed concern with the needs of 'strangers' would seem to require, at the very least, some acknowledgement of them.

Detached commiseration is the keynote of the opening pages of the book, where Ignatieff weaves Foucauldian reproaches against the impersonality of the welfare state into autobiographical comment on street life near his home in North London. For the 'strangers' he encounters are not those who 'have' – and 'on whose behalf' social workers, nurses and the like perform their welfare duties – but the respectable poor who rummage for curtains outside his door, 'beating down the barrow man's prices, scrabbling for bargains like crows pecking among the stubble'. 'In my name,' writes Ignatieff, 'the social worker climbs the stairs to their rooms and makes sure they are as warm and as clean as they can be persuaded to be.' But this is actually an extremely prejudicial way of stating the matter, for it is, of course, not *only* in his name but in theirs as well, since even the sick and destitute recipients of welfare benefits are to be numbered among those 'on whose behalf' the State impersonally administers its aid. The bias of Ignatieff's writing invites us to confound the formal and indifferent relations of the welfare state – from whose standpoint we are all equally abstract and anonymous entities – with an 'estrangement' resulting from differences of income.

Again, when he claims that we can only bear the reality of our actual reliance upon each other by complexly mediating it through the 'numberless capillaries of the State', Ignatieff seems to imply that the underlying relations needing to be masked are those of charity. 'They are dependent upon the State,' he writes, 'not upon me and we are both glad of it.' But pensioners are not merely beneficiaries but erstwhile toilers and benefactors themselves; and in speaking of a 'transference of some tiny portion' of his income into the pockets of those less fortunate than himself, Ignatieff overlooks the transference of some rather less than tiny portion of the revenue of their labours that in turn enables the fortunate to remain fortunate.

Ignatieff's regrets over the impersonality of welfare provision stem from his conviction that it is impossible to treat individuals both equally *and* as persons. 'To treat men equally – only as men', he tells us, 'is to deny them the respect due to their humanity.' It is to this 'paradox' that he turns in his second chapter, using as his vehicle for discussion a highly contentious reading of *King Lear* as a 'tragedy of need' centred upon the King's incestuous longing for Cordelia. Let us pass over the not inconsiderable objection that to treat any such obsession as a 'need' ought (surely to goodness) to have been ruled out by Ignatieff's earlier insistence that needs are to be distinguished from 'urgent desires' in coming with entitlement to their satisfaction. For there is worse confusion to come. If we take his claim that individuals fail to 'prize equality' and value only social needs of 'merit, rank or status', while holding him to his definition of needs as entitling, Ignatieff must be credited with the astounding proposition that all such 'social needs' should be treated as having a right to gratification. Indeed, it is precisely this viewpoint which Ignatieff claims to be propounded in Lear's speech 'O reason not the need!'[5] The crux of Lear's demand, he tells us, is that 'what a man needs is his due, and what is his due, he needs'. So just as Lear his retinue, so the Earl his family seat, the magnate his private jet, the developed world its affluence? Perhaps not. Ignatieff, as indicated, can be very slippery. We have, apparently, been speaking only of Shakespeare's time, whereas for us today not only is Lear's idea that dignity reposes on difference 'very unfamiliar', but 'our profoundest political ideas of human dignity are paired with those of equality'. And yet it *was*, surely, we moderns who but ten pages previously were failing to prize equality and whose need for differentiation was to be found exemplified in Lear's history?

Clearly it is Ignatieff's fear that, in according people equal treatment, we eradicate the differences between them.[6] But individuality persists in fact, even in differences in physical needs, and to deal with persons equally is not to suppress it but to abstract from it in respect of certain goods (those, for example, of rank, station or income). To distribute income equally would be to give each individual an entitlement to the same portion of social wealth; it would not abolish all divergencies in their needs or deprive them of the means of individuation. To do away with rank and social hierarchy would be to treat persons as on the same footing in respect of their claims to be respected; it would not remove the grounds for respect – unless it is assumed *a priori* that there are no other reasons than those of income and social status for us to value individuals.

These arguments, of course, have a familiar ring to them. Ever since Marx inveighed against Stirner in *The German Ideology* for confusing individual freedom and fulfilment with the pursuit of utilitarian egoism, Marxists have been quick to point to the actual 'indifference' of market relations to personal differences, and to deny the equivalence between socialism and self-abnegation. It is, nonetheless, true that Marx's diagnosis of the forces in capitalist society which limit individualization is more compelling than his recipe for correcting them. Ignatieff is right that Marx pays too little attention to the political institutions required to realize 'all-round individuality' in a society of equals. (At times he even seems to suppose that he has proved its possibility simply by positing it as the formal antithesis of the 'abstract individualism' of bourgeois society.) It is also true that Marx is too inclined to solve questions of conflict between our needs by wishing them away in a productive plenitude. But it was not wholly chiliastic on his part to assume that human needing might one day transfer its energies from the sphere of commodities to the sphere of self-cultivation; I think, in fact, it will have to. And however sketchy and open to criticism Marx's conception of communism may have been, he was never so pious as to aspire to a 'state of social unity in which each private self would feel its choices ordered and confirmed by the general will'. He would, I feel, have been extremely acerbic about such a notion.[7]

Third World Strangers?

A reluctance to acknowledge the true nature of dependency between rich and poor pervades Ignatieff's treatment of global relations no less than it does his discussion of welfare provision. Certainly, he shows himself quite ready to recognize both the brutality and the interconnectedness of a world order in which 'so innocent an act as the consumption of a cup of tea in London implicates us in the oppression of tea-workers in Bangladesh and Sri Lanka'. Yet his tone is one of pity rather than anger. It is to the pathos of Third World conditions, or to the blight they cast upon the pleasures of our own consumption that he refers us rather than to the urgency of the struggle to overthrow them.

In this context, too, we find that the 'strangers' are not 'ourselves', the privileged inhabitants of the First World who barged in, ransacked what they could, and still claim rights to the oil, timber, uranium, even territory of 'host' countries to whose efforts they largely owe their flourishing; they are, on the contrary, those outside 'our zone of safety' who stand 'hands outstretched, gaunt, speechless or clamouring in the zone of danger'. Ignatieff would insist, no doubt, that to portray these victims of exploitation as 'strangers' is precisely to draw attention to the fact that we have too little in common with them to acknowledge them as our own. Other than our existence as 'bare, forked animals', there is nothing, he claims, to link us to our fellow creatures, and this is too brute a universality to unite us across differences of nation, tribe and class. Once again, an example is made of King Lear – who learns too late that when you are out 'on the heath', with no State, army, community or neighbourhood to enforce your claim to need, then it is power and violence, not obligation, that rule the day.

In the penultimate – and most explicitly political – chapter of the book, this lesson is applied directly to our own times, and the conclusion again reached that difference must predominate over identity: it is only when our 'murderous desire' for national or tribal belonging has been assuaged that any common identity might begin to find expression. Though we may share the threat of ecological and nuclear disaster – a threat which of its nature can only be met through collective action – the claims of tribe, race, class, region and nation seem all too likely, says Ignatieff, to triumph over any common sense of humanity.

One can share Ignatieff's pessimism as to our chances of escaping global conflict and destruction, but one can scarcely subscribe to his reasoning on the matter. In the first place, one must object to the illicit mapping of attributes he claims to discover in individuals onto social groupings: the conflicts of the latter are not directly accountable to individual patterns of need, and to present them as if they were is to abstract from their real – and usually very complex – causes. Secondly, to assimilate such divergent groupings as those of class, nation, tribe, region and the like, in terms of their satisfying a desire 'to belong', is to obscure the highly varied nature of their interests and struggles. More – and far less abstract – categories than those of 'difference' and 'identity' are needed if we are to distinguish between a chauvinist or racist confederacy and the partisanship of those who seek to transcend existing political divisions. The struggle of the black community in South Africa, for example, can hardly be said to be opposed to the cause of humanity as a whole. Nor, indeed, can that of the striking miners in this country, since their strivings to preserve their own community have taken the form of resistance to an economic rationality supposedly in the 'national interest' but in reality profoundly disintegrative in its effects both nationally and globally. An appeal to the voguish notion of 'difference' has here stood in for any serious political analysis of the causes and possible outcomes of existing world tensions.

'On the Heath'

One of the less acceptable devices of the book is the multi-purpose use made of the notion of the 'heath'.[8] Turn by turn, this becomes a metaphor of the 'vast grey space of confinement' of our psychiatric hospitals and prisons; of the concentration camps where millions stripped of their 'retinue' of rings, spectacles, hair, clothing were broken down into 'unaccommodated humanity'; and finally – as we have seen – of the Third World itself. But do we want so readily to assimilate the convicted murderer to the inmate of Auschwitz or of the Soviet prison camp? And if the 'heath' is indeed a realm 'beyond reason, law and duty', then let us admit that much of the barbarism of First/ Third World relations is to be found not 'out upon it' amid the begging bowls and Oxfam queues, but at the heart of the metropolis, in the insatiability of capitalist accumulation, the nonchalance of a consumption that knows no tomorrow and the deliberate decisions of those who rule in the 'zone of safety' to tighten the screws on their 'debtors' in the 'zone of danger'.

Humanity's needs are arguably just as reduced in the free 'Rumbletums' cereal bowl on offer from Kellogg's as they are in the outstretched hand of the Ethiopian peasant. And those on the outside, looking in upon the *gemütlich* tavern scene of First World affluence, are looking in upon a carnival whirling us beyond all reason and control. Where, in any case, shall we place Bhopal, or the forests of Czechoslovakia dying of acid rain, or Greenham Common? Locked as these are into the needs of modernity, it hardly seems right to relegate them to the territory of unaccommodated man; yet the blind victims of Bhopal have paid, like Gloucester, for their loyalty to civilized enterprise. Our trees are dying from an excess of it, our nuclear arsenals stand ready to extinguish it.

In the course of his investigation into what Christian theology (especially Augustine) and Bosch (especially his *Haywain*) have to teach us about the conflict between carnal and spiritual need, Ignatieff reminds us of the prelapsarian paradise of plenitude 'glimpsed at the beginning of Western culture'. A place beyond hunger, thirst, lust, pain, decay and death – this, he claims, is our first image of transcendence, our first acknowledgement of alienation and the central reference point of all subsequent utopias. Yet I think this is not quite true: today we are not sufficiently beckoned by a paradise wherein we shall be freed from lack. If need tended to figure as pain in the iconography of pre-industrial societies, that was due no doubt to the uncertainty of its gratification. Today, at least in the developed world, where goods are guaranteed in plenty, it has come to be experienced as itself a pleasurable herald of future satisfaction. It is not to an Eden of satiety that modern culture aspires, but to an indefinite multiplication of the sources of pleasure – and it is this dynamic conception of needing that was central both to Adam Smith's defence of the market society and to Marx's critique of capitalism.

Ignatieff argues, in fact, that both Smith and Marx offer inappropriate arguments for our times. But he condemns them not on account of their productivist conception but for their failure to appreciate its social implications: Smith sought vainly to sustain a market without the invidious effects of inequality and competition; Marx equally vainly to combine socialist egalitarianism with the indefinite expansion of needs. But it is the appropriateness to our times of the productivist argument itself that must now be called in question. Ignatieff dismisses this idea, too, as utopian. It is, he suggests, as unrealistic to attempt to curb consumption as it is dangerous to abandon the 'freedom' of the market in favour of socialist planning. A 'republic of needs', such as Rousseau imagined, would not only risk economic stagnation but would involve such constraints on personal desire that it would be bound to end in a tyranny of consumption. But the argument from 'economic stagnation' is in no sense a theoretical objection to the Rousseauan conception since it quite arbitrarily presupposes the continuation of a capitalist economy. It is in fact a fetishized notion – though one retailed as much on the left as on the right – that it is only through economic 'growth' that we shall continue to be able 'to afford' such 'scarce' goods as health, education and a measure of free time.

Nor should we accept uncritically the supposition that to place constraints on material consumption is necessarily to curb the scope of self-fulfilment or to curtail individual freedom. Admittedly, if the factitious and emulative drive of *amour propre* is intrinsic to our nature,[9] then it will always seek some outlet. But that it attaches to the differentiation provided by wealth and status is surely a reflection upon the failure of contemporary societies to offer sufficient other channels for individuation. 'A market society,' writes Ignatieff towards the end of his book, 'leaves it up to each of us to find work capable of satisfying our needs for purpose and meaning.' It does indeed. It has also rendered the quest increasingly futile for most people. Here we confront another 'paradox'. We live in a society that offers so little diversification in the way of work and creative activity that consumption comes to figure as the main vehicle of self-expression. Yet the same processes of rationalization responsible for tedious work tend to make conformists of us at the level of consumption. The market may offer a degree of 'freedom of choice', but it scarcely encourages eccentricity or cultural diversity.

There is much to quarrel with Rousseau about, and Ignatieff may be right to accuse both him and Marx of utopianism in the sense that it will prove impossible to mobilize sufficient numbers quickly enough around the idea of a more restrained and egalitarian consumption of material goods. But it is no longer utopian, if it ever was, to present that idea for consideration. It is not 'putting the clock back' to want to secure a just and reasonably enjoyable future; and to be sure now of any future at all, we need to become less scornful of those evoking the old-fashioned notion of plenitude as the feast of sufficiency. Ignatieff tells us that insatiability is indissociable from modernity. But if this is true then it is also the curse of our times. Here I am put in mind of another lesson glimpsed early in our culture: that of Erysichthon, condemned by Demeter, goddess of fertility, to perpetual hunger however much he might eat, for daring to cut down the trees of her sacred grove in order to provide timber for his banqueting hall.

Happiness and Modern Life

There is a further question raised by all this, and it bears directly on Ignatieff's discussions of our 'spiritual' needs: even if it were to prove possible indefinitely to sustain the way of life of the industrialized nations, would this secure our happiness? I suspect not. I suspect, on the contrary, that many who seek to assuage a *'fureur de se distinguer'*[10] in further material consumption end up feeling strangely cheated of their goal. Less boring work, less time spent on it, less pollution, more space, the removal of the threat of war – many, I believe, both West and East, would if given the chance opt for these conditions of self-realization at the cost of an increase in more tangible gratifications.

Nor is it clear that even our purely physical well-being is promoted by increased material consumption. In his final chapter Ignatieff evokes the pleasures of urban *anomie* itself, a certain vertigo of city life, the almost ineffable bonds of shared ephemerality that link the Walkman-wearers passing on the escalator.[11] There is, so he claims, a belongingness that desperately calls for expression even in the nomadic and solipsistic existence to which contemporary capitalism compels the individual. But in acknowledging what one might call an 'anti-camaraderie' among the isolated monads of London and Los Angeles, we should not overlook the rather hellish and utterly unglamorous forms of separation imposed by the twin symbols of urban existence: the skyscraper and the motor-car. Ignatieff puts great, indeed exclusive, emphasis on the need for a *language* of contemporary need; he is certainly right that values that are not spoken for are not in play, and that an essential element of material change is talk about how the future could be. But to stress the importance of language without specifying the agents and mechanism of change, or the more concrete directions it should take, is to annul too much of reality. There is no change merely of language or sensibility that can abolish the gulf dividing the loneliness of the child in the high-rise block from the solitude of Wordsworth's boy who 'Had run abroad in wantonness to sport,/A naked savage, in the thundershower.'[12]

Children cannot forget themselves in play, parents cannot forget them, neighbours cannot be neighbourly, when there is a six-lane throughway to the very door, and juggernauts racing past it. Industrialization is rendering it increasingly impossible to satisfy even such simple, basic needs as these. In the same process, a 'need for nature' in its more metaphysical aspect as a source of spiritual renewal and solace, is first deprived of satisfaction, then progressively blunted, then lost to us altogether.

Ignatieff concludes his account of body and soul by

suggesting, rather against the grain of his earlier insistence upon the tragedy of spiritual longing, that earthly need provides a quite adequate metaphysic of everyday life. *Pace* Bosch, Augustine, Pascal, Erasmus *et alii*, 'the simplest pleasure has the capacity to produce more genuine assurance of the worth of existence than many a tortured chain of reasoning about God's ultimate purposes for humankind'. Ignatieff tells us this not to lament it, but rather to deplore the 'loss of nerve' of those who prematurely announce the death of the spirit or glibly condemn the materialist aspiration of capitalist society. Somehow, amid all this purely carnal self-sufficiency, he manages to imply, we are still seeking the way of the spirit: instead of being astonished at the spiritual emptiness of our times, we should rather be amazed that individuals manage to find sufficient purpose and meaning.

This might strike some as tortuous reasoning (if not the verbal holy water whereby the agnostic sanctifies the heartburn of the expense-account dinner!). But if we follow through the argument, it comes to rest in fact not on the claim that the goods of the flesh are all that the spirit needs (which, if true, would seem to make it gratuitous to refer to them as 'spiritual'), but on the more interesting suggestion that what has for long distinguished us from the 'primitive' is the belief that we can establish the meaningfulness of our private existence in the absence of any collective cosmology or teleology. The search for spiritual fulfilment has for some time been left to the individual – who seeks it 'in the logic of childhood, dreams and desires'. Psychoanalysis is the ultimate guide in this quest; those, like Adam Smith and David Hume, who tried to imagine a society 'without confessional unity or shared belief', its original pioneers.

Whatever construction we may want to put upon the distinction between 'carnal' and 'spiritual' need (and· *are* the two in fact separable?), we may still agree that Ignatieff is right to associate the period of the Enlightenment with a shift away from pregiven assumptions about the 'meaning of life' towards the idea of the individual as responsible for providing it. He is right, too, of course that many today live without religion and in that sense without any 'shared cosmology'. But many also share their secular ideologies, and commit themselves to common purposes – sometimes, indeed, with 'murderous desire'! Nor should we assume that the disbeliever lives the more autonomous life. Ignatieff makes much of Boswell's horror at the serenely atheist manner of Hume's death; and he suggests that it is Boswell, the man of religion beset by existential doubts, rather than the autarkic and worldly Hume who best understood 'the loneliness of the modern self in its hour of need'. But to die without God is not necessarily to be cast back exclusively on one's own resources; it may be to die in desperate reliance upon those supplied by others.

On the other hand, what is perhaps most painful is not that we die alone but that we die in the midst of those we love, and that those we love die in our midst. It is the intensity of our emotional bonds with others that makes death terrible, as much as the fact that we go through it alone. Nor should we underestimate the importance of the continuity that others – strangers included – provide in reconciling us with our own rupture with life. The most awful death in many ways is the one that we do not go through alone. Such would be the death within the total annihilation of nuclear war – a death that would disarm us of all the usual means by which we come to terms with our individual mortality precisely because it would be coincident with the destruction of everything that would otherwise outlive us.

Perhaps this is one of the hitherto 'unimaginable' deaths at which Ignatieff hints? He does not say. He certainly hopes to avoid it. Hence the *deus ex machina* of an argument he introduces in the closing pages, where suddenly he flies in the face of his earlier insistence upon the futility and abstraction of any humanist doctrine of 'universal needs or rights', in order to address us as the 'first generation to have seen our planet under the gaze of eternity ... revolving mist-wrapped in the cobalt darkness of space', and speculates upon the emergence within us of feelings of 'real identification, not with this country or that, but with the earth itself'. But then he also tells us, in less lyrical vein, that 'the heath must be ploughed up, put under the sovereignty of a nation armed and capable of protecting its people'. Nor can one forget the reference to 'loss of nerve' at the march of progress, suggestive as this might be that we should not quail at where our nuclear age may take us. Ignatieff is certainly not an apologist for the Cold War, so one can only regret the similarity of this imagery to that used, across the Channel, by André Glucksmann, to taunt faint-hearted members of the European peace movements who cannot stare unblinkingly into the abyss of total human destruction.[13]

Notes

1. *The Needs of Strangers*, London 1984. The book has recently been reissued by Penguin. Ignatieff is also the author of *A Just Measure of Pain: the Penitentiary in the Industrial Revolution, 1750–1850*, London 1979, and (with Istvan Hont) of *Wealth and Virtue: the Shaping of Political Economy in the Scottish Enlightenment*, Cambridge 1983.

2. E.P. Thompson, *The Poverty of Theory and Other Essays*, London 1978, p. 355; cf. p. 302.

3. Actually, reflections on the reflections of a number of other writers – all of them male – on human needs. They include Shakespeare (*King Lear* – especially the speech beginning 'O reason not the need'), Augustine, Hieronymous Bosch, Erasmus, Pascal, Hume, Boswell, Adam Smith and Rousseau.

4. Thus he writes that 'any purely secular morality is an ethics without ultimate forgiveness' (p. 99), and argues, counter to liberal humanism, that no protection can be afforded by abstract doctrines of universal human needs and rights (pp. 52–3).

5. Again, one can dispute the interpretation. I myself construed Lear's speech rather differently in *On Human Needs*, Brighton 1981, pp. 17f., taking it to be an acknowledgement of the difficulty of justifying any claim to need. What counts as a 'true' need, asks Lear, and why? Cf. E.P. Thompson, *ibid.*, p. 338, who acclaims in King Lear a 'great proto-Marxist' critic of the utilitarian concept of 'need'.

6. Cf. Marx in the *Critique of the Gotha Programme*, where the concern is rather that equal treatment would prove unfair in privileging natural endowment: 'This *equal* right is an unequal right for unequal labour. It recognizes no class differences, because everyone is only a worker like everyone else; but it tacitly recognizes unequal individual endowment and thus productive capacity as natural privileges. *It is, therefore, a right of inequality, in its content, like every right*' (*Selected Works*, London 1968, p. 320).

7. It is no doubt true that Marxists have paid too little attention to these transhistoric determinations in their zeal to establish the historically developed nature of needs. The work of the Italian Marxist Sebastiano Timpanaro has, however, gone some way to rectify this neglect (see, for example, his work *On Materialism*, London 1975). See also Norman Geras, *Marx and Human Nature – Refutation of a Legend*, London 1983; in arguing that Marx possessed a concept of human nature, Geras provides theoretical grounds for defending Marx against the kind of Promethean aspirations attributed to him by Ignatieff.

8. The underlying problem with the image of the 'heath' is that it implies an absence of social relations between those upon it and the 'civilized' world – interestingly enough precisely the message drawn by Jeremy Waldron, who writes in the course of a review of *The Needs of Strangers* (*Times Literary Supplement* 21 December 1984): 'The experience of the Ethiopian famine has shown that people do respond, however half-heartedly and hypocritically, to an image of the pressing necessity of others on the heath with whom they have no social relations at all.'

9. I myself have argued that it is – see *On Human Needs*, pp. 155–63.

10. '*O fureur de se distinguer*' – writes Rousseau in his *Discourse of Inequality* – '*que ne pouvez-vous point!*'

11. This is my own rather than Ignatieff's imagery, but I think it conveys something of his sense. For illustration of the 'language of the joy of modern life', he refers us to the painting of Edward Hopper and to the writing of Joyce, Musil, Bellow and Kundera – all of whom, it is true, do have the virtue of taking us beyond easy laments about alienation. Yet what they have celebrated about city life may already now be passing or in decline. Ignatieff's discussion owes a good deal, as he acknowledges, to Marshall Berman's *All That Is Solid Melts Into Air: The Experience of Modernity*, London 1983. Cf. the exchange between Perry Anderson and Berman in *New Left Review* 144, March–April 1984.

12. Wordsworth, *Prelude*, 290f.

13. André Glucksmann, *La Force du vertige*, Paris 1983.

PART TWO

Morals, Politics and
the Subject

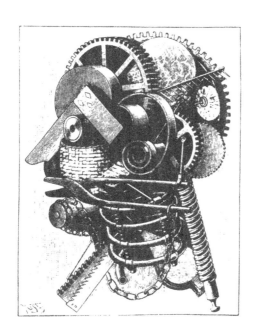

4

The Socialist Humanism of E.P. Thompson

The term 'socialist humanism' has an ambiguous history, as Edward Thompson himself has said.[1] Many and various are the parties that have laid claim to it.[2] But for Thompson it has throughout meant one thing only – the movement of communist libertarian opposition to Stalinism which first took root in Europe in the late 1950s.

The core themes of the 'socialist humanism' defended by Thompson at that time were the rejection of the antithetical 'philistinisms' of social democracy and Stalinist communism; the insistence that the sole route to genuine socialist emancipation lay on a course between the two; and the affirmation of our moral autonomy and powers of historical agency. Together these have provided the unbroken thematic thread of all Thompson's writings. The early study of William Morris and the critique of Stalinism in the 1950s, the wrestlings with labour movement reformism in the 1960s, the polemic against Althusser and his assaults upon the erosion of civil liberties and the manufacture of consensus in the late 1970s, and – perhaps most pressingly of all – the denunciation of Cold War stasis and the 'exterminist' logic of the arms race in the 1980s, have been part of a singular project: to rescue the 'moral imagination' from 'philistinism' (the disposition to accept and defend any existing reality as immutable necessity), and thus to check the mindless drift towards the obliteration of all human culture.

In charting Thompson's 'socialist humanism' we are therefore charting both a 'moment' in his political thinking, (one which also belonged to a larger 'moment' of European history), and the conceptual framework within which that thinking has always been cast. But while this framework has proved a constant, Thompson has not shown himself disposed to cling to the early formulae of his 'socialist humanism' as if their ritualistic repetition could ward off all diabolisms, whether of left or right. On the contrary, they have been continually modified and reformulated as new circumstances have come into being, requiring different emphases, struggles and polemic. Sulk in his tent as he has at times, Thompson has also always emerged again to renew the dialogue, to hassle again with history, and to put veteran arguments to work for new campaigns. In this sense, his socialist humanism has a history of development within its relative fixity of outlook.

Out of Stalinism

Thompson has always maintained that the crucial inaugural date for socialist humanism was 1956. In reaction to the revelations made at the Twentieth Congress of the CPSU and the Soviet invasion of Hungary, the term, he tells us:

> arose simultaneously in a hundred places, and on ten thousand lips. It was voiced by poets in Poland, Russia, Hungary, Czechoslovakia; by factory delegates in Budapest; by Communist militants at the eighth plenum of the Polish Party; by a Communist premier (Imre Nagy), who was murdered for his pains. It was on the lips of women and men coming out of gaol and of the relatives and friends of those who never came out.[3]

In actual fact, the movement of anti-Stalinist rebellion had arisen somewhat earlier if we count as its first manifestation the uprising in East Germany which took place almost immediately upon Stalin's death in 1953 – an uprising which was crushed, we might add, in a way premonitory of later events in Hungary.[4] But

Thompson is certainly right to suggest that what happened in 1956 proved more catalytic for the emergence of a distinctive 'socialist humanist' formation. In Britain the key factors in its making were the massive resignation from the Communist Party (one third of its membership) occasioned by the suppression of the Hungarian revolt, and the subsequent regrouping of former communist dissidents and others into the 'New Left'. The twin journals of this new movement – *The New Reasoner*, coedited by Thompson and the main organ of his political writings in the late 1950s, and the more universities-oriented and less politically heavyweight *Universities and Left Review*[5] – were both explicitly committed to the promotion of 'socialist humanism'.

Disillusionment with Soviet communism was not, it should be said, the sole motive behind these developments – which were inspired also by fears of a wholesale rejection of socialist argument. In a cautionary anecdote related in the first issue of the *The New Reasoner*, we are told of the *Daily Worker* subscriber who in the wake of the Hungarian massacre opened the door to her usual deliverer of the paper with stony refusal rather than her accustomed welcome. No explanation was forthcoming until finally a voice from within shouted 'go away – we don't trust you'. By defending the 'socialist humanist' impulse of the Hungarian rebellion, the New Left hoped also thereby to retain a foot in the door of the former *Daily Worker* reader. For if left to itself, demoralization might well lead to a slamming of doors on any form of socialism. Abhorrence at what 'Marxism' had come to encompass, anxiety lest disenchantment lead to its complete abandonment: these were the impulses of the New Left in general and of Thompson's argument in particular.

In line with this, the New Left conceived its task in actively political terms: the aim was to build a nationwide campaigning base for socialist renewal (hence the importance attached to the formation of the network of New Left clubs). Its critique of Stalinism and the British CP was also immediately political. As Thompson himself describes it, it was concerned with the structure and organization of the Party, the control of the membership by the full-time apparatus, the Moscow orientation (and training) of that apparatus, and the self-perpetuating modes of control ('democratic centralism', the 'panel' system, the outlawing of 'factions', etc.).[6] The larger themes of the 'return to man', cultural creativity, a respect for individuality, and so on, that were so central to 'socialist humanism' in continental Europe were by no means absent; but the more concrete conception of its political mission does seem to mark out the British New Left.

Rather in contrast to this emphasis, the socialist humanist revolt on the continent was much more directly associated with a flowering of Marxist philosophy based on a reappraisal of Marx's debt to Hegel and an awakened interest in his early texts. New readings of Hegel were of critical importance in this process,[7] as was the influence of the 'humanist-Hegelian' Marxism first developed in the interwar years by Gramsci, Korsch and, above all, Lukács. As a philosophical critique, in fact, we can think of socialist humanism as comprising rather more than Thompson mentions – including for instance, the existentialist Marxism of Sartre, Merleau-Ponty and de Beauvoir, a good part of 'Frankfurt School' argument, the *Praxis* group in Yugoslavia, the Christian-ized Marxism of writers such as Calvez, Bigo and Rubel, as well as the somewhat disparate arguments to be found in Erich Fromm's large volume of socialist humanist writings.[8]

The broader the church, however, the more rudimentary tends to be the creed uniting the communicants. This is certainly true of socialist humanism in this larger definition. For Marxist humanists have occupied a range of epistemological positions and diverged widely on such crucial issues as the nature of the dialectic or interpretation of the theory of alienation. On the other hand, where they have found agreement is in their critique of positivistic metaphysics and their rejection of deterministic interpretations of historical materialism. Hence the stress placed on *praxis* as purposeful human action, and its role in the creation of social processes and institutions.

Though the general claim of these humanists was that they were doing no more than reassert the authentic Marxist dialectic of human beings as both 'made' by historical circumstances and active in their making, it was inevitable – given the mechanistic orthodoxy to which they were reacting – that they placed the stress on the active and creative component. At times this brought them close to a denial of economic or ideological determination altogether, a denial associated in the existentialist argument with a tendency to recast relations of production as interpersonal relations, and thus to put in question the whole idea of 'unwilled' social forces possessed of their own dynamic and exigency. At the same time, and incompatibly in some ways, there was an emphasis on *alienation*, a process associated with the failure of individuals to perceive the social source of the value of commodities (fetishism) or to understand the true nature of social relations and institutions.

The tension between these emphases is reflected in a certain polarization of Marxist humanist argument. On the one hand, a more Hegelian–Lukácsian school of thinking points to the importance of generalized processes of reification and alienation as the 'theft' of our humanity, but encounters difficulties in consequence when it comes to specifying the means of escape from these. (Thus Lukács was led to posit a hyperorganic collectivity – the proletariat in its 'ascribed' consciousness – as the universal 'subject' of history, and to view its project in directly Hegelian terms as the realization of an immanent historical reason.) The existentialist tendency, on the other hand, has emphasized the irreducibility of conscious, or 'lived' experience, and insisted upon the intelligibility of history as aggregated human *praxes*. This is an argument which rightly regards history as made by real men and women rather than by hypostatizations, but has difficulties in reconciling these themes with the recognition by historical materialism of 'alien' or 'unwilled' social forces possessed of their own intrinsic order.

Turning back to Thompson, where upon this spectrum should we place his socialist humanist argument? Nearer to the existentialistic pole than to the Hegelian–Lukácsian in the stress it places on conscious experience, it should nonetheless be distinguished from both, not only on account of its sharper political focus and moral passion, but also by what might be described – though not without ambiguity – as its resistance to 'philosophical anthropology'. The first point is the easier to state: Thompson, as most would agree, has brought an urgency and clarity to the socialist humanist argument missing from more abstract, and often rather pious, effusions penned in its name. As Thompson himself wrote in 'Outside the Whale', at a certain point in the postwar declension towards Natopolitan quietism the 'blaring moral loudspeakers ("progress", "humanism", "history" and the rest) were simply switched off with a tired gesture'.[9] Among the many who turned them on again in 1957, Thompson was one of the relatively few who managed to make them sound both interesting and morally compelling.[10] These features of his writing have their bearing on the other and more complicated factor differentiating his position from that of his European counterparts. As a historian by training and inclination, rather than a philosopher, his encounter with Marxism was mediated not primarily through Hegel, Husserl and Heidegger, but through the very English figure of William Morris: as we shall see, this has had a definite impact on the tenor of his humanism. At the same time – and herein lies the ambiguity of suggesting any anti-philosophical bent – his analysis of agency and of the nature of historical process is without doubt 'philosophical', and invites direct comparison with the argument of continental theorists, and most notably Sartre.

In what was to prove a seminal article in the first issue of *The New Reasoner*,[11] Thompson wrote of 'socialist humanism':

> it is *humanist* because it places once again real men and women at the centre of socialist theory and aspiration, instead of the resounding abstractions – the Party, Marxism–Leninism–Stalinism, the Two Camps, the Vanguard of the Working-Class – so dear to Stalinism. It is *socialist* because it reaffirms the revolutionary perspectives of Communism, faith in the revolutionary potentialities not only of the Human Race or of the Dictatorship of the Proletariat but of real men and women.

And he proceeded to defend it as the truth of Marxism which Stalinist 'ideology' had systematically distorted and betrayed.[12]

The rejection of the Trotskyist critique of Stalinism implicit in this position was made explicit in Thompson's curt and dismissive references to Trotsky ('the anti-Pope to the Stalinist Pope').[13] What was also implied – and again made explicit in the 'Epistle' – was the exoneration of Marxism of any blame for the Stalinist deformation.[14] However, this position was swiftly revised in the light of Charles Taylor's insistence that there were roots for the distortion in Marx's conception of the proletariat as the 'class that suppresses all classes'.[15] Expressing a good measure of agreement with Taylor, Thompson wrote in reply that he now saw more clearly that 'if Stalinism is a mutation of Marx's ideas, the very fact that they are capable of undergoing such mutation while remaining in a direct line of relationship indicates an original weakness which goes beyond mere ambiguity'.[16] The weakness in question here was the implicit determinism of the 'base–superstructure' model – its invitation to view economic activity as a separate 'level' causing a certain set of automatic effects at another 'level' ('superstructure'). Thompson rejected this suggestion on two main grounds. First, he argued that it misrepresents the essential imbrication of economic, legal, political and cultural relations in any actual society;[17] second, it denies human agency, treating consciousness and affectivity as the unmediated reflex of – seemingly quite autonomous – social structures. However, what has not been made clear in Thompson's discussion of this 'determinism' is how far he regarded the base–superstructure metaphor as itself to blame for it, as opposed to those economic functionalists from Stalin through to Althusser who interpret it substantively. In this sense, the question of classical Marxism's responsibility for its Stalinist 'ideology' has been given no unambiguous answer in his work.

However, it can be said that Thompson's criticism of Marx has become sharper over time. Thus *The New Reasoner* articles read into Marx's commentary on the relations between 'being' and 'consciousness' an account of the mediating role of experience which in reality was almost entirely his own;[18] but in *The Poverty of Theory* he finds Marx himself guilty of encouraging Althusserian rationalism by his silence on the crucial category of experience. The same goes for the Althusserian reduction of the moral and affective component of experience to the status of ideology: for that, if for little else in the 'orrery', says Thompson, there is indeed a valid licence on offer from Marx.[19]

But these are essentially changes of emphasis, and in the end what Thompson has wanted to maintain is the fertile because ambiguous nature of the pronouncements of Marx and Engels on the relations between 'being' and 'consciousness'. These pronouncements were 'socialist' in their recognition of the socially conditioned nature of 'consciousness' and 'humanist' in their refusal to treat the latter as wholly predetermined. In defending this account of the relations of structure and agency Thompson places himself firmly within the camp of Marx's humanist interpreters, all of whom regard a dialectical approach of this kind to be indispensable to any coherent conception of socialism. As they have justly argued, the treatment of individuals as passive 'supports' or 'effects' of social relations must render any socialist project both impossible and pointless. The anti-humanists, in short, are trapped in a dilemma. Either we are no more than 'supports' or 'effects', in which case no political theory, their own included, can have any bearing on what we do; or else we are the kind of creatures for whom anti-humanist argument could have political relevance, but in that case we are not really the 'supports' or 'effects' figuring in the theory.

Yet the humanist alternative *is* an ambiguous dialectic with its own difficulties. There is the theoretical problem of how an ambiguity of this kind can be registered other than through a fluctuation of stress, falling now on the conditioned, now on the creative dimensions of experience. There is also the related difficulty of juxtaposing 'humanism' and 'socialism' as if these were two clearly complementary impulses of a single *political* strategy.

To take the second point first. No sooner had Thompson formulated the argument for 'socialist humanism' than the charge of idealism – and thus evasion – was laid against it from both sides of the political fence. The more liberal critics suggested that 'socialist humanism' was all very fine as an aspiration, but Stalinism had made clear the impossibility of any such route to communism, and therefore commitment to the latter had to be rethought anew. The more 'Stalinist' argument was that it was simply unrealistic to suppose that a movement committed to the interests of a particular class could hope to proceed to its goals without offending against a 'humanist' regard for all individuals 'as such'. In short, a class-based morality was incompatible with any humanist ethic, and the linking of the two purely verbal: 'socialist humanism' offered no guide at all on the crucial issue of the means that communists could justifiably use in pursuit of their ends. As one of the 'liberal' critics, Charles Taylor, put it:

> the ideal conjuncture of events, whereby humanity as a whole will accept spontaneously the end of class society is not likely ever to be realised. The question remains: What value has a man, even unregenerate and obstinately resisting the most elementary social justice? This question is a crucial one for humanism.[20]

Thompson's general line of reply to all this (though never as fully articulated as it might have been) was that so abstract and stark a posing of the 'question' was itself an evasion of the socialist humanist response – which was precisely to the effect that no general guidance on the application of its principles could be given. The particular constraints of each situation had always to be taken into account in assessing the justice or morality of acts. As Thompson put it, humanist attitudes should find expression 'whenever and to the degree that contingencies allow'. As he later admitted, it was a clumsy formulation but an unavoidable one: 'what else can one say? That they must always find expression irrespective of contingencies?'[21]

The implication here was that the charge of 'contradiction' laid against the socialist humanist argument was inappropriate, since the appeal was not to a seamless theoretical unity but to a certain sensibility or instinct: we know very well what we are talking about when we call for a more democratic and humanist socialism, and we also have a pretty good idea what sort of practices conform to it; but to attempt any rigid specification of those principles and practices would be to betray the very spirit of flexibility which they oppose to communist dogma.

That said, it cannot be denied that a 'socialist' recognition of the class-conditioned nature of experience and affectivity is in uneasy tension with Thompson's 'humanist' appeals to a more universal and apparently 'natural' moral sense. The problem can be formulated thus: if this morality is genuinely universal (i.e. to be human is to be possessed of it) then how do we explain evil except as a form of corruption accountable to social conditioning? But to explain it in that way would appear to deny the essential element of moral autonomy central to the 'humanist' case. If, on the other hand, we take the view that individuals are morally autonomous, and thus good or bad 'in themselves', it is not clear why 'humanists' should be so concerned to defend the principles of the moral equality of persons. Nor can we allow, it would seem, for the possibility of moral error. There are passages of Thompson's writing in the 1950s which bring this problem very forcefully to mind: arguing against Arnold Kettle, John Gollan and their ilk, he wrote that 'wrong theories do not frame up, slander and kill old comrades, but wrong men, with wrong attitudes to their fellow-men'.[22] And he went on to insist that no amount of speculation upon intention (Stalin, Rakosi, Beria, etc. 'believed' they were defending the interests of the working class ...) could mitigate the horror of trials such as that of Kostov (the Bulgarian Party Secretary shot in 1949):

> Those moral values which the people have created in their history, which the writers have encompassed in their poems and plays, come into judgement on the proceedings. As we watch the counsel for the defence spin out his hypocrisies the gorge rises, and those archetypes of treachery, in literature and popular myth, from Judas to Iago, pass before our eyes. The fourteenth-century ballad singer would have known this thing was wrong. The student of Shakespeare knows it is wrong. The Bulgarian peasant, who recalls that Kostov and Chervenkov had eaten together the bread and salt of comradeship, knows it is wrong. Only the 'Marxist–Leninist–Stalinist' thinks it was – a mistake.[23]

I am inclined to agree. But it should also be remembered that it was one of Stalinism's more malevolent moves to dismiss any plea of 'intention' or 'belief' when it suited *its* purposes: hence its identification of moral turpitude with what was objectively 'counter-revolutionary'. Thus the case of Bukharin: persuaded that speculation on his intentions could not 'excuse' the outcome of his acts, he came to 'confess' to charges that were obviously false.[24] In other words, the construction that people put upon their acts is surely of relevance to our assessment of them. Inversely, it must be allowed that wrong acts can be committed by those convinced of their rightness and acting with the best intention. An inherent moral sense of the kind invoked here by Thompson may be the only guide in the end as to what is right and wrong. However, it can never be a guarantee against our acting badly; at least not if we accept, as Thompson appears to do, that the consequences of our acts, and not merely our beliefs about them, have to enter into consideration of their ethical status.

But if we acknowledge that individuals can make moral 'mistakes' of this kind, then moral consciousness must be open in some sense to forces it cannot grasp and to which its response is 'irrational'. In fact, some recognition of this was implicit in Thompson's claims regarding the 'ideological' status of Stalinism. For to treat it as an 'ideology' was to imply that it was not so much a deformed moral character but the grip of false ideas that drove the Stalinists to their crimes. Thompson was critical of the view (attributed to the Trotskyists) that Stalinism was a 'hypocrisy' rather than an 'ideology' on the grounds that this underestimated its strength, inner logic and consistency, and so reduced it to a matter of 'personality'.[25] But in the passage cited above it is significant that he spoke of 'hypocrisies': the logic of his argument implies that a much more central role should be accorded the moral 'personality'.[26]

This may be compared with the argument of *The Poverty of Theory*, where Thompson is well aware of the potential conflict between his insistence upon the irreducibility of 'lived experience'[27] and the acceptance of certain Marxist categories (e.g.

'alienation', 'fetishism', 'ideology') by many Marxist humanists on the continent. For instance, he writes:

> It is not true that Marx passed over in innocence the need to provide his theory with some 'genetics'. He attempted such a provision, first, in his writings on alienation, commodity fetishism and reification; and, second, in his notion of man, in his history, continuously making over his own nature ... Of the first set of concepts I wish only to say this: they propose to supply a 'genetics' – to explain how history is determined in ways which conflict with the conscious intentions of subjects – in terms of mystified *rationality*. Men imprison themselves within structures of their own creation because they are *self-mystified*. While historians may find these notions suggestive in certain areas (as in the study of ideologies), they would argue – I certainly will argue – that, in more general application, they are the product of an overly-rational mind; they offer an explanation in terms of mystified rationality for *non*-rational or *ir*rational behaviour and belief, whose sources may not be educed from reason. As to the second set of concepts (man making over his own nature), while they are important and point the right way, they remain so undeveloped that, in effect, they do little more than restate the prior question in new terms: we are still left to *find out* 'How'.[28]

The possibility of systematic misunderstanding of social relations along lines argued for by Marx is here more or less ruled out. Experience is itself a form of truth, and if we 'handle' it irrationally, that is not due to misconceptions about its causes or consequences but to our own intrinsic (affective, moral) being. Women and men, that is to say, are not only, or even primarily, ignorant or ideologically determined, but good or evil; they do not simply act in error, they act well or badly. Here again, then, as in the 1950s articles, the individual's 'moral character' is presented as a kind of baseline grounding the assertion of human agency which lies at the heart of the socialist humanist critique of Stalinism.

Part of the reason, one supposes, for Thompson's resistance to the idea of 'self-mystification' is that it appears to rely on the idea that consciousness can be moulded by forces that it cannot know. This was very much Sartre's objection to the Freudian unconscious, and it is curious that Thompson appears so little inclined to recognize any intellectual kinship here. For Sartre is not of the party of the anti-humanists, as Thompson is wont to imply,[29] but is at one with Thompson in rejecting the idea of 'unconscious' forces which are excluded from experience while determining its content. For Sartre 'lived experience' is all there is; consciousness is translucent and the individual capable in principle of total self-understanding. Yet 'lived experience' is also a 'mystery in broad daylight'[30] since it has no means to express what it 'sees'. It *comprehends* totally, but lacks the conceptual means and reflexivity to articulate that comprehension in the form of *knowledge* or *intellection*. Through this concept of 'lived experience' and the associated epistemological distinction between 'comprehension' (an understanding of human action in terms of the intention of its agents) and 'intellection' (an under-standing of human action without necessary reference to inten-tion), Sartre has attempted to account for the opacity of experience to itself in a manner that avoids recourse to the notion of ulterior and radically unknowable forces controlling it. In other words, he has attempted to preserve the possibility of human emancipation based on rational understanding. Indeed Sartre suggested that what was wrong with the existentialism of *Being and Nothingness* was that it could not account *rationally* for those processes 'which are "below" consciousness and which are also rational, but lived as irrational'. The concept of 'lived experience' represents, by contrast:

> an effort to preserve that presence to itself which seems to me indispensable for the existence of any psychic fact, while at the same time this presence is so opaque and blind before itself, that it is also an absence from itself. Lived experience is always simultaneously present to itself and absent from itself.[31]

How far Thompson would want to go along with this more complex conception of 'lived experience' is not clear, given his warnings against seeking explanations of 'irrational' behaviour. On the other hand, it is surely something much more like the Sartrean conceptual framework that is needed to do justice to that favourite of Thompson's quotes from Morris – that men and women are the 'ever-baffled and ever-resurgent agents of an unmastered history'. Indeed, one might almost claim that the *Critique of Dialectical Reason* is an extended gloss on that remark; in other words, that it is a sustained attempt to theorize (through the concepts of 'lived experience', 'the group', 'seriality', 'the practico-inert', 'alienation', 'alterity', etc.) the Vico–Marx–Engels–Morris–Thompson conception of history as a humanly created but largely unauthored (in the sense of unintended) process.

What is more, Sartre insisted that this is a process in which action is both conditioned and free (by which he means that it is able to transcend or 'totalize' existing experience). 'Subjectivity', as he wrote, 'is neither everything nor nothing; it represents a moment in the objective process (that in which externality is interiorized), and the moment is perpetually eliminated only to be reborn'.[32] Out of the dead ashes of the 'practico-inert', the pheonix of human freedom continually rearises – or so Sartre would have us believe. Is this so very different from Thompson's faith in the ever possible resurrection of the 'moral imagination' from the deadening processes of bureaucratization, State encroachment, the arms race and media manipulation?

Out of neo-Stalinism

It was, of course, precisely because he felt a need – two decades on from 1956 – to reaffirm this 'moral imagination' and to rescue it from the deadening effects of Althusser's structuralist Marxism, that Thompson wrote *The Poverty of Theory*. For younger readers of the book are not, he tells us, the 'post-Stalinist' generation they fondly imagine themselves to be. On the contrary, Stalinism as *theory* and attitude still 'weighs like an alp' on the brain of the living; the agenda of 1956 is still to be completed; the 'post-Stalinist' generation yet to be born.[33] Thompson proceeds to call for 'relentless war' upon the Althusserians, for they are the latest representatives of that current of Marxism against whose inhumanity and irrationalism the agenda of 1956 was originally drawn up. The book ends, in effect, with a call to all Marxist intellectuals to come out of their academic ivory tower to renew, in 1978, the programme of the (old) New Left sketched in the original 'Epistle' of 1957.[34]

In *The Poverty of Theory* all the main themes of the socialist humanist polemic against Stalinism are reenacted but in the form of an attack upon its theoretical legitimation rather than directly upon its practice. As might be expected, the argument converges in an assault on Althusser's anti-humanist denial of agency. But directly associated with that, and equally repugnant to Thompson, is the downgrading of ethical protest to the status of ideology. This is indeed an important move to contest, for it is by means of it that Althusser is able to assimilate the humanist defence of morality to 'moralism'. That is, Althusser invites us to suppose that those who offer moral protests are assuming that moral argument is sufficient to bring about political transformation. And by highly selective quotation of a passage from *The German Ideology* he would persuade us that this was Marx's own position.[35] My own view is that, when read in full, the passage in question tends otherwise: the burden of Marx's attack was not upon the making of value judgements as such but upon the idealism of supposing that it is *values themselves* which determine the degree to which they are realized in actuality. Whether or not I am right to impute this distinction to Marx, it is an important one for humanists to defend.[36]

The distinction is also very relevant to the reproaches levelled by Perry Anderson against socialist humanism. Adopting a somewhat bibliocentric viewpoint, he has argued that no special significance attaches to 1956 since the protest movement it generated issued in no substantial studies on the USSR in the Khrushchev years, an analytical dearth which he attributes to the 'merely moral' nature of the socialist humanist critique.[37] The fault of Thompson and of the old New Left in general was a substitution of 'moralism' for historical materialism. This, suggests Anderson, is the central point from which radiate all the oppositions of outlook dividing the 'old' New Left from the grouping, led by himself, which took over the editorial direction of *New Left Review* in 1962. As one reads through Anderson's punctilious charting of their disagreements on historiography, Marxism, philosophy, internationalism and political strategy, a series of antinomies and equations impresses itself upon one: moralism versus historical materialism equals empiricism versus rationalism equals humanism versus anti-humanism equals reform versus revolution equals the parliamentary road versus (probably violent) class struggle equals the Labour Party versus international communism. In short, the issue of 'moralism' appears to carry a heavy load.

But whatever the strains and stresses of the socialist humanist argument, it is simply not true that Thompson and the old New Left were guilty of 'moralism' in the sense of supposing political action to be exhausted in moral protest. In the discussion of '1956' one cannot help feeling that Anderson has uncritically adopted the same reductive attitude to moral criticism that Thompson justly objects to in Althusser. And yet elsewhere in *Arguments within English Marxism* Anderson states explicitly that he does not think Thompson's engagement with Communist morality can be reduced to a mere 'moralism', or that we can dispense with moral critique.[38] Thus he writes that

> the dominant emphases in the writing of the 'old' and 'new' levies of the New Left should be complementary rather than conflictual ones. Strategy without morality is a machiavellian calculus, of no interest or use to a real socialist movement. Stalinism did indeed reduce Marxism to that, power without value, in its time: men like Rakosi or Zachariadis are the malignant momentoes of it. Morality without strategy, a humane socialism equipped with only an ethic against a hostile world, is doomed to needless tragedy: a nobility without force leads to disaster, as the names of Dubček and Allende remind us. Thompson's formula for William Morris furnishes the fitting synthesis: what revolutionary socialism above all needs today is *moral realism* – with *equal* stress on each of the terms. For that kind of

synthesis to start to emerge, here or anywhere, initial divisions of labour on the Left must connect into eventual forms of active cooperation.[39]

This is certainly a more even-handed appraisal of the contribution of the 'old' New Left. One can note too that some new and different dialogues have been taking place, whether or not they properly represent the synthesis Anderson calls for. One index of this was the publication of *Exterminism and Cold War* in 1982: among those paying tribute to Thompson's 'key' essay was the allegedly arch 'neo-Stalinist' Etienne Balibar.[40]

Has it all, then, been a matter of emphases, and the furore around Althusser a storm in a tea cup – one, moreover, largely whipped up by Thompson himself? Yes and no. For Althusser was not calling for 'equal stress' on both the terms of 'moral realism' but ejecting the moral component itself. Nor was the bias of *The Poverty of Theory* misplaced given the relentless war that was waged at the time by the Althusserians against the merest intrusion of anthropology. No doubt we are talking about a handful of Marxist intellectuals, but Thompson's diatribe has been of critical importance in restoring some balance to their outlook. On the other hand, *The Poverty of Theory* is a very uneven piece of work, at times intemperate and frequently unfair in the impression it promotes of Althusser's arguments and intentions. Anderson has rightly wanted to defend Althusser against the wilder charges of Thompson. He has also homed in unerringly on some of the weaker links in *The Poverty of Theory*'s own chain of reasoning.[41] To Anderson, too, must go credit for placing Althusser's attack on socialist humanism in its correct context – the Sino–Soviet dispute of 1960–64.[42] As he points out, in 1960 the USSR revised its position: the 'class humanism' which it had been defending in the 1950s against Marx's 'revisionist' detractors ceded to a 'personal humanism' based on the slogan 'Everything for Man!'. This signalled four years of contumely on the part of the Chinese against what they regarded as the opting by the USSR for 'revisionism' and 'bourgeois humanism'.[43] Since he does not take any account of this, Thompson fails to appreciate that Althusser is writing as a Maoist sympathiser and thus remains 'deaf' (as Anderson puts it) to the irony of his commentary on the Soviet Union. But while it is true that Thompson misjudged the real target of Althusser's polemic, it is not clear why Anderson should suppose that in revealing Althusser's Maoist leanings he has vindicated him of the charges laid against him by Thompson. Moreover, Anderson is surely mistaken in suggesting that we should interpret the irony of Althusser's remarks as a veiled rebuke of the USSR for its failure to practise the principles of socialist humanism that it was preaching in the official 'ideology'. If that were the case then Althusser would have subscribed in secret to the very critique of Stalinism that he dismisses as 'bourgeois' moralism, as the 'obsession' with ethics,[44] of those Western 'humanist' intellectuals of whom Thompson was certainly one in 1956.

Out of Apathy

In 1960 Thompson looked back upon the 1950s as a decade of apathy in which only the alarm call of CND had seriously disturbed public complacency. Capitalism had been left to rot on the bough, and Britain was overripe for socialism. Yet never had the orthodox labour movement shown itself less concerned to foster the immanent growth.[45]

Along with this gloomy retrospection went a distinct change of emphasis. The call was not for communist renewal but for a socialist 'revolution' in Britain, and it was directed primarily at members and fellow-travellers of the Labour Party rather than to disaffected Communists. It is as if accounts had been settled with Stalinism, at least for the time being. The immediate task was to correct the flight from humanism of 'Natopolitanism', not communism.

This really amounted to an admission of defeat for the original socialist humanist project: the pattern of the 1930s *had* been followed in that disenchantment had indeed only served to 'fatten the whale' of capitalism. What is more, responsibility for this retreat from the left (which Thompson acknowledged had become a rout during the 1950s) was now laid directly at the door of the Russian Revolution, which had made the concept of *any* transition to socialism 'appear synonymous with bloodshed, civil censorship, purges and the rest'.[46]

In a climate which Thompson himself had defined as one of apathy, the call for 'revolution' was a bold (even a presumptuous?) move. For who was to be its agent? The question can be put of course to Thompson's argument more generally. For his tendency has always been to assume a 'moral community for socialism'[47] while remaining rather vague about its specific political form. In the writing of the early 1960s, this vagueness was exemplified in the terms in which he redefined the political struggle: the battle was less between 'workers' and 'ruling class' than between 'the people' and 'monopolies', between the 'common interest' and the 'business oligarchs'.[48] At the same time, the more orthodox Marxist categories were still providing the basic framework of his argument. For while he agreed that it would be foolish to dispute the evidence of working-class adaptation to capitalism, he yet argued that changes brought about by automation (displacement of primary workers into secondary occupations, etc.) would shatter not the 'working class' but traditional notions of the working class as a fixed, unchanging category with a definite consciousness and immutable forms of expression. Clearly Thompson still intended the abolition of capitalism to be the aim of a new consciousness, less cloth-cap and class bound; and while he rejected the Trotskyist reliance on the traditional 'working class' as the agent of change, he also rejected Wright Mills's alternative of the 'intellectuals' with its Fabian overtones. Yet there is more than a hint here that the task of socialists was less to foment revolutionary desires than to adjust to the new 'common interest' of 'the people' at each stage in the development of affluence. At the same time, and not entirely consistently with the more pragmatic conception of the task of socialism, he was arguing that

we can *fix* this new working-class consciousness and give it goals.

More than that, I am saying that it is the constant business of
socialists to endeavour to fix this consciousness, since – if we do not
do it – the capitalist media will 'fix' it for us. Political consciousness
is not a spontaneous generation, it is the product of political action
and skill.[49]

The argument is not necessarily in conflict with the earlier
defence of agency: as a socialist rather than liberal humanist,
Thompson had always recognized that ideas do not arise spontaneously. But there is a change of emphasis here – from
consciousness as an active 'handler' of experience to consciousness as 'passively' moulded by cultural forces. And while in *The
New Reasoner* Thompson remained vague as to where ideas did
come from, here he gave a more definite answer, and one more
in line with his comment in 'Outside the Whale' that 'the shape
of cultural history is determined by minorities'.[50]

Here then, in the article of the early 1960s, we encounter the
same tensions in the socialist humanist argument, the same
difficulties in sustaining its 'ambiguous' dialectic – but now
viewed, as it were, from the opposite pole: where the former
stress on the irreducibility of moral feeling and consciousness
had the cost of not making proper sense of the notion of cultural
conditioning, the later stress on the openness of consciousness to
manipulation put in question the assertion of our moral autonomy. But a certain vacillation between these poles is, as I have
suggested, inevitable. It should be noted, too, that these theoretical difficulties were due in part to a preparedness to question
the traditional Marxist wisdoms in the face of new historical
developments. In that sense, they were the problems of any
socialist analysis sensitive to the problems posed by the transformation and breakup of the traditional working class under
conditions of relative material comfort. The New Left was not
alone with its dilemmas, nor was Thompson the only Marxist at
the time to be accused of abandoning faith because he questioned the continuing validity of some of its categories. At around
the same time in the USA Herbert Marcuse (of whom
Thompson has been markedly critical) was writing:

> *One-Dimensional Man* will vacillate throughout between two contra-
> dictory hypotheses: (1) that advanced industrial society is capable of
> containing qualitative change for the foreseeable future; (2) that
> forces and tendencies exist which may break this containment and
> explode this society. I do not think that a clear answer can be given.
> Both tendencies are there, side by side – and even the one in the
> other.[51]

And both these 'tendencies' were registered turn by turn in
Thompson's writings of the period. On the one hand, 'revolution' is said to be in prospect, and the continued possibility of
socialist transformation justified by reference to 'the long tena-
cious revolutionary tradition of the British commoner'.[52] On the
other hand, we are reminded of how easily the revolutionary
impulse is contained and defused by the 'fixing' of popular
consciousness and the systematic manipulation of opinion. At
the same time, and overarching any such sociological
accounting, we are offered an argument of an altogether
different, and more deeply pessimistic, temper, one that invites
us to think in terms of the failure of the socialist project as such:

> it is not Stalin, nor Khrushchev, nor even Gomulka who must be seen
> to have failed, so much as the entire historic struggle to attain a
> classless society with which the particular, and more or less
> ephemeral, system of Communist Party organisation and doctrine
> have been associated. What must be seen to have 'failed' is the
> aspiration itself: the revolutionary potential – not within Russian
> society alone – but within *any* society, within man himself.[53]

Here, revolution is no longer presented as an issue of rulers and
ruled nor even of 'oligarchs' and 'people'. It is rather that human
nature in some more collective, trans-class, trans-individual, even
trans-historical sense has 'betrayed' itself, and we are all –
exploited and exploiters, manipulated and manipulators – to
blame.

The note of pessimism continued to sound throughout the
1960s[54] and into the writings of the 1970s, where a deep and
sometimes even despairing concern with the encroachment of

State power, the erosion of civil liberties and above all with the sclerotic effects of the Cold War, came to take precedence over the defence of Marxism or the advocacy of revolution. Maybe even, Thompson suggested at one point, we have been passing through a counter-revolution.[55] Together with pessimism went a relative retreat from political action and, it has been said, a lessening of interest in the affairs of the Communist nations. Anderson claims, pointing in particular to Thompson's low profile during the Vietnam Solidarity Campaign, that 'when the challenge of '56–'58 faded, his interest correspondingly waned'.[56] But to suppose, as Anderson implies, that this represented a falling off of socialist commitment is disingenuous. For the issue had never been purely one of the strategy alone, but concerned the extent to which the existing 'socialist' nations could still be conceived as providing any sort of model for socialism. As a 'socialist humanist' Thompson has always opposed American imperialism and favoured the overthrow of capitalism; but he has also, as part of that same identity, persisted in his criticism of the Soviet Union, and been wary of all political organizations and strategies that would bring him into alignment with it. This, one feels, is the real significance of 1956: that it marked the beginning of Thompson's long and unswerving pursuit of a nonaligned programme of socialist renewal. 'Socialist humanism' thus understood does not simply amount to a Eurocommunist endorsement of the parliamentary road to socialism; it is also distinguished by its hostility to the methods and ideologies of both the superpowers, and by its demand for the transcendence of the bloc system as such.

Out of Cold War

In the early 1980s as the peace movement surged again in response to the agreement on INF deployment, this demand for an end to the Cold War and the dissolution of the blocs assumed central political importance. It became the major theme of all Thompson's political writings and the core of the political agenda to which he has devoted unremitting energy for the better part of a decade.

But sounded as it was with a new urgency and with a definition which obviously reflected the specific historical moment, the 'out of Cold War' politics of the 1980s must also be seen as a continuation of a central motif of the 1950s 'socialist humanism'. From the beginning, in fact, Thompson's major fear was that the Cold War would preempt all moves towards an authentically democratic socialism in Eastern Europe: a fear which issued in numerous warnings of the repercussions this would have on socialist projects in the West, and reminders of the common interest of the opposed Soviet and US elites in repressing popular initiatives.[57] It is true that nothing in the earlier argument matched the bitterness and irony with which he was in his later 'exterminist' writings to illustrate this 'mirroring' of Soviet attitudes in Western postures.[58] But the call of these writings – for European Nuclear Disarmament, for a movement 'beyond the blocs', for active British neutrality and the uncoupling of Europe from superpower domination, for solidarity with independent peace initiatives in Eastern Europe, and for resistance to pro-Sovietism in the Western movements – this is of the same logic which lay behind the initial demand for a 'socialist humanism' as a mid-course between the opposing but complementary philistinisms of Soviet socialism and complacent anti-communism.

In more marked contrast, perhaps, was the quality of the response to the rallying-call of the early 1980s. Anyone involved in the early days of the peace movement renaissance is likely to have felt the historical significance of Thompson's opening of the classic disarmament argument to the European dimension and the politics of the Cold War and in particular, perhaps, of the 'moment' of *Protest and Survive*,[59] with its insistence on the importance of consolidated pan-European opposition to the warmongers, its visionary sense of the alternative to their 'degenerative logic', and its signalling of the emergence of the 'All-European Appeal for END'. Individuals do not make history, but some more than others help it on its way, and to Thompson must go some of the credit for shoving it minimally towards the END end rather than the other end.[60]

That there has been a very significant swing of the needle away from the pole of 'exterminism' is undeniable, even if a great deal of the disarmament agenda still remains to be completed. Movement there has been, but into a transition period in which we must pit the 'positives' of the advent of democracy in Eastern Europe, of the signing of the INF treaty, of the current moves towards strategic weapons agreement, and of the fast developing East–West economic and cultural detente against a number of negatives: the more globally confrontational and self-regarding US policy which may follow from the breakdown of Atlanticism and redeployment of US forces from Western Europe to more volatile areas; the parallel commitment of the West European NATO powers to economic expansion and to the strengthening of their influence elsewhere in Europe; and the instability of the Gorbachevian programme given the extent of Western resistance to further demilitarization and the growing ferment for ethnic and national self-determination in the USSR itself and other Warsaw Pact countries. That said, it would be absurd to deny that there has been a vast improvement in East–West relations since the beginning of the decade.

Paradoxically, however, it is precisely this degree of movement beyond the stasis of Cold War which has led some to call in question the adequacy of the 'exterminist' thesis with its emphasis on the role played by social movements and citizens' initiatives – and hence, by implication, to cast doubt on the contribution of the peace movement itself (especially in its END formation) in bringing about these changes in international relations. The 'exterminist' vision, it has been suggested, with its portrayal of the blocs as locked into reciprocal antagonism, formulated the dynamic of arms accumulation and of peace movement opposition to it in terms which excluded the possibility of state-led initiatives to break the impasse. Since this perception has been self-evidently wrong-footed by the INF agreement, it must be seen to have offered no more than a superficially plausible account of the politics of the Cold War.[61]

This argument seems to imply, however, that in stressing the role of social movement (rather than class) struggle and of a 'citizens' detente' rather than state initiatives, END politics was operating some sort of historical veto on these other forms of intervention: had these alternative distraints on the arms race been obviously forthcoming at the beginning of the 1980s no one would have been more pleased than Thompson and his fellow campaigners (who would probably have cast doubt themselves, in the light of it, on the appropriateness of the 'exterminist' image). Secondly, it mistakenly suggests that END politics was exhausted in unofficial inter- or trans-bloc citizens' dialogues when in fact a great deal of energy went into pressurizing East European officialdom and influencing Western governmental and opposition parties precisely with a view to bringing about some state-led defence and foreign policy initiatives. Thirdly, it tends to a hypostatization of the 'state' as an 'agent' constantly out-manoeuvreing peace movements and other naive forms of citizen protest in the pursuit of an overarching and always perfectly coherent historical rationality. In reality states muddle along much as do peace movements (who also, incidentally, have played no small part in more recent governmental confusions ...). But finally, all these other mistaken tendencies derive from the fundamental error of interpreting Thompson's arguments about 'exterminism', the mirroring of the blocs and the self-sustaining dynamic of the arms race in too literal a fashion. The 'exterminist' account was surely never offered as a finished conceptual analysis, but rather as a heuristic formula, and above all as a parable to capture the political imagination at a moment when the maximum mobilization of opposition to the deployment of INF was clearly called for.[62]

That the first measure of nuclear disarmament has come about through state negotiation is therefore by no means an embarrassment to the 'exterminist' thesis, or its falsification. Or it is not unless it is assumed that either the thesis was a profession of nihilism (when in fact as everyone knows it was a summons to humanist resistance), or else that it implied that the 'people' themselves would physically dismantle the weapons systems without the mediation of any governmental or institutional forces at all, which is plainly absurd.

It is true that there can be no certain pronouncement on the respective role played by peace movement pressure (as opposed, for example, to that of economic reformist pressure within the USSR) in bringing about the sequence of moves which led on to *glasnost, perestroika,* the INF agreement, and everything which has followed thereafter, but this is a rather separate issue from that of the plausibility of the 'exterminist' argument and strategy. (Even if the peace movement had had minimal impact on the change of direction issuing in the INF Treaty – which of course cannot be established – it would not invalidate END politics unless it were known for sure – which it cannot be – that some other politics would have had at least the same or greater impact.) Of one thing, however, we may be fairly confident, and that is that the initial changes of direction of Soviet defence and foreign policy were assisted rather than disabled by the nonaligned policies pressed for by Thompson and his END supporters – and this has been acknowledged of late even in Soviet official circles.[63]

What then of the other more directly 'socialist humanist' aspect of Thompson's END politics?: the suggestion, that is, that democratic socialist developments in both halves of Europe were blocked by Cold War and advanced by its erosion? Can it be argued that this too made unwarranted assumptions which recent history has tended to confound?

So *in media re* are we still that it would be falsely knowing to speak on these matters with any confidence. It is true that the end of the Cold War is being acclaimed by many on both sides of the old divide as a victory for 'Western' values and as heralding the final demise of socialism. But given that we are so freshly emergent from the period of East–West confrontation, and that the unfreezing of Europe has opened up so many new possibilities for reshaping its political life in the years to come, it may be imprudent to make any very definitive judgements on the future of socialism at the present time.

This is not to deny the gravity of the crisis through which socialism is now passing in Eastern Europe as a result of the collapse of its Stalinist version, or the many signs in Western Europe that it no longer commands any significant political support. Even if in the West there are some indications that the tide of support for neo-conservatism is beginning to ebb, it will hardly be in favour of any very oppositional policies, at least as far as the economy is concerned. In Britain, on the contrary, the 'new realist' turn of the Labour Party has brought a very noticeable acceleration of the general drift away from any serious socialist commitment which has characterized its policy in the postwar period. Indeed, if we think of the values for which Thompson and the New Left stood in the 1950s – anti-nuclear,[64] anti-nationalistic, anti-capitalist, and anti-consumerist – then we must acknowledge that the record has been generally counter-vailing for some thirty years now, and has probably never shown fewer signs of reversing this tendency than at the present time. Indeed, the leadership of the Labour Party celebrated the INF agreement by ditching the one commitment it had made which brought it more in line with New Left demands – that of unilateral nuclear disarmament. Finally, it must be admitted that despite present attempts to reaffirm socialist policies and to develop an international opposition to counter the prevailing directions of West European politics, much of the former radical anti-capitalist sentiment has gone into a 'consumer communist' style very much at odds with that of the original New Left. Meanwhile, in the newly democratized societies of Central and Eastern Europe, we have yet to see what political formations will prove most popular with the electorates, but the signs suggest that 'socialism' is too discredited for anything associated with that idea to have majority appeal, and that the option (at least in Hungary, Poland, Czechoslovakia and the GDR) will also be for some form of social democracy rather than for any strongly anti-capitalist programme of social renewal. In this sense, we may have to recognize that democratization in Eastern and Central Europe is going together with forms of economic restructuring whose effect will be to hand over these societies to the inherently undemocratic and inegalitarian control of market forces.

None of this, however, exactly invalidates Thompson's thesis about the inhibiting effects of Cold War on the development of democratic socialist politics. Indeed, it may even be said to confirm the truth of it, for we may argue that Thompson's warnings have been all too much to the point, and that it is only now, as we are finally emerging from the Cold War period, that we are in a position to appreciate how far this deformation may have deterred or stunted the growth of other, more progressive, political forms in either half of Europe. Of course, we can also argue, in more optimistic vein, that it follows from this same analysis that if such growths are ever to flourish again, then the transcendence of the politics of Cold War will have been the necessary, if not the sufficient, condition of their doing so, and that in that sense Thompson's targeting of the bloc system as the obstacle to all progress was always justified and has been absolutely vindicated by recent political events. We may insist, too, as part of the same argument that not only was the diagnosis essentially correct, but so also was the remedy, and that whatever now ensues in Europe, there can be no gainsaying the prescience of END's linking of the possibilities of demilitarization of the continent to de-Stalinization in Eastern Europe, and of the emphasis it placed on the contribution to that process of every reduction of East–West tension. It will be said, of course, that the Gorbachevian liberalization can in no way be regarded as a *response* to a relaxation of Western hostility, but has rather to be seen as an accommodation to its sheer intransigence. But even if this too crude analysis is allowed, it does not confound the logic of the mutually reinforcing nature of disarmament and democratization, which precisely pointed the finger at the impasse of Cold War politics so long as both its superpower parties were incapable of seeing the wisdom of a more conciliatory approach. Mr Gorbachev may well have launched the USSR on the path of glasnost and perestroika for primarily domestic reasons. But he knew, too, that the disarmament and improved international climate essential to the success of his reforms could not be brought into being through the continued pursuit of Brezchnevian Cold War foreign policy – and he therefore took the appropriate measures to sidestep its implacable logic.

Moreover, as suggested earlier, even as we acknowledge that at the present time the dynamic of glasnost and perestroika is threatening the engulfment by capitalism of the East European societies rather than carrying them in the direction of a democratic socialism, let us also acknowledge the element of political uncertainty which has been introduced by the extension of the space for a more pluralistic politics: an uncertainty which has been seeded now even in the USSR itself and may eventually take it in directions which transcend at least some of the philistinisms of either capitalism or Stalinist communism. Equally, in the established pluralist society of the West, the same element of uncertainty – which arises ultimately from the failure of people ever quite to comply in their moral outlook and political choice with the deterministic conceptions of an anti-humanist theory – makes it impossible to say finally that no form of democratic socialism will ever flourish on its soil.

Indeed, just as one is about to yield to pessimism on this score, one is given cause to reflect again in the sudden flurry of concern for Third World suffering and exploitation manifest in the response to Live Aid and Band Aid; in the emergence of all sorts of half-articulated conflicts about needs and lifestyles; in new laments for the loss of old communities; in the unease about the new-right celebration of greed; and above all, perhaps, in the growing alarm about the environment and ecological sustainability.

Reflecting himself on this disquietude in 1985, Thompson spoke of the need for the 'whys' of the people to be reasserted against the 'hows' of the television experts, who

> go on and on, in these frames, to the point of tedium, with the *how* questions only. How do we get inflation down? How should we cut up the defence budget between Trident and the fleet? A national 'consensus' is assumed – but in fact is manufactured daily within these frames – as to questions of *why* and *where*.... But across the world people are asking questions of *why* and *where*? Do we have the right to pollute this spinning planet any more? To consume and lay waste resources needed by future generations? Might not nil growth be better, if we could divide up the product more wisely and fairly?[65]

Without pretending that the alternative values embodied in these 'whys?' and 'wheres?' have any very effective support at the present time, it has to be said that they are implicitly being espoused in any expression of 'green' concern – and that this concern has moved sharply up the political agenda since Thompson penned those words.

Indeed the ecological crisis is so alarming, the 'green' response to it so obviously rational, and capitalism so clearly unhelpful in countering environmental degradation and resource attrition, that in the coming years a renewal of a much stronger greened socialist movement in Western Europe remains a distinct possibility. Should it emerge, it will have the advantage of the parallel ecological concern of increasing numbers of citizens in Eastern Europe, and their complementary recognition that neither the orthodox communist nor capitalist models will be adequate to the solution of the dilemmas posed by the shared East–West commitment to current forms of growth and industrialization.

Rather than speculate further on these issues, however, let me conclude simply by pointing to the way in which any such 'greening' of the socialist outlook would be a realization of Thompson's earliest political aspirations, insofar as these were based around a union of the wisdoms of Marx and William Morris. In other words, the same Marx/Morris argument which has been 'working inside' Thompson for some thirty years now – and it was, he has said, upon Morris's modes of perception that he fell back in 1956[66] – would now seem, in updated form, to be 'working inside' a good part of the left also. With what outcome we cannot as yet say. But in this longstanding commitment to the Marx/Morris nexus, Thompson must surely be allowed to have had a certain prescience about the outlook and preoccupations of any movement laying claim to be both 'socialist' and 'humanist' as we approach the end of the century.[67]

Notes

1. E.P. Thompson, *The Poverty of Theory and Other Essays* London 1978, p. 326.

2. Cf. Louis Althusser, *For Marx*, Harmondsworth 1969, pp. 221–2; 236–41; and see above, p. 92.

3. Thompson, *Poverty of Theory*, p. 322.

4. The rebellion erupted in June 1953 and was put down with the aid of Soviet troops.

5. Cf. Raymond Williams's account of the character of these journals in *Politics and Letters*, London 1979, pp. 361–2. Both journals were founded in 1957. They merged in 1960 to form *New Left Review*, edited by Stuart Hall with a large editorial team drawn from both previous journals. Shortly after Hall's resignation as editor in 1961, editorial direction passed into the hands of a small group led by Perry Anderson.

Copies of *The New Reasoner* and *Universities and Left Review* are extremely difficult to come by these days. I should like to express my gratitude here to Robin Blackburn and *New Left Review* for allowing me to remove their 'not to be removed' copies from the *Review* office.

6. Thompson, *Poverty of Theory*, p. 326.

7. Those of the Frankfurt Institute theorists before the war and the very influential lectures given by Alexandre Kojève in France in the 1930s deserve particular mention.

8. Erich Fromm (ed.) *Socialist Humanism*, London 1965.

9. Thompson, *Poverty of Theory*, p. 10. (The essay was first published in E.P. Thompson (ed.) *Out of Apathy*, London 1960.)

10. He was one of the *few* to do so, but by no means the only one, as is evidenced by the poets and authors already cited. Among the philosophers, special mention should be made of Leszek Kolakowski, to whose voice in the 1950s Thompson pays such well-deserved tribute. (See 'An Open Letter to Leszek Kolakowski', reprinted in *Poverty of Theory*.) Kolakowski's remarkable polemic, 'Responsibility and History' (first published in *Nowa Kultura* 1957) is included among other of his essays of 1956–8 in *Marxism and Beyond*, London 1969.

11. 'Socialist Humanism, an Epistle to the Philistines' (henceforth referred to as 'Epistle'), *The New Reasoner* 1, Summer 1957, pp. 103–43.

12. *Ibid.*, pp. 109ff. By 'ideology' Thompson meant 'a constellation of partisan attitudes and false, or partially false, ideas with its own inner consistency and quasi-religious institutional forms'. See 'Agency and Choice', *The New Reasoner* 5, Summer 1958, p. 95.

13. 'Epistle' pp. 139–40; cf. pp. 107–8. Perry Anderson has suggested that Thompson's war experiences, and their formative influence on his Communism, may have contributed to his hostility to Trotsky, who

condemned the war as an 'inter-imperialist struggle'. (See *Arguments within English Marxism*, London 1980, p. 154.) This may certainly have shaped Thompson's original attitude to Trotskyism, but the persistence of his antagonism has more to do with what he regarded as the sectarianism and dogmatism of the Trotskyists.

Anderson goes on to charge Thompson with a 'repression' of Trotsky's writings, (*ibid.*, pp. 154ff.), suggesting that this is all the more surprising since not only did Trotsky provide the most durable Marxist theory of Stalinism – the prime object of Thompson's concern after leaving the British CP – but was also the first great Marxist historian. Certainly Thompson offers no systematic review of Trotsky's work, expressing such criticisms as he has in a vague, offhand kind of way. But we should recall that Trotskyism was a fairly marginal phenomenon in Western Europe until the late 1960s, and that Trotsky's writings were largely outside the effectively available stock of political theory until then. (Anderson admits as much in his *Considerations on Western Marxism*, London, 1976, p. 101.) In any case, 'repression' is too strong. Thus in the 'Epistle' (p. 108) Thompson writes: 'In understanding the central position of the Russian bureaucracy, first in developing and now in perpetuating, this ideology, i.e. Stalinism, we have a great deal to learn from the analyses of Trotsky and even more from the flexible and undogmatic approaches of Isaac Deutscher and others.' Deutscher is saluted again in *The Poverty of Theory* along with Victor Serge, and so too are the 'old comrades' of *Socialisme ou barbarie*. See *Poverty of Theory*, pp. 329, 360.

14. 'Epistle', pp. 111–12.

15. Charles Taylor, 'Marxism and Humanism', *The New Reasoner* 2, 1957. Taylor was the most cogent, and at the same time the most sympathetic of Thompson's critics during this period. In the same issue Harry Hanson charged him with 'romanticism' and 'utopian socialism'. These responses to the 'Epistle' were followed by contributions from Tim Enright, John St. John and Jack Lindsay in *The New Reasoner* 3, 1957–8. Thompson's 'Agency and Choice' was offered in reply to these critics.

16. 'Agency and Choice', p. 96.

17. On this, see Ellen Meiksins Wood's recent discussion of Thompson's argument on 'base and superstructure' in K. McClelland and H. Kaye (eds) *E.P. Thompson: Critical Perspectives*, Oxford, 1990, pp. 125–52.

18. 'Epistle', p. 132f. Cf. *Poverty of Theory*, p. 357f.

19. *Poverty of Theory*, pp. 364–5, but see also the whole of section XV.

20. 'Marxism and Humanism', p. 96.

21. 'Epistle', p. 128; 'Agency and Choice', p. 103.

22. 'Epistle', p. 119; Kettle was a literary critic and leading CP intellectual, Gollan a full-time Party official.

23. 'Epistle', p. 119.

24. Cf. Merleau-Ponty's comments in the 'Bukharin and the Ambiguity of

History': 'the true nature of the tragedy appears once *the same man* has understood both that he cannot disavow the objective pattern of his actions, and that the motive of his actions constitutes a man's worth as he himself experiences it.' *Humanism and Terror*, trans. J.O. Neill, Evanston 1964, p. 62.

25. 'Epistle', p. 107.

26. Stalinism, however it is finally understood, was not the coherent and seamless fabric that the term 'ideology' implied. On the contrary, it was as inconsistent in its 'anti-moralist' stance as it was in its economism (from which, of course, Stalin's own ideas were exempted ...) and in its actual political strategies. Charles Taylor made the point in his reply to Thompson that Stalinism combined unbridled voluntarism with economic determinism. Isaac Deutscher conveys a very powerful sense of the role played by the sheer *inconsistency* of Stalin's policies in creating the disaster of 'Stalinism' in his 'Tragedy of the Polish Communist Party' (in R. Miliband and J. Saville (eds) *The Socialist Register 1982*, London 1982).

27. Interestingly enough, Thompson refers us to Merleau-Ponty when he invokes this term in *The Poverty of Theory* (p. 366), yet he employs it not so much as a technical term in phenomenology, but as more or less equivalent to the ordinary concept of 'experience', which in the 1950s articles and elsewhere in *The Poverty of Theory* he seems to find quite adequate.

28. *Poverty of Theory*, p. 357.

29. In his 'Open Letter to Leszek Kolakowski' Thompson associated Sartre with Althusser as part of the same Parisian culture with which he cannot hope to compete (*Poverty of Theory*, p. 104), and the same lumping together of 'Western Marxists' as denying human agency and creativity recurs in his review of Perry Anderson's *Considerations on Western Marxism* (*The Guardian* 16 September 1976). Sartre, however, wrote as a fellow 'socialist humanist' in *The New Reasoner* 1, Summer 1957, pp. 87–98.

30. See David Archard's *Consciousness and the Unconscious*, London 1984, pp. 50–52.

31. Jean-Paul Sartre, *Between Marxism and Existentialism*, trans. John Matthews, London 1974, p. 42.

32. Jean-Paul Sartre, *The Problem of Method*, trans. Hazel E. Barnes, London 1963, p. 33n.

33. *Poverty of Theory*, pp. 331–3.

34. *Ibid.*, p. 383.

35. *For Marx*, pp. 236–7.

36. What is under attack in the passage from *The German Ideology* (in Marx–Engels, *Collected Words* London 1975–, vol. 5, pp. 431–2) is Stirner's reduction of 'the world historical struggles' between classes to a clash of concepts, not the ideological status of the concepts themselves. There are, of course, passages where Marx does appear to disown morality and to argue for its ideological status (cf. *The German Ideology*, pp. 184, 247, 254, 285) and it is no doubt on the

basis of these remarks that Thompson has seen fit to concur with Althusser's assessment of Marx on this issue. But against his professions of moral relativism must be set Marx's recognition of 'desires which exist under all relations, and only change their form and direction under different social relations' (p. 256), and the fact that he clearly regarded hitherto existing societies as 'inhuman' because they were based on the oppression of one class by another, and thus on the exclusion – be it under capitalism, feudalism or slavery – of one class from development.

37. 'The mainstream of '56 proved in the end surprisingly thin, and left rather little trace.' *Arguments within English Marxism*, p. 120; cf. pp. 116–20.

38. In fact Anderson has apologized for his suggestion in 1966 (in 'Socialism and Pseudo-Empiricism', *New Left Review* 35, January–February 1966) that 'Thompson's most distinctive political concerns could be reduced to the category of "moralism"'. He associates this misconstruction with his failure to appreciate the real force of Thompson's engagement with Communist morality in his study of William Morris. (See *Arguments within English Marxism*, p. 157.)

39. *Arguments within English Marxism*, p. 206.

40. Etienne Balibar, 'The Long March for Peace' in *Exterminism and Cold War*, ed. *New Left Review*, London 1982. In the introduction to this work, the editors wrote of Thompson's intellectual role in the revival of the peace movement following the NATO decision to deploy Cruise and Pershing missiles in Europe as 'an act of public service with few comparisons in the recent history of any country' (p. ix). Thompson's article, 'Notes on Exterminism, the Last Stage of Civilization' appeared originally in *New Left Review* 121, May–June 1980.

41. For example, the equivocation as to whether we are indeed free agents or must only think ourselves to be so; the multivalent notion of 'experience': see *Arguments*, pp. 16–58.

42. *Arguments*, pp. 105–7.

43. Some flavour of this is provided by a speech given by Chou Yang in 1963: 'The modern revisionists and some bourgeois scholars try to describe Marxism as humanism and call Marx a humanist.... In particular they make use of certain views on 'alienation' expressed by Marx in his early *Economic and Philosophic Manuscripts, 1844* to depict him as an exponent of the bourgeois theory of human nature. They do their best to preach so-called Humanism using the concept of alienation. This, of course, is futile.' Cited in Raya Dunayevskaya, *Philosophy and Revolution*, New York 1973, pp. 181–2.

It should be said that there were some definite political motives for this 'philosophical' dispute, since the Chinese were hoping to establish an alliance with the Indonesians as a 'third force' to which all those genuinely opposed to American imperialism might turn for leadership.

44. *For Marx*, p. 239.

45. *Out of Apathy*, pp. 9–10.

46. *Out of Apathy*, p. 11.

47. I owe this phrase to Keith McClelland. One might argue that this trust in the existence of such a 'community' reflects at the social level Thompson's faith in the essential 'humanity' of the individual.

48. 'Revolution Again! Or Shut your Ears and Run', *New Left Review* 3, 1960, pp. 19–31. Cf. 'Commitment in Politics', *Universities and Left Review* 6, 1959.

49. 'Revolution Again!', p. 28.

50. *Poverty of Theory*, p. 21.

51. Herbert Marcuse, *One Dimensional Man*, London 1964, p. xv. Thompson's differences with Marcuse were stated in 'An Open Letter to Leszek Kolakowski': see *Poverty of Theory*, pp. 141–2, 174.

52. *Out of Apathy*, p. 308.

53. 'Outside the Whale', *Poverty of Theory*, p. 11.

54. Thompson did, however, continue to press for a gradual and non-violent 'revolutionary' transition to socialism in his 'The Peculiarities of the English' (1965 – now included in *The Poverty of Theory*). He was also a contributor to the New Left 'May Day Manifesto' which urged a similar policy in 1968 – (see Raymond Williams (ed.) *May Day Manifesto 1968*, Harmondsworth 1968). For the French 'events' of May 1968 Thompson did not express any great enthusiasm, either at the time or later.

55. 'The State of the Nation', in *Writing by Candlelight*, London 1980, p. 252. (The series of articles comprising 'The State of the Nation' were first published in *New Society* between 8 November and 13 December 1979.)

56. *Arguments within English Marxism*, p. 151. Thompson still resists any 'canonization' of the VSC and, he has written, dissents 'sharply from the analysis of Anderson and others which tends to demote CND (pacifist, neutralist, middle-class "failed")': *Exterminism and Cold War*, p. 33 n.48.

57. The role of the Cold War in crushing socialist initiatives both East and West is one of the major themes of Thompson's article on 'The New Left' in *The New Reasoner* 9, 1959, and was repeated in 'Outside the Whale' the following year. Cf. also 'Agency and Choice', p. 94; *Universities and Left Review* 4, 1958; and 'The Doomsday Consensus', in *Writing by Candlelight*, p. 273 – where Thompson himself remarks on the persistency of his warnings since 1958.

58. But see 'An Open Letter to Leszek Kolakowski': 'the failure of "1956" was in part a failure imposed by "the West". The West as anti-communist aggression; and the West as inadequate socialist response. Suez consolidated Soviet reaction; Kennedy's dance of death during the Cuban missile crisis precipitated the pragmatic Khrushchev's fall; the bombs falling in Vietnam were a background to the occupation of Prague' (*Poverty of Theory*, p. 168). This was echoed in his call for European Nuclear Disarmament in 1980: 'The hawkism of the West directly generated the hawkism of the East.... On the Cold War billiard table, NATO played the Cruise missile ball, which struck the Afghan

black, which rolled nicely into a Russian pocket' (*Writing by Candlelight*, p. 278).

59. This was first issued as a pamphlet in 1980 by CND and the Bertrand Russell Peace Foundation, and later included along with writings by other authors in the Penguin edition of the same name (Harmondsworth 1980). Nothing here should be taken to imply that Thompson was the sole initiator of the END idea or unaided architect of its organization. For an account of the origins of the 'European campaign' see James Hinton's *The British Peace Movement*, London 1989, and for a sense of the currency of 'END' ideas in left political parties at the time and of the role of the Bertrand Russell Peace Foundation, see Ken Coates (ed.) *Detente and Socialist Democracy*, Nottingham 1975, and *Listening for Peace*, Nottingham 1987.

60. Cf. *Protest and Survive*'s closing words: 'The acronym of European Nuclear Disarmament is END. I have explained why I think that the arguments of Professor Howard are hastening us towards a different end. I have outlined the deep structure of deterrence, and diagnosed its outcome as terminal. I can see no way of preventing this outcome but by immediate actions throughout Europe, which generate a counter-logic of nuclear disarmament. Which end is it to be?'

61. For an elaboration of some of these themes, see Simon Bromley and Justin Rosenberg, 'After Exterminism', *New Left Review* 168, March–April 1988.

62. Bromley and Rosenberg seem partially to admit this at one point (*Ibid.*, p. 78), but only at the cost, one feels, of undermining a good part of their earlier analytic critique.

63. Cf. the interview with Tair Tairov of the Soviet Peace Committee, in *END Journal* 36, Autumn 1988.

64. It should be noted, however, that the attitude to nuclear *power* was generally favourable: one reads now with shock and a sense of datedness remarks such as that Marx 'pointed to the kind of unitary consciousness which is alone adequate to grasp and handle the secrets of material transformation such as nuclear fission, and to express the human unity of world-brotherhood' (Jack Lindsay, 'Socialism and Humanism', *The New Reasoner* 3, 1975–8, p. 96). One cannot but feel that Thompson might have preferred to do without this kind of thing.

65. E.P. Thompson, *The Heavy Dancers*, London 1985, p. 3. (The title essay from which this quotation comes was first delivered as a television talk in 1982.)

66. E.P. Thompson, Postscript to *William Morris. Romantic to Revolutionary*, 2nd edn, London 1977, pp. 810.

67. For some more contemporary comments, see his introduction to Rudolf Bahro, *Socialism and Survival*, London 1982, pp. 7–8, and his tribute to Lucio Magri's definition of the possible relationship between the European peace movement and the Third World in 'Europe, the Weak Link in the Cold War,' in *Exterminism and Cold War*, p. 347. Magri's very fine essay, 'The Peace Movement and Europe', is included in that volume, pp. 117–34. Cf. also

Thompson's resistance to any dismissive attitude to green-type sentiments and his support for those who would affirm 'life values' against 'rationalized career values' (see 'An Open Letter to Leszek Kolakowski', p. 176; cf. p. 170).

5

Marxism and Morality

Marx's vision of communism is of a society that has transcended morality. Such a society is not only impracticable but inconceivable, since social and moral conflict requiring the arbitration of ethical rules will be an invariant feature of any human community however saintly one assumes its individuals to have become. Marxism therefore rests on a conceptual incoherence that renders the 'higher' society to which it aspires an indefensible social and political goal. Such, in essence, is the argument at the centre of Steven Lukes's *Marxism and Morality*.[1] A similarly negative verdict is delivered on the book's subsidiary concern: the record of Marxism as a practice. Here, too, Lukes finds the Marxist position deeply flawed, indeed vitiated by its disdain for the 'humanism' with which liberals have approached the question of 'means and ends', and by its generally cavalier attitude to matters of morality. There is, of course, nothing very new in the general substance of these charges. That Marxism is deficient, if not downright unscrupulous, in its approach to morality is, after all, one of the most frequently cited reasons for rejecting its doctrine. At the same time, many of those who are sympathetically inclined to the political argument of Marxism have found much to trouble them in this area. Indeed, the question of Marx's and Marxism's attitude to morality, and whether it constitutes a 'strength' or a 'weakness', has from the outset been a major bone of contention among Marxists, one might even say the key issue around which the interpretative disputes splitting the Marxist camp have perennially revolved. Nor does anyone need reminding of the traumatic impact upon these debates of the disasters perpetrated and legitimated in the name of Marxism.

Yet if the fundamental arguments pursued in *Marxism and Morality* have little novelty in themselves, they are formulated by Lukes with a precision and directness that are not so common. And they are presented with an understanding and appreciation of the strengths of the Marxist reasoning that makes the case moved against its acceptance the more commanding of respect. There is, moreover, a certain opportuneness about this book, appearing as it does in a climate of opinion less susceptible than that of a decade ago to the lure of an 'anti-humanist' Marxism and more ready to allow questions of ethics to emerge from the penumbra of their structuralist and poststructuralist eclipse. Nor is it simply a case of growing scepticism about these erstwhile wisdoms. There is also abroad, one senses, a new openness towards dimensions of Marxist argument that cannot be disconnected from the discussion of morality, but which, unlike the latter, have received rather scant consideration. I have in mind here the greater readiness to query long accepted nostrums about communism (as a society of 'abundance', of 'rich individuality', of 'distribution according to need', etc.) and to ask what precisely it is that these formulae, which have tripped so lightly off the Marxist tongue for so long, can mean and imply. I am thinking also of a new preparedness in certain sections of the left to challenge the orthodox Marxist veto on blue-printing; to ask whether the dismissal of 'utopian socialism', together with its 'moralism' and its 'nostalgic-romantic' hesitations about industrialism, has not worked in certain ways to the disadvantage of Marxist aspirations: for has it not provided reasons to evade a whole range of questions (about needs, the political role of moral feeling, the ecological and human consequences of industrial expansion) that must command the attention of anyone seriously interested in promoting socialism today? Or again, I am thinking of recent attempts[2] to spell out the kind of economic and political institutions that would go into the making of any authentically socialist society – endeavours which call in question the further tendency, undeniably present in Marx's writing, to portray communism as transcending not only morality but the domain of politics itself.

For all these reasons, then, Lukes's books is to be welcomed even if, in my case, it is with some regrets: first, that so little attempt is made to link its argument to these other debates and agendas, or to offer any positive speculations about the kind of practices and institutions that would be essential to any realizable socialist or communist form of existence; secondly (as should emerge more clearly in what follows) that it pays so little attention to the 'Marxisms' that share their name with the orthodoxy it is attacking even as they depart so widely from that in their approach to questions of moral and political responsibility.

The Central Paradox

Lukes begins where any unprejudiced reading of Marx is likely to begin, with an acknowledgement of what he calls the 'paradoxical' stance of Marxism towards morality: on the one hand, it presents morality as nothing more than bourgeois prejudice, a form of ideology that is social in origin, illusory in content, and serving class interests; on the other hand, Marxism continually implies and often explicitly invokes moral concepts and categories in its critique of capitalism and advocacy of communism:

> From his earliest writing, where Marx expresses his hatred of servility through the critique of alienation and the fragmentary visions of communism in the Paris Manuscripts and *The German Ideology*, to the excoriating attacks on factory conditions and the effects of exploitation in *Capital*, it is plain that Marx was fired by outrage and indignation and the burning desire for a better world that it is hard not to see as moral.[3]

And yet Marx just as constantly suggests that all moralizing and moral vocabulary must be expunged as unscientific and prejudicial to proletarian revolution. Nor is such inconsistency simply a quirk of Marx; it is equally to be found (as Lukes amply illustrates) in the position of Engels, of Lenin, of Trotsky, and indeed of the Marxist tradition in general, where passionate denunciation of the evils of capitalism has always combined with equally fiery polemics against 'all ethical standpoints'.

Few, I think, would want to dispute the existence of this 'paradox', and Lukes's assessment of the material assembled in evidence of it is generally compelling. My only reservation concerns the pertinence to any interpretation of Marx's writing on ethical issues of the distinction – acknowledged by Lukes but never fully explored[4] – between 'morality' and 'moralism'. For one can uphold 'morality', that is, one can have a general belief in the importance and validity of moral values and judgements, without committing oneself to the 'moralism' of those who assume that adherence to moral values is in itself sufficient to their realization. There is no space here to argue the point in detail, but my own sense is that there are certain texts of Marx which have commonly been taken as indicative of outright rejection of morality, where the burden of the attack is not so much upon the holding of moral positions themselves but upon the idealist conception that it is values themselves which determine the extent to which they are realized in practice. Thus, for example, the charge brought against Stirner's 'egoism' or the pieties of Feuerbach and the 'True' socialists in *The German Ideology* is not so much that any and every moral concept is of its nature ideological, but that it is ideological (and the classic move of Hegelian idealism) to treat all actual struggles and conflicts as if they involved no more than a clash of moral concepts and were resolvable within the realm of ideas alone. This is not to deny that if Marx had meant us to understand that his attack was not against morality as such but against the idealist overestimation of its powers to change the world, then he should have said so much more explicitly than he did, and offered an altogether more qualified discourse about morality. It is only to insist that there may be *some* places at least where Marx and Engels are being condemned for condemning morality when what is really under attack is 'the vain intrusion of moral judgements in lieu of causal understanding',[5] as Perry Anderson has put it – a formula I would be prepared to accept providing it is made clear that moral feeling and judgement have themselves an efficacy and that their causative role and specific effects must form part of any concept of 'causal understanding'.

In the end, however, what is at issue is less the interpretation of this or that particular text than the overall imputation of inconsistency, which I would not wish to contest. Nonetheless, it is, Lukes tell us, only an apparent inconsistency, since it is ultimately explicable in terms of a distinction (which, it is implied, Marx *was* consistent in drawing) between a morality of *Recht*, which he condemned, and a morality of 'human emancipation', which he approved. Drawing on texts such as *On the Jewish Question*, where the doctrine and rhetoric of the rights of man are denounced as ideological, and their merely 'political emancipation' opposed to the genuinely 'human emancipation' that consists in freedom from *Recht* and from the conditions of bourgeois society which call it into being, Lukes argues that the Marxist critique of morality is essentially a critique of *Recht*: an exposure of the socially derivative nature of so-called natural rights and of their ideological service in maintaining and defending the divisive, egoistic and utilitarian relations of bourgeois society. *Recht*, in short, from the Marxist point of view, is simply a means of stabilizing certain relations of production by presenting the interests they serve in the guise of eternal principles of justice, equality and fraternity, principles which therefore can have no rationally compelling force for Marxists.[6] We should recognize furthermore, says Lukes, that in the attack on *Recht* Marx is also rejecting the almost universally held assumption that, given the inherently conflictual nature of human societies, moral principles function as a necessary constraint on human conduct: 'It is a peculiar and distinctive feature of Marxism,' he writes, 'that it denies the conditions of *Recht* inherent in human life – denies that scarcity, egoism and social and moral antagonisms are invariant features inherent in the human condition.' Hence, he goes on, 'Marxism is virtually innocent of any serious consideration of all the interpersonal and intrapersonal sources of conflict and frustration that cannot, or can no longer, plausibly be traced even remotely to class divisions.'[7]

It is unfortunate, however, that Lukes does not spell out certain distinctions that would have enabled his reader to know exactly what construction was to be put on these arguments. For the claim that societies must necessarily embody antagonistic social relations is one thing; the claim that all sources of interpersonal conflict are eliminable is another. Moreover, even if we suppose that Marx adhered to both, I do not see why that in itself justifies the conclusion that Marx conceived of communism as a society dispensing with all principles of equity and justice. That Marx rejected the idea that antagonistic social relations were an essential feature of any human community (and with it the view that civil and political institutions serve a primary 'policing' function) is undoubtedly true. Indeed it is definitional of Marxism that the conflicts which the tradition of liberal political theory made accountable to 'human nature' are social in origin – and therefore removable in principle. Repudiating any Hobbesian conception, historical materialism assumes instead, as its premise, the possibility of what Sartre has called 'reciprocity' in human relations. One can certainly challenge this assumption, but it would clearly be begging the question to do so inductively by pointing to the fact that conflict has been a feature of all societies hitherto, since Marx himself would be the first to agree while insisting that nothing followed from that as to the possibility of alteration in the future. It is, in short, of the essence of the Marxist case that the major antagonisms of society have their root in forms of economic exploitation that can – and ought to – be removed. To speak, for example, of 'scarcity' as if it were an ineradicable and universal obstacle to the removal of conflict seems perverse in a world where the subsistence needs of some are only denied because of the excessive consumption of others and the massive waste of resources on a superfluity of arms.

That said, I would agree that certain sources of tension in human relations are not traceable to economic causes – or only so remotely that to accommodate them in such terms would be to deny them their particular character and specificity – and that these would persist even in societies that had corrected major iniquities and forms of exploitation. I think it is true, too, that Marx (along with much utopian argument with which he himself took issue on other grounds) failed sufficiently to acknowledge these tensions – even if it might be mistaken to conclude that he regarded them as eliminable. But whether he did so or not, I certainly find such a presupposition as problematic as Lukes does, not only on the grounds that it is impractical to suppose that a perfect harmonization of wills within society is realizable, but also because it is *dys*topian to aspire to it. In other words, were we, *per impossible*, able to excise all such forms of tension then we would have extirpated much that lends human life its meaning, vitality and interest. 'Why,' asks William James, 'does the painting of any paradise or utopia, in heaven or on earth, awaken such longings for escape?'[8] precisely because, I suggest, it typically seeks to entice us with an image of uninterrupted accord, when what we really yearn for, if we are honest, is something more complex: a form of community where, certainly, we are no longer beset by endless fear, violence and oppression, but where despite that (even because of it?) we are still able to enjoy the stimulus of cultural and personal difference and even abrasion. It is not, perhaps, the elimination of all tension that we ultimately desire, but the provision of means to experience it constructively, a form of society that frees us from the *bellum omnium contra omnes* without committing us to the *taedium vitae* of perfect accord.

Utopianism and Anti-utopianism

It is a 'sub-paradox' of Marxism, says Lukes, that it is both 'utopian' and 'anti-utopian', both scathing of all ideal visions of the future and motivated by its own vision of an emancipated world latent in the present. The negative consequence of such ambivalence, he suggests, is that it has enabled Marxism to evade two crucial tasks – that of justifying the 'higher' or more emancipated nature of the coming future, and that of detailing the types of institutions and forms of social intercourse essential to the realization of that future. I agree with this, and have already suggested that opportunities for clarifying and furthering socialist ideas have been inhibited as a consequence. There is undoubtedly something inconsistent in the scorn that Marx pours on the 'utopian socialists' for their lack of realism in failing to see that the only possible future is that already immanent in the present, when he himself suggests that human nature will have been so transformed under communism that no argument from its present character has bearing on the realizability of that 'higher' society. If, as Marx and Engels imply, a materialist perspective on the future must look to the potentialities 'emerging in the womb' of the actual, then this must surely apply at the level of moral and affective feeling as much as it does to economic arrangements. What is mistaken about the assumption that the structure of 'bourgeois' feeling offers no yardstick whatsoever from which to assess the virtue or practicability of any future society is not simply that it serves as an excuse to avoid the concrete task of elaborating upon realizable alternatives to the present, but that it imposes an impossible conceptual demand: it asks us to acknowledge that a certain form of society is an improvement on what it supplants while feigning ignorance of the kind of persons whose needs and desires it supposedly accommodates.

To the extent that Marx rests some of his 'anti-utopianism' on this kind of assumption, I believe he is guilty of a *theoretical* incoherence from which he cannot be rescued. But in *practice*, of course, Marx *is* influenced by contemporary values in his conceptualization of communism,[9] and thus is not open to the charge that his defence of the 'higher' status of communism makes no reference to the morality of his day. It is clear that the appeal of communism lay for him in the greater freedom, equity, individuality and justice it would promote, all of these being values that any bourgeois liberal would approve. It may well be that Marx was not fully aware of the nature of the moral grounds upon which he was commending communism, or fully prepared to acknowledge them. But to maintain, as Lukes does, that Marx actually managed to conceptualize the 'higher' status of communism in a manner that 'went beyond' all moral frameworks, is another question altogether, and not an achievement (if that is the word for it) which can plausibly be attributed to him. In other words, whatever view one takes of the degree to which Marx explicitly admitted it, his arguments in condemnation of capitalism and in defence of communism invoke principles that are recognizably moral.

The point may best be illustrated by reference to the notorious passage in the *Critique of the Gotha Programme* where Marx discusses the distributive arrangements of 'first stage' socialism and 'second stage' socialism (i.e. communism). Marx's general argument here is that the contribution principle employed in 'first stage' socialism, where each receives in accordance with labour input, is an advance on the arrangements of bourgeois society since 'principle and practice are no longer at loggerheads', but nonetheless embodies a 'right of inequality' insofar as it 'tacitly recognizes individual endowment and thus productive capacity as natural privileges.' Such privileging, he concludes, can only be corrected by the distribution according to need of 'second stage' socialism. Lukes (who sees this passage as a key to Marx's views on justice)[10] interprets Marx as claiming that any system of rules specifying justifiable claims must treat persons unequally since, by its nature, it applies a common standard and thus considers them under one aspect only. From this he concludes that Marx regarded any social system of general rules as undesirable – because it would necessarily abstract from differences between persons and thereby overlook the absolute individuality of the person. Not only will there be no more bourgeois right under communism, but no rule of morality or law at all. The perspective of the *Critique of the Gotha Programme* has 'gone beyond' justice and injustice.

But this cannot be right. For what else can Marx mean when

he says that it is a defective principle which abstracts from natural differences between persons except that to distribute in that manner is unfair – unjust? Is not Marx's point precisely that a truly just society only treats its members as socially equal when it treats them as naturally unequal? Where Lukes goes wrong, I think, is in assuming that the principle of distribution according to need invokes no common standard and therefore cannot qualify as a moral rule. But what else does the principle tell us to do, if not to distribute according to a common criterion of neediness, in other words, to treat that as our standard? It is true, of course, that such a distribution would involve a non-equivalence in the share of resources accorded each person. But, as Norman Geras has pointed out:

> the same applies to absolutely every substantive conception of social justice or principle of equality. If distribution is according to some standard of need, then people who make the same labour contribution, or people for that matter of the same height or born under the same astrological sign, may well not receive equivalent resources. But likewise if distribution is according to some standard of achievement or merit, then those with identical needs or who have made similar efforts may just as well find that their needs are not equally provided for or their efforts not equally rewarded, as the case may be. It is indeed a truism of the philosophical analysis of both justice and equality that the *formal* principle involved here – 'Treat like cases alike and different cases commensurately with their differences' – is practically useless until one has specified *substantive* criteria regarding which likenesses and differences are morally relevant; what kind of quality it is, in other words, that matters. Marx, for his part, comes down in favour of need, and against 'individual endowment', as the decisive criterion.[11]

Agreed, he does. On the other hand, there is no doubt about Marx's reluctance to acknowledge the normative status of the distribution principle, to acknowledge, that is, that it must rest on some common agreement as to what is to count as a need. As I have written elsewhere:

135

whatever way we turn it about, we can make no sense of distribution according to need unless we assume what Marx appears precisely to want to avoid assuming by his appeal to that notion, namely a criterion of need, a concept of value, and thus in turn political decisions about what it is that it is 'good' for society and its individuals to consume, and therefore what it is worth producing.[12]

Indeed, for me the fundamental problem of Marx's arguments in the *Critique of the Gotha Programme* is not so much that he fails to make explicit the principle of equity that in fact underlies any distribution according to need, but that he appears to recognize no other criterion for assessing differences of need than that provided by 'nature'. Even if it were conceded that individuals had some common agreement as to what constituted the relevant natural differences between them, such that they could agree about differences in their needs, this would still presume that needs were natural attributes of persons – a presumption I would have thought we ought to be rather reluctant to impute to the founding theorist of historical materialism. In other words, is not Marx here flying in the face of all his own arguments about the 'historic' nature of our needs, about their socially instituted content, and about the dominance of production over consumption, in order to inform us that under communism 'needs' are pre-found as natural givens marking the differences between individuals?[13] The problem, then, is not that the argument of the *Critique of the Gotha Programme* dispenses with any principle of justice, but that it fails to acknowledge that decisions about what constitutes a truly human consumption (about what we ought, as opposed to what we are able, to produce and consume, about the organization of work in the 'good' society, about the right use of its natural resources, and so on) are necessarily *political* in character and cannot be resolved by reference simply to differences of natural need.[14]

It is true that Lukes implicitly raises some of these questions about needs and capacities when he asks what Marx can possibly have meant by a 'humanly emancipated' society. But he does so only to illustrate and reinforce his claims about the incoherence of a society that has abandoned principles of *Recht*, taking communist society as depicted by Marx to be precisely such a society. My position, by contrast, is that Marx does not project such a picture, but argues for communism in the conviction that it would prove more equitable and just. What he does lose sight of, however, is the fact that the relations of communism will continue to require the mediation of political institutions, and that even distribution according to needs will depend on social agreement on the criteria of needs and capacities in accordance with which it is equalizing between persons.

I have argued, counter to Lukes, and against the grain of some of Marx's own polemic against *Recht*, that Marx does not think 'outside' or 'beyond' the terrain of morality, but remains, at least implicitly, committed to some of its fundamental values and principles. I would not want to deny that such an interpretation imputes to Marx a tacit acceptance of certain positions that many would insist are ruled out by historical materialism. It is to suggest, for example, that Marx is caught up in assumptions that commit him, if not directly to some form of Kantian argument, at least to postulating the existence of a common and trans-historic moral sensibility – and that, of course, is a postulate at odds with the 'anti-essentialism' on human nature so often ascribed to Marxism. It would mean accepting, in other words, that Marx did, if only rather implicitly, understand there to be features universal to us in virtue of our being human, and that a certain moral sense (as the condition of the emergence of moral principles) is one of them. Now, these are obviously quite controversial issues which there is no space to enter into here.[15] I cite them only in order to bring out the difficulties of discussing Marx's stance on these fundamental questions of morality, when he has so little explicitly to say about them, and certainly nothing of any philosophical sophistication. The point here, I think, is that when we say 'Marxism has no ethics' we can mean one of two things: either that it has no recourse to ethical argument (which, as I have suggested, is mistaken), or that it offers no ethical philosophy (which I think is true).

Whatever view we take of these matters, and even if it is

conceded that Marx does not altogether escape the framework of conventional moral reasoning, it remains true that Marx is very far removed from what we ordinarily think of as the 'bourgeois' moral position. One of the ways he differs is in the emphasis placed on the changing and historic content of morality – on the fact that the behaviours which are accounted 'just' or 'equitable' differ between societies despite a transhistoric and common adherence to the formal principles of justice and equity. There will be those, of course, who will insist that Marx recognizes no such 'common adherence', and that in denouncing bourgeois moral discourse as 'ideology' he exposes the falsity of thinking in terms of any kind of moral absolutes at all. But the overall coherence of his arguments is, I would argue, vastly improved if we take him to be contesting not so much the validity of moral values as such, but the refusal of the bourgeois moralists to distinguish between the abstract moral principle and its historical application. The weight of his critique would then fall on the failure of the bourgeois moralists to recognize that the content given to any moral principle must always be related to the differing conceptions that different societies entertain as to who qualifies as 'human' for the purposes of allocating rights and duties. It would be a critique not of the 'false' or 'ideological' status of 'justice' itself, but rather an argument that brought out the intimate relationship between what happens to be accounted 'just' in any society at any point in time and who happens at that time to be accounted truly 'human'. Slave society, for example, can seem just only to the extent that the slave is not accorded a properly 'human' status (and similar points might be made about the complacency with which women, or particular ethnic groups, have been discounted as relevant moral subjects in many a community priding itself on the 'universal humanism' of its moral values). Such a position would also be critical of any society which, even if it recognized the formal equality of all its members in respect of the rights it advocated, engaged in practices whose reproduction of inequalities directly contradicted its formal moral aspirations.

Now it follows, I think, from any such position that the

morality of acts cannot be judged solely in terms of what one might call a 'first level' adherence to the abstract rights and principles professed by one's society. In E.M. Forster's *Passage to India* the 'humanism' of Fielding's moral championing of Doctor Aziz in the face of colonialist persecution is indisputable, but he himself is culpable at another level as a colonialist in the employ of an oppressive and right-denying system. As Sartre wrote apropos of Algeria:

> I should like to make you see the rigour of colonialism, its internal necessity, how it can lead us exactly where we are, and how the purest intention, if it is born in this infernal circle, dies immediately. For it is not true that there are good settlers and others who are wicked: there are settlers, that's all.[16]

Where, then, the Marxist perspective arguably differs from the liberal is in the importance it attaches to this 'second level' morality, and to the responsibilities that individuals incur in regard to it. For the Marxist (or at any rate the 'humanist' Marxist) would argue that we have responsibilities not only for how we act individually within a given system, but for the system itself in which we are participant. The fact that we deplore Third World exploitation, for example, and attempt to comport ourselves in ways that minimize our individual complicity in it, does not, on this argument, exonerate us of responsibility either for that part of our consumption which is inextricably caught up in it at the present time, or for its overall functioning. The liability remains, and with it the duty to do more than deplore: to act to change it. One of the reasons why so many liberals are resistent to the 'two-tier' morality I have sketched is that it commits us not only to 'being moral' but to political activism.

Means and Ends

Up to a point, this seems to be recognized by Lukes, at least in the sense that he credits Marxism with a much richer conception of freedom than that associated with liberalism's doctrine of rights. And yet when he turns in his penultimate chapter to the problem of 'Means and Ends' there is very little indication that it is no less exigent for the liberal than for the Marxist, given their respective conceptions of freedom. To avoid misunderstanding, I should say that I find many of the Marxist arguments reviewed in this chapter as unsatisfactory and repugnant as Lukes does, and regard all glib dismissals of the question of means as guilty of precisely the kind of abstract moral platitude that Marxists are so quick to condemn in the mouths of the bourgeois ideologues. That said, there is something very questionable about the prevalent treatment of 'means and ends', as if it were a moral Achilles heel peculiar to Marxism and without any relevance for other theory and practice. For not only are many of the 'ends' pursued under cover of liberal morality (economic prosperity, competition, nationalism, market freedom, etc.) of dubious ethical status, but the 'means' adopted towards these ends do not always look so morally healthy either. What is more, liberals frequently invoke the very same 'means–ends' argument they deplore in Marxism in justification of their own behaviour. Is it not a commonplace that the industrialist who scruples over the 'means' will simply go out of business? That the 'ends' of national defence cannot be realized by the nuclear planner who loses sleep over the 'collateral damage' his strategic 'means' must be prepared to inflict? That the 'freedom fighter' or 'anti-terrorist' who worries overly about civilian casualties will also have to refrain from many acts (the mining of Nicaraguan ports, perhaps, or the targeting of Tripoli barracks) deemed essential to their larger purposes?

Such irony is misplaced, Lukes might insist, since nothing of his criticism of Marxism implies a validation of what is done in the name of 'liberalism'. Let us grant him this, then, and accept that we are concerned here not with the practical records of Marxism and liberalism, but with the claim that the liberal principle of respect for the immediate short-term interests of the individual is always to be preferred to the 'long-term consequentialism' advocated by the Marxist. In the concluding pages of his book he writes:

In what respects is Marxism morally blind? What does the Marxist version of consequentialism rule out or ignore in the assessment of human action and character? A general answer is: all that it holds to be irrelevant to the project of human emancipation; and, in particular, the interests of persons in the here and now, both victims (intended and unintended) and agents, in so far as these have no bearing on that project.

This, he suggests, is why Marxism has so little to say about the sphere of personal morality and interpersonal relationships; why it identifies all obstacles to progress at the social and historical, rather than psychological and anthropological level; why it is ambivalent about the domain of *Recht*; and why, finally, 'Marxism has never come to grips with the means–ends issue, and the problem of dirty hands.'[17]

That there is a good deal of truth in this 'general answer', I would not deny. What is less easy to assent to is the implication that liberalism *has* got to grips with the problem of 'dirty hands', and even provided a generally compelling and morally sanitary reply. According to the liberal argument, our first concern must always be for the dignity of the person, whose rights are such that no social end, however laudable, can justify or exculpate a crime against them. Furthermore, since all individuals possess these rights simply in virtue of their humanity, there can be no exception to the obligation we have towards them. But the problem here is that no sooner have we sketched the theoretical principles of the liberal position than a host of practical situations spring to mind in which we would deem it morally very problematic, if not repellent, to apply them – and problematic and repellent precisely because of our general respect for the principle of individual rights! Is it right, we ask ourselves, to concern ourselves too much with the dignity of the person threatening rape or murder? How far should we respect the wishes of the followers of a religious cult persuaded that salvation lies in administering cyanide to their children? Or, to invoke a more immediately pressing example, are we happy to accept the consequences of the application of the liberal principles in the case of South Africa today – where respect for the dignity of all individuals (at least in the sense of refraining from acts of violence against them) would seem to condemn the black community to an indefinite deprivation of their fundamental rights as persons?

If liberal 'rules' regarding means and ends are just as problematic as Marxist exemptions when we come to implement them in practice, this certainly does not imply that we can simply override the claims of the individual; nor does any socialist humanist think that one should. However, the rule we might do better to follow is the rule that no absolute rule applies; that all situations requiring moral decision are concrete and have to be judged on their merits; and that in making such judgements what counts morally more than any adherence to principle is our possession of a certain moral intuition or sensibility. To act morally, I would suggest, is often to act in a regretful spirit of compromise: it is to be aware of what kinds of things in general are right and wrong, and in that sense to act in the light of general rules; but it is also to be aware that some of what we shall actually feel called upon to do will be in contradiction with one or other of those principles. I am put in mind here of E.P. Thompson's recommendation that humanist attitudes should find expression 'whenever and to the degree that contingencies allow', and of his comeback to his exasperated critics: 'what else can one say? That they must always find expression irrespective of contingencies?'[18] The argument seems clumsy, somehow unsatisfactory – yet in essence I think it is the right one.

On the other hand, the morality it implies is not easy to formulate or render into a coherent whole, since it requires us to combine respect for the individual with an agreement to waive that respect in certain conditions. Perhaps all one can say in mitigation of such ambivalence is that if one is a socialist in outlook then one feels obliged to recognize that individuals not only have immediate personal rights and duties but are also answerable for the larger social consequences of their collective individual acts, and that consistent failure to act on the obligations incurred at the social level is legitimate ground for challenging their entitlement to respect for their personal rights.

The morality in question here is one that recognizes the worth and importance of the individual, while at the same time insisting that individuals always function in groups and classes such that they have responsibilities not only for their 'private' acts but for the 'public' history they are collectively making. Marxists must accept that respect for the person, along with freedom of speech and other 'liberal' rights, are not to be dismissed as mere bourgeois hypocrisies, whatever injustices may have been perpetrated in their name, and however difficult it may be to know how to apply the liberal principle on any particular occasion. But liberals equally must recognize that in an age of impending nuclear catastrophe, of massive economic exploitation, and ecological destruction, there seems something increasingly immoral about the refusal to extend the domain of the 'moral' beyond interpersonal relations.

The work that immediately comes to mind in this connection is Sartre's *Critique of Dialectical Reason*, which is surely the most serious attempt hitherto to introduce some system and coherence into the 'ambiguous ethic' of the socialist humanist position.[19] Whether or not Lukes would accept Sartre's claim to be 'Marxist' I do not know, but it is surprising, and also disappointing, that one finds so little discussion in *Marxism and Morality* of the Sartrean argument or of other attempts by humanist Marxists to construct a morality that attempts to combine the more positive aspects of both the liberal and the Marxist argument. One thus comes away from a reading of the book with a sense that it, too, embodies a paradox – and in a double sense: for not only does it spend much time criticizing Marx for having successfully conceptualized a transmoral position which Lukes insists is inconceivable; it also contains the larger paradox of being about Marxism – and not being about Marxism.

Notes

1. Steven Lukes, *Marxism and Morality*, Oxford 1985.

2. See in particular the debates on 'market socialism' (Alec Nove, *The Economics of Feasible Socialism*, London 1983, Boris Frankel, *Beyond the State*, London 1983, and the exchange between Nove and Frankel in *Radical Philosophy* 39, Spring 1985), as well as the contributions of Bahro, Gorz and other 'blue-printers', and the agendas and discussions of 'The Other Economic Summit'. P. Ekins (ed.) *The Living Economy*, London 1986, contains a collection of contributions to T.O.E.S. conferences.

3. *Marxism and Morality*, p. 3.

4. In the context of a very brief discussion of the exchange between E.P. Thompson and Perry Anderson on the question of Marxism and morality. See *ibid.*, pp. 25–6.

5. Perry Anderson, *Arguments within English Marxism*, London 1980, p. 98.

6. Hence it follows, so it is said, that it makes no sense for the Marxist to criticize capitalism for failing to live up to such principles. Lukes makes no mention of Critical Theory in this connection, but it is precisely the problem raised here – the problem of conducting any immanent critique of bourgeois society – that has so taxed the Frankfurt theorists, and which emerges also as the central dilemma in the current debate on Marx and justice (apropos of which, in fact, Lukes does argue for the relative validity of an immanent critique – see *Marxism and Morality*, ch. 4). For a full bibliography of the 'Marx and Justice' debate, see Norman Geras, *New Left Review* 150, March–April 1985, pp. 48–9.

7. *Marxism and Morality*, p. 35.

8. William James, 'The Dilemma of Determinism', in *The Will to Believe and other Essays on Popular Philosophy*, New York 1987, p. 167.

9. Indeed, one could well ask how he could not be if his own theory is correct.

10. *Marxism and Morality*, pp. 55f.

11. Geras, *New Left Review*, p. 81.

12. *On Human Needs*, Brighton 1981, p. 208.

13. Similar points can be made about 'capacities' – which can hardly be a function simply of natural attributes in any society beyond a minimal level of technological development.

14. It is true that the 'naturalization of needs' I am imputing to Marx here is not in any sense an explicit message of the *Critique of the Gotha Programme* (a passage which, given its brevity and polemical purpose, has been asked, perhaps, to bear too much interpretative weight) and that I do not intend to imply that Marx is guilty overall of any such simple approach to needs. Indeed, I am emphasizing its uncharacteristic bias in this respect. Nor, I should add, am I claiming that Marx everywhere directly associates communism with an

'end of politics', though I think this strand of thinking does have more textual support elsewhere – for example, in *The German Ideology* and *The Poverty of Philosophy*, where there is an undeniable discrimination against the 'merely political' and a tendency, by contrast, to present communism as freed of the mediation of political institutions.

15. For a sense of their controversial nature and of the issues relevant to any assessment of Marx's views on 'human nature', see the challenge to 'anti-essentialist' interpretations of Marx in Norman Geras, *Marx and Human Nature, Refutation of a Legend*, London 1983.

16. J.P. Sartre, 'Colonialism is a System', *Situations* 5, 1947, p. 27.

17. *Marxism and Morality*, pp. 146–7.

18. 'Socialist Humanism, an Epistle to the Philistines', *The New Reasoner* 1, Summer 1957, p. 128, and 'Agency and Choice', *The New Reasoner* 5, Summer 1958, p. 103.

19. For an interesting 'analysis' of the dialectical moral argument of the *Critique* see Thomas R. Flynn, *Sartre and Marxist Existentialism – The Test Case of Collective Responsibility*, Chicago and London 1984.

6

Constructa ergo sum?

I am sure that I am a discursively constructed subject. No matter under which aspect I conceive myself, whether as gardener or philosopher, cyclist or political activist, pianist or parent, matron or child, writer or reader, lover or friend, I see most clearly that I am the site of intersection of a multiplicity of social discourses and practices which have made me who I am. Whether in my everyday pursuits or in my more studied commitments: whether it be a matter of parsnip seeds or of my mode of sexual relating, of forms of transport or forms of loving, of what I say in public or discuss in the pub, of reading my bank statement or writing this article: I am aware that I am not an autonomous subject, but relating and deciding, feeling and reacting only through a grid of discourse and practice which I myself have not created. I cannot be without this grid, yet its 'thought' nonetheless comes to me from elsewhere. What am I, then? I am a *res cogitata*.

And yet I think to myself, who is it who is certain of this? Is the sense of certainty of my own constructed status itself a constructed effect? And is it a further constructed effect that I should question the constructed status of my certainty of my constructed status? I fear I have arrived upon a regression, from which, lacking Descartes' self-confidence, I may be unable to return. Perhaps I should go and plant my new strain of Victorian parsnip seeds. Or is it that insofar as I am certain of my constructed status, I am aware of a self who is constructed: *constructa ergo sum?*

These meditations are too private. Let me remove them to a wider register by recalling that I am only having them in virtue of those social currents of discourse assembled under the notion of 'postmodernist' theory. I am being thought even as I think, by certain meditations on the fragmented subject. And yet, of course, there is a self who is thinking the relationship to the discourse of the fragmented subject, and what is more in thinking it is thinking the paradox of postmodernism in its relations to the subject.

Let me discuss this paradox in ways which relate it more nearly to the ethical issues with which I shall here be primarily concerned. For I suspect that one of the achievements of postmodernist critiques is that even as they have converged in an assault upon the autonomy of the moral subject as traditionally conceived in ethics, they have brought us back to the question of ethics. Not brought us back in the sense that at the level of 'lived experience' we ever ceased to relate to ourselves as moral persons, who attended to the voice of conscience, acted in accordance with a sense of right and wrong, felt ourselves responsible for much of our action, and spoke in the language of ethics. But brought us back in the sense of inviting us to think again about the coherence of remaining in any kind of critical engagement with our times while espousing ethical relativism and refusing credence to the notion of an autonomous moral sensibility.

Postmodernist theory has insisted that 'lived experience' must be viewed as itself a 'living out' of various discourses and cultural modes through which the subject is 'individualized'; it has rejected the idea of some prior moral self who is selecting between and responding to various cultural and moral influences, and argued that it is only as points of contact for a complex of such influences that we attain a selfhood; it has asked us to think of ourselves as having 'moral choice' only in the sense of participating in various discourses – including that of ethics itself – which speak to us of our choice and freedom; and it has presented these discourses themselves as entirely relative.

And in all this, it has confounded the whole idea of moral

'truth' or 'identity' construed in the traditional sense of that which provides our continuity and solidity as persons, defines our projects as particularly ours and grounds our response to the world about us.

Herein, then, lies the paradox, for if postmodernism does bring us back to ethics conceived not merely as discursivity but as a fundamental and irreducible dimension of human existence, it does so very much against the grain of its own explicit commitments. But I would say that it does so also in part *because* of its commitments, since these in fact go well beyond a diagnosis of the world as textuality within which human subjects are simply coopted pawns in the game of proliferating 'knowledges' and circulating codes of speech. For the truth is, that much of postmodernist theory is also in critical engagement with the conditions it diagnoses. And critical theory, if it is to prove coherent, requires as its complement the subject whose feelings or moral sense are being ignored, or oppressed or abused by the rationalities condemned in its critique.

It is true that used simply as a descriptive term to capture our contemporaneity or 'spirit of the age', 'postmodernism' carries no critical import. But postmodernism as a reflection on these times is marked by its openness to difference, its resistance to systematizing or 'totalizing' argument and a refusal to sanctify the traditional scientific and philosophical quests for presence, objectivity and truth – and in this mode is certainly critical (of systematization, 'identity' thinking, etc.).

The deconstructive impulse of postmodernism was, moreover, not simply critical but progressively so. It was indeed important to question the nineteenth-century legacy of scientistic, humanistic and progressivistic ideas: we needed, and still do need, to challenge the faith in science and technology and the conceptions of human progress and guaranteed amelioration which they inspired. Equally, we did and still do need, to challenge the 'humanist' idea in the sense of being alert to the groups and communities which are actually being excluded or marginalized under the universalist pretensions of the term. And such questioning and deconstruction of our former vocabularies and metaphysical confidences has given us some of the more enlightened social movements of our times. Without a deconstruction of the humanist subject we would not have feminism; without a deconstruction of the modernist faith in science and its 'productivist' and 'technocratist' rhetorics (including those of Marxist Prometheanism) we would not have the green movement and eco-socialist rethinking on the left.

In these respects, the impulse to assert difference over identity, to expose the colonizing tendencies of humanist discourse, to raise the problem of the 'totalitarianism' inherent in totalizing theory, to alert us to the inadequacy of seeing language as simply the medium for expressing a reality 'out there' rather than as playing an active role in the creation of our social and cultural universe: all these have been important and relevant arguments for our times. We can see, however, that our 'paradox' has already surfaced within them. For why concern ourselves with the exclusions from the 'humanist' universal of women, or blacks or gay people or the insane, or any other oppressed or marginalized group, except on the conventional ethical grounds that all human beings are equally entitled to dignity and respect? Why concern ourselves with the 'totalitarian' implications of theory if not out of a belief in the value and importance of human freedom?

This paradox continues to dog the postmodernist argument even as it has moved into a kind of overdrive through which the logic that challenged certain kinds of identity thinking, deconstructed specific notions of truth, progress, humanism and the like, has pushed on to question the very possibility of objectivity, or of making reference in language to that which is not itself the effect of discourse. We have seen the initial impulse propelling the postmodernist argument develop a momentum which in the name of 'difference' and the supposed mistakenness of any recourse to 'identity' now invites us to disown the very aspiration to truth as something unattainable, no longer even a regulative idea. And in doing so, it has also disallowed any reference to a common, transcultural or transhistoric sensibility as the ground of moral or aesthetic response. Equally, it has called in question the idea of political consensus, and hence that of collective political endeavour. Pushed to its uttermost, the logic of 'difference' rules out any holistic and objective analyses of societies of a kind which allows us to define them as 'capitalist' or 'patriarchal' or, indeed, 'totalitarian', together with the transformative projects such analyses might recommend. The result, then, is that we are offered not new identities, not a more considered understanding of the plural and complex nature of society, but only the hyperindividualism of proliferating 'difference'.

But even in this overdrive deconstruction retains its ethical gesture. For why want to disturb the tyranny of 'identity' thinking and its binary logic, if not in order to reclaim for attention – to have us identify – the 'difference' or 'otherness' it forecloses? Why, for example, hint at the 'utopias' of 'difference' (the Derridean universe of 'in-difference', Foucault's 'different economy of bodies and pleasures') if not because it is thought that therein something richer in the way of individualization will flourish – that a fuller identity can be found in a world that has broken free of the constraints of the 'constructed' subject? Who is being appealed to in these imagined scenarios, who is enjoying the escape from the tyranny of binary straitjackets, if it is not the subject in the Enlightenment conception?

If, then, postmodernist argument is to remain loyal to the normative dimension implicit in these and similar arguments;[1] if it is to retain its critical edge, and not flip over into a validation of the existing plurality together with all its actually very conformist and homogenizing pressures;[2] if, in short, it is to avoid the collapse into positivism, then there is surely no way it can avoid being shadowed by the traditional moral subject.

This ethical paradox within postmodernism, I now want to suggest, has a familiar ring about it. For despite the rejection of the Marxist tradition within the postmodernist camp, it is difficult not to sense in it a 'post-socialist' repeat or extension of a longstanding equivocation around issues of morality within left-wing theory. This equivocation has its roots in a central dilemma of Marxist (and by association socialist) thinking, which has been given a recent and lucid airing in Steven Lukes's work on

Marxism and Morality:[3] how far can any consistent ethical critique
of society be offered within the general framework of an argument which treats morality as an ideological precipitate of
bourgeois relations, and would explain all so-called 'immoral'
acts in terms of economic and social conditioning? But it is found
at a less academic, and more immediately practical-political level
in a general reluctance on the left to address the question of
individual moral responsibility. The temptation, on the contrary,
has always been to evade any direct confrontation with that issue,
and to concentrate instead on the environmental conditions
(economic circumstances, ideological formations ...) disposing
people to behave in the ways they do. Only in the crudest
versions of the argument are these environmental factors
presented as actually *determining* the responses of individuals or
classes of individuals. But even the more qualified – 'dialectical'
– presentations of the relationship between circumstances and
their effects at the level of individual behaviour tend to focus on
the conditions or influences imposed or exerted by the former,
and say rather little about the subjective side of the dialectic –
about, one might say, the vice or virtue of the soul which is
experiencing and reacting to these cultural pressures.

Now, this emphasis has indeed been perfectly understandable
as a response to the 'personalism' of a right-wing moral argument which has wanted to present behaviour as accountable to
nothing but the 'vice' or 'virtue' of an autonomous moral subject.
The predilection of the right for presenting all forms of personal
trouble or antisocial behaviour as the 'responsibility' of the
individual concerned (no one is a victim of circumstances, but
only of their natural laziness, or non-conformism, or perver-
sion ...) quite clearly and justifiably invites the environmentalist
response associated with the socialist tradition. Moreover, environmental explanations of this kind undoubtedly find much
empirical backing: the urban deprivation, lack of educational
opportunity and cultural and material impoverishment which
are always features of highly economically divisive societies, are
most certainly linked to drug abuse, vandalism, domestic violence, street crime and other forms of destructive behaviour.

But there are difficulties nonetheless about the reliance on environmentalist explanations, since these are open to objections which the average intelligence is quite capable of perceiving: the objection that individuals subject to very similar environmental conditions behave in vastly differing ways; that many crimes are committed by relatively affluent members of society; that the explanations themselves are not always internally coherent. It has been pointed out, for example, in regard to child abuse, that if it were true, as some have claimed, that abusers are typically victims of abuse themselves, then two-thirds of them should be women, whereas in fact over 90 per cent of them are men.[4]

Of course, to meet such objections, one can always extend the range of environmentalist explanation to cover less directly material influences on the development of the personality. One can argue, for example, that centuries of patriarchal culture have conditioned men to assume the sexual identity which may issue in sexual abuse. But again, it is only a small minority who are guilty of sexual offences, whereas all men are subject to this cultural influence; and in any case, the theorist can expand environmentalist accounting along these lines only at the cost of denying the element of individual autonomy of social condition-ing which seems essential to changing the patterns of social influence themselves. For if it is true that subjects are entirely coopted by society, then where does one locate the emancipatory impulse to free people from the cultural forms which it is implied by the theory are 'responsible' for their cooption?

It is not that environmental explanations of this type are without their importance. It is rather than they generate a kind of slippage in their treatment of the moral subject: just as the emphasis on personal autonomy of a right-wing ethics tends towards the extreme of an absolute 'personalism' in which even poverty is regarded as a fault of the soul, so conversely, the emphasis on environmental conditioning tends always to the extreme of denying all autonomy to the subject altogether. Or if this is not directly denied, it becomes a site of theoretical prevarication. And, I suspect, of a prevarication which works against the grain of the intentions of the environmentalist objections to preempt the development of a really forceful oppositional argument to that of new-right 'personalism'. I have already suggested, moreover, why the postmodernist criticisms of the Marxist–socialist position do little to correct this explanatory imbalance. For while it is true that these take issue with what is seen as a deterministic 'economism' in the Marxist linking of the ideological formation of subjects to their infrastructural circumstances, they do so, of course, not in the name of the 'humanist' subject but in virtue of commitments to a theory of discursivity whose logical correlate is an uncompromising ethical relativism. Or if it is objected that postmodernism in its 'new times', *Marxism Today* formulations[5] has offered a 'left' counter to right-wing 'personalism' in focussing on individual needs for self-realization and personal expression long neglected by the socialist tradition, then one can only repeat that insofar as this may be true, it is at odds with the postmodernist emphasis on the constructed subject.[6]

Today one senses that the extreme 'personalist' ethic associated with neo-conservatism is no longer in the ascendency. One can detect perhaps the emergence of a moral argument rooted in a less evasive treatment of the subject. But I think this can only flourish in and through a direct engagement with the equivocations I have tried to illustrate here in both the socialist and the postmodernist responses to our times. What this amounts to saying is that if both socialist and postmodernist critiques of prevailing rationalities depend for their very coherence on an appeal to an element of subjective freedom – to a potentiality for transcending the forces by which we have been culturally constructed – then this should be openly acknowledged.

This does not mean denying the role played by environmental factors in determining behaviour, or the extent to which we acquire our selfhood in and through the complex grid of practices and discourses which constitute our society at any given moment. But it does mean recognizing that selves are not automatically instituted, that there is a self which is *in relationship* to the world by which it is constructed, and that even as we acknowledge our own dependency on a social universe which always comes to us in conceptualized form, this conceptualization is dependent on subjects who are reflecting upon and constantly renegotiating the forces of construction. In short, what has to be recognized is that an element of moral and aesthetic autonomy is an essential precondition of the formation of a distinctively human culture and environment, and of a distinctively human responsiveness to the conditions it imposes on the subject.

But another way of putting this would be to say that it does not need to be recognized because it is daily confirmed in our experience of ourselves. Feminist discourses, for example, have 'raised the consciousness' of many men and women, and in doing so have paradoxically made them more deeply aware of how much of their consciousness has been patriarchally constructed and remains patriarchally complicit. But in this very process we have also been made aware of a new range of moral dilemmas and of the opening up of a new space in which we are called upon to exert our powers of moral agency. Even as we recognize the weight of the past upon ourselves we see the emergence on the horizon of new choices. Even as we recognize that in a sense we have no choice – short of insanity or total loss of ego identity – but to live within some of our 'constructed' desires and modes of relating, we are engaging in forms of reflection, and submitting ourselves to forms of existential anguish and decision, which are altering the discourses and practices through which desire and communion between the sexes will be 'constructed' in the future.

Let us accept, then, that there is no limpid pool of nature in our soul: that we are driven, thought and spoken by the artifice of culture, and that no matter how hard we peer into the depths of the inner self we seem to find only the opaque sedimentation of its historical influence.[7] But let us also accept that we cannot dispense with personality: that the layering of this sedimentation is never identical; that an archaeology of its formation would never reveal the same cross-section, and that it is subject to seismic disturbances, shifts and eruptions which are uniquely our own. To do this, however, is surely to assent to the idea of a self which is actively involved in its own evolution, which is layering the layers even as it is moulded by their deposit, and which in that sense is always – as Sartre has suggested – making more of the self than what we are made of.[8]

The moral implications of this position are very complex for they require us to reconcile the moral autonomy of the subject with recognition of the cultural relativity of values. It requires us to give due weight to the fact that moral choices are not made in a vacuum, but always within a context of prevailing ideas of what constitutes good or bad behaviour, and to that degree under their influence. In this sense, the exercise of moral responsibility is culturally formed and culturally dependent: we cannot decide on our responsibilities, or even conceive what it might be to have them, except in relation to a socially instituted value system. This value system, moreover, is to a significant degree temporally and culturally specific; and also, at least in some of its rulings and valuations, being continually contested within any particular society or milieu. All these are reasons why we should be very hesitant about speaking of the 'natural' vice or virtue of human actions. Actions or attitudes which in one culture may be regarded as virtuous may in another be regarded as of dubious worth, if not positively pernicious. If, then, we see 'vice' or 'virtue' as revealed in the final decisions we make about our actions (decisions to engage in or refrain from 'immoral' or 'antisocial' behaviour), we must not overlook the extent of the differences which exist within and between societies, as to what constitutes 'immoral' or 'antisocial' conduct.

But the fact that our choices are made in relation to a contestable code or set of conventions as to what is 'good' or 'bad' does not in itself detract from the element of autonomy in the choice. The fact that we are disposed by our culture to think of certain acts as right or wrong does not make it any less our own decision whether we engage in them or not. In fact, it is arguably only because we are capable of moral autonomy that we can be subject to moral conditioning, since to be subject to what are distinctively moral rules and codes of conduct is to be subject to principles which it is up to us to decide about. In other words, it is only because we are not simply programmed or 'constructed' by our moral codes to behave in the ways that we do that it makes sense to speak of these as moral: a code of behaviour which no one was capable of infringing would arguably not be an ethical code. Even in regard, then, to those acts, such as murder, which most of us find it most 'impossible' to commit, I think it would be mistaken to suggest that we are more constrained by our moral conditioning than someone who has proved capable of the act: leaving aside other environmental influences on behaviour, we must say that the element of freedom is being exercised in both cases; and that if we can speak of the 'vice' or 'virtue' of the decision to murder or not, it is because, *ceteris paribus*, we are all equally free to murder in a way that we are not free to stop breathing. What prevents us doing so (if it is not simply fear of the law) is that we have no inclination for the act and feel moral revulsion for it. Now, it might be said that this lack of will or revulsion are themselves socially inculcated. But even if we grant that this is true up to a point, the constraint imposed on us by that moral education is very different from the constraint imposed on us in virtue of the biology of respiration.

Moreover, if we are free in this sense, despite the intensive moral conditioning of our culture, even in regard to the most entrenched prohibitions (such as upon murder or rape), then I think it follows that we are even more clearly autonomous in our decisions across a range of more transient and less deeply embedded codes of behaviour. These, too, play their role in constructing our responses even if only in the form of the social difficulties caused by dissenting from a widely held convention of conduct. (One may think it immoral to stand for the National Anthem, but still find it embarassing to remain seated in a crowded auditorium.) But it is also, of course, precisely in regard to this range of social norms that people are most continually exercising their powers of moral choice, and in doing so collectively changing the conventions themselves.

I have sketched a picture of our moral autonomy as residing in our ultimate freedom to concur with or dissent from socially inculcated norms and values. Although our culture may exert an enormous influence on what we feel ourselves able to do or not to do, it cannot finally determine our conduct. Nonetheless, it may be objected that this picture is consistent with allowing moral feelings (of disgust or approval) which deter us from antisocial behaviour to be a matter of personal good fortune rather than possessed of any obvious moral worth. Recognizing to the extent I do that the 'vice' or 'virtue' of acts is culturally relative, ought I not also to accept that there is no basis for discriminating between vicious and virtuous acts except in terms of their conformity to a prevailing moral code, and that if this comes easier to some than to others by reason of their revulsions and inclinations, then it is problematic to accord it any special moral superiority. Unless it be because of the 'absolute' rightness of the act, or the 'natural' goodness of the soul approving it, how can something we have no problem in doing be accounted 'virtuous'?

To address these questions is to open up a further implication of the position I have been arguing for: that it does, in fact, commit us to a degree of moral absolutism. If it is the autonomy of our moral decisions which provides the grounds for us to accord responsibility for them (and hence to treat them as 'vicious' or 'virtuous' regardless of other environmental factors in their making), then this autonomy must be premised on the idea of a sensibility which we deem to be held in common by all those we account as moral subjects, and which we invoke as the grounds for arriving at any kind of moral agreement whatsoever.

But it may be said that there is too little evidence of any agreement of this kind for this to be a viable premise. Given the divergence of moral codes what grounds have we for attributing any universal sensibility of a kind to which appeal could be made in justifying our moral preferences or according moral value to any individual act (whether it conform to or dissent from a particular moral code)? Now it is certainly very difficult to defend a case for moral absolutism in the face of the disparity of cultural practices; but I would argue that it is even harder to sustain an argument for an uncompromising moral relativism.

157

A first point which may be made is that in revealing disparities in cultural practice we are often discovering a measure of moral agreement at a deeper level (and are even tacitly acknowledging it in our selection of the contrast in the first place). Herodotus has an anecdote of some relevance in this respect. It tells of the horror-struck reaction of some Indians at the court of the Persian king when asked by the king for what sum they would be induced to forego their usual practice of burning the bodies of their dead and inter them instead. The Indians pleaded with him never to mention such an idea in their presence again. Later, the king mischievously confronted them with the equally horrified reaction of some African envoys also present at court and whose practice was to bury their dead by asking them at what price they might be prepared to cremate them instead. At one level this looks like an illustration of moral relativism. At another, however, it speaks to the shared strength of their desire to give all due respect to their dead.

But a second point to be made is that there would seem to be a range of behaviours towards which we encounter a considerable degree of transcultural and transhistoric moral disapproval. Murder, massacre, torture, rape: the moral repugnance at these is not universal, the rules prohibiting them are all too frequently broken, the interpretation of what comes under these descriptions differs somewhat historically and culturally – but there is no denying that the repugnance and the prohibition have been sufficiently widespread to make it important to distinguish their status from that of more temporally or culturally specific norms of behaviour. They are manifestations of something more universal in our moral responses than can be done justice to in an uncompromising moral relativism. Of, if it is insisted that acts of this kind have always been condoned when perpetrated against certain sections of the community (Jews under Hitler, blacks in South Africa, etc.) and that in that sense their condemnation has always been extremely partial, I think it may still be said that there is a sufficiently extensive agreement that to do these kinds of things to people is to do something worse than, for example, to lie to them or verbally abuse them, for us to speak of some communality of moral outlook in this area, however flagrantly it has been breached.

This, perhaps, is not to say very much. Everywhere else we look, whether it concern sexuality or slavery, forms of punishment or freedom of speech, the treatment of animals or the rights of the unborn, we seem to find only a ramifying moral relativism. But the point I think, here, is not that there are not numerous examples of the moral relativity of human societies. They are legion, and the exponents of cultural relativism have in this sense no problem at all in finding exceptions to the rule of moral universalism. The point is rather that if we can discover any rule at all then an extreme moral relativist position is defeated; and that one need no more deny the existence of ethical differences in asserting a measure of moral universalism than one need deny the role of environmental conditioning on behaviour in asserting a degree of moral autonomy.

But this degree of moral communality would arguably not be possible were it not for a degree of common sensibility, and it is this sensibility which finally grounds the possibility of discriminating between good and evil action, and hence allows us to insist on an element of moral 'naturality' or autonomy. If we approve the moral feelings which deter us from certain kinds of acts, it is surely because, even as we recognize the extent to which this moral conscience is a social construct, we are also acknowledging that there would be no shared conventions of morality at all were it not for this element of moral affectivity: an affectivity which is 'natural' or autonomous in the sense that it is not ultimately manipulable by cultural conditioning or 'moral' indoctrination. It is this autonomous feeling which makes people stand fast (when they do) to certain values, under whatever duress and no matter how subject to influence to the contrary. And when we discover virtue in this steadfastness it is because there is a fairly widespread understanding that it is defending a formal quality of feeling which grounds the possibility of any moral community at all; and also, importantly, because we treat it as a moral stance in principle available to everyone. In other words, unless it is premised on some supposition of common moral feeling which we credit people with having the freedom to respond to, it is difficult to see how any moral judgement can be consistently defended. If, for example, we denounce Muslims who are committed to hounding down and killing Salman Rushdie, then presumably it is because we credit them with being more than the mechanical constructs of Islamic fundamentalist ideology and discourse: because we think they are capable of appreciating the rationale of other moral values and able to opt for them if they so choose. In short, and to make an obvious point, it is clearly absurd to pass moral judgement (as opposed to judgements of insanity or the like) on those we regard as beyond the reach of any common moral sensibility and unable to exert any degree of moral choice in the light of it.

To conclude, then, by coming back to our point of departure, we cannot critically discriminate between the different rationalities in play in our times if we do not treat human beings as potential victims or beneficiaries of these. But we cannot so treat them unless we also accord them an element of autonomous feeling (which is denied or enhanced by these rationalities); and to treat them as autonomous in this way is to refuse to account for them purely as constructs of their culture. Cultures therefore construct subjects to the extent that they do only against a background of a more universal, transcultural sensibility. It is this sensibility to which appeal is made in the denunciation or approval of any norm or moral ruling. But if we emphasize only difference and plurality, then we are logically disarmed of the possibility of making these judgements, and in the process, moreover, disarmed of any grounds for defending the emphasis in the first place.

Notes

1. Arguments very relevant to the development of this point are to be found in Peter Dews' discussion of the tensions to which Foucault's position is subject in its critical and prescriptive aspects. See 'The Return of the Subject in late Foucault', *Radical Philosophy* 51, Spring 1989, where Dews extends on similar

themes discussed in his *Logic of Disintegration*, London 1987.

2. One of the central weaknesses of the postmodernist celebration of 'difference' is its failure to address the huge pressures for sameness in consumption and lifestyle resulting from the integration of capital and the extension of the world market. The major urban areas of Western Europe have already become depressingly similar to each other, and the visiting tourist will find very little on offer in them which is not to be found on the high street back home. Such standardization will be accelerated as the EEC moves to break down national barriers to a free market in trade and movement of capital. In the rush, then, to assert the heterogeneity of our 'postmodernist' times, let us not forget how far this present is the product of the erosion of past differences.

3. Steven Lukes, *Marxism and Morality*, Oxford 1985.

4. The point is made by Julie Burchill, *New Society* 24, July, 1987; cf. David Edgar, 'The Morals Dilemma', *Marxism Today* October 1987.

5. See in particular *Marxism Today* October 1988 and January 1989.

6. For in what sense can we speak of a 'constructed' subject as having an 'identity' or 'individuality' of a kind that has not already found 'expression'? And how, come to that, is the very notion of 'self-expression' to be reconciled with the rejection of the metaphysics of 'presence'? Some similar problems, I think, attach to Foucault's rather different call for individual self-realization in his advocacy of an 'aesthetics of existence'; cf. Dews, 'Return of the Subject' and *Logics of Disintegration*.

7. My use of the term sedimentation reflects my debt to Merleau-Ponty's philosophy of subjectivity.

8. This is the central theme of the argument for a dialectical conception of human freedom developed in Sartre's *Critique of Dialectical Reason*, London 1976.

9. Such a common sensibility must surely be related to our shared capacity to experience pain and humiliation and hence to know what it is like for these ills to be inflicted on others.

PART THREE

Feminist Frontiers

7

Patchwork Dragon Power?

The general thrust of much anti-militarist argument in recent years might be said to find expression in the call for there to be 'womanly times'. It is a compelling rhetoric in some ways, but it also gives me pause. For what are its underlying implications? That women are by nature pacifist or possess some special vocation for peace? That this disposition derives from their maternal function or goes along with some spiritual affinity to nature and its life forces denied to men? That there is some distinctively feminine ('emotive', 'intuitive') way of behaving and thinking that can – and should – be opposed to masculine ('analytic', 'instrumental') modes of action and cognition? That a masculine 'rationality' must yield to, or be tempered by, a feminine 'irrationalism'? Well, possibly all these things are implied. And do I endorse them? Well, possibly, yes and no ...

Let me offer an autobiographical anecdote in illustration of this ambivalence. It will take us back to that extraordinary gathering of women at Greenham, 12 December 1982. Much of what served to make that demonstration original: the decoration of the perimeter fence with personal memorabilia, the symbolic knitting and weaving, the bodily embracing of the base by a human chain, the candlelit vigil with its monotonous chanting and wailing, the siren whoop that alerted the outsider to the doings of the military within the base – all this has since become the stock-in-trade, as it were, of anti-nuclear protest, whether separatist or involving men as well as women.

At the time, however, it did seem, indeed it was, exceptionally innovative, and its potency and creativity impressed one as a very suitable tribute to the inner powers and sources of energy the peace-campers had obviously managed to generate within themselves as a condition of sustaining their mode of life at the base. It felt to me, in fact, as if I were attending at the advent of a new style of political protest: here imagery and symbolism were being used to wonderful effect; here a determinedly non-political discourse – a discourse resolutely disdaining to speak of anything but 'life', 'love' and 'peace' – had been answered by an emergency parliamentary debate; here we had a politics in which the anarchic ideal of order without externally imposed discipline, organization without leaders, had somehow been realized; here the creative means had been found, against all the odds, to convey in highly persuasive form a message directly challenging the prevailing values of our culture.

'Here', as I wrote enthusiastically at the time, 'were women in their thousands warning the world off from the warmongers at the door, and darkly hinting to the warmongers themselves that there are wiles and stratagems that can undo the best-laid plans of men.' And I went on to suggest that this was a mode of protest in which all those, both women and men, committed to the struggle against militarism, might find themselves increasingly involved as they moved into the 1980s.

Over the next year, however, my enthusiasm waned somewhat. In the first place, counter to what I had hoped, and half expected, men were not to be drawn into the protest at Greenham. On the contrary, the separatist tactics were reaffirmed in the ensuing period and became, so to speak, institutionalized. Second, I jibbed at a certain strain of mysticism which began to creep into communications issuing from Greenham and to become associated with the peace camp.

My growing unease with this came to a head with the invitation to all those who had been present in December 1982 to return at midsummer (or some other propitious time like the full moon, I can't now remember) to celebrate the festival of the 'Rainbow Dragon'. Through invocation of the 'Rainbow

Dragon' we would reawaken buried feminine forces of such puissance that no nuclear arsenals could prevail against them. As part of the rituals we were to bring bits of cloth and whatever materials we had to hand to contrive a patchwork effigy of this ancient matriarchal icon.

My rationalist hackles went up. I penned an aggressively ironic item to *The Guardian*, suggesting that if women behaved like this they had no right to object to the charge of irrationalism, and arguing that such antics could only bring the peace movement into disrepute, thereby undoing all the careful work that had been built up over the last two years. Fortunately, *The Guardian* would have none of it. I say 'fortunately' because within days I came to feel ashamed of the arch, poker-faced 'common sense' of the piece.

It was not that I underwent any sudden conversion to mysticism, but I realized that my sense of affront had something in it of the same unthinking arrogance about the superiority of scientific fact, the same instrumental rationality and no-nonsense approach to 'nature and her mysteries', that I myself detected so easily and found so deplorable in the nuclear militarists and technocrats. The upshot of all this was that I came to view the whole issue of 'peace and gender' as not only very highly charged politically, but also exceedingly complex – indeed as concentrating within it key issues at stake in the politics of feminism generally.

For it seemed to me that no sooner did one start thinking about the issue of women and peace than one was forced to confront an entire tradition of oppositional categories within which sexual difference has been discussed and supposedly accommodated – and to decide where one stood towards it. In other words, associated with, and in some sense underpinning, the idea that peace is a 'womanly' disposition, we find a whole series of polar concepts, metaphors and symbolisms of the male–female distinction (active–passive; cultural–natural; logical–intuitive; cognitive–emotive; head–heart; light–dark; sun–moon; day–night, etc.), many of them figuring in the arguments of feminists themselves, and all of them demanding further scrutiny and evaluation.

And this is where my mixed feelings come in. For while I fear that our culture is unlikely to flourish, or even survive, unless there is some definite shift in values towards the pole accounted 'feminine', I am also very reluctant to accept the implied opposition between the 'feminine' and the 'rational', or the notion of a distinctive feminine essence or nature which the call for 'womanly times' might seem to invoke.

The problem here is not simply academic, a problem about where one takes one's intellectual stand between scientism on the one hand, and mysticism on the other; it is also a matter of practical politics. Indeed, my feeling is that all thinking about the kind of future we want (about peace, ecology, relations with the Third World, about the family, the care and upbringing of children, the patterning of sexual relations, and so forth) must now register, and somehow come to terms with, the tensions at the heart of these gender antitheses. Equally, when we turn to the strategies to be adopted in pursuit of our goals, our attitudes to these oppositions and what they signify will be found to affect our thinking. They will be involved, for example, in the decisions we make about the wisdom of separatist campaigning, about whether violence of all kinds must be condemned, about the kind of ideology we want associated with our protest, and so on.

At this point, however, I should like to make it clear, to avoid subsequent misunderstanding, that in speaking of 'masculine' and 'feminine' perspectives, I am not assuming that these are perspectives automatically adopted by actual men and women. I use the terms, in other words, as 'gender' categories, that is, as referring to values, behaviours and attributes culturally associated with the male and female biological sexes respectively, and I do not presume any necessary coincidence between sex and gender. Nor shall I be concerned here with the vexed issue of how far gender attributes reflect natural predispositions.

I think there probably is some – fairly minimal – degree of conditioning and reinforcement between that component which is genetically determined in virtue of biological sex, and the characteristics that come to be culturally aligned with the male and female sexes respectively. Indeed, were this not the case, it is not clear how the process of 'genderization' could have attained any cultural significance in the first place. But even if there is a degree of, for example, genetically determined aggression in men, I cannot accept that this is in any sense a cause or adequate explanation of such phenomena as rape or the extreme violence of war. I no more see an inevitable transition from aggression 'in the nursery', as it were, to the 'maturity' of the nuclear arsenal, than I do from the existence of maternal instincts in women to the economic dependency, domestication and cultural devaluation that has been their historical lot.

I should also say that I am well aware what a conceptual hornets' nest is stirred up when one starts invoking (as I have) notions of the 'rational' and 'irrational' in connection with gender issues. The main question here is how far one can use these terms as if they were neutral, how far they themselves belong to an already gendered vocabulary. I do not think this is an easy question: thus, as I have indicated, certain strands of feminism, assuming the 'gendered' nature of these terms, now celebrate the feminine 'irrational' as an intuitive, diffuse, non-analytical form of thinking to be counterposed to a 'masculine' reason – the latter thereupon becoming for them the pejorative 'other' of a laudable feminine unreason.

But to take that line is, of course, to burn the bridges across which one might otherwise have passed in order to congratulate the women at the peace camps for the sanity and reason which they oppose to the madness of the arms race, or to approve the rationality of the feminist response against the sheer irrationality of the nuclear technocrats.

Hitherto, I have highlighted my ambivalence towards the call for 'womanly times'. But this is not to contest the very real sense in which women can be said to be the 'pacifist' sex. Even less is it to disparage them for being it. Certainly, the majority of women today (as in the past) follow the pattern of the majority of men in seeming to have no very special concern with promoting peace. Nevertheless, no one would sensibly want to deny the very extensive involvement and high profile of women within the contemporary peace movement, or the very distinctive – and positive – role that 'feminine' ideas and values have had in shaping its politics and image over the decade.

Equally undeniable is the extent to which this involvement continues a very long tradition of linkage between feminist and anti-militarist causes whose basis and rationale is to be found, at least in part, in the nurturing role of women. In other words, I think there is a measure of truth in the standard explanation for the 'pacifist' tendencies of women – namely that as those who conceive and give birth to life, and who have been almost exclusively responsible for the care of the young, women are bound to deplore anything that tends to the violent destruction of life.

There is surely much truth, too, in one of the implications of this account: that had more men been more directly involved in the intimate day-to-day caring of children, militaristic values might have become less prevalent and esteemed in our culture. Insofar, then, that the call for 'womanly times' is interpreted as a demand that a much more respectful hearing be given to the arguments against war of those most directly responsible for the reproduction and nurturing of the human species, then it seems to me uncomplicatedly valid.

I would insist, too, that never have these arguments been more pertinent or deserved more serious attention than at the present time – when what is at stake in any recourse to arms on a global scale is the very continuation of life on earth. In the past, the general devaluing of the nurturing role has allowed 'feminine' attitudes to war to be standardly associated with a contemptible 'familiocentricity' and hence not regarded as seriously challeng-ing.

Women have been viewed as incapable of transcending the concerns of the immediate family circle in order to involve themselves in matters of state and 'public life', and hence to arrive at an understanding and appreciation of the more universal values that issues of national defence and foreign policy bring into play. Ignorant of these realities, and unheeding of 'King and country', women, so this story has it, have been opposed to war simply because it threatens the destruction of their nearest and dearest.

This is, of course, an ideology which feminists would want to challenge, on many grounds, but I shall here limit myself to one or two points of particular relevance to the cause of the peace movement. Firstly, even if we accepted that it is a loyalty to kith and kin rather than a concern for the 'public interest' that is reflected in women's attitudes to war, it is, of course, only from a standardly 'masculine' conception of the 'public interest' – a conception that is singularly inappropriate in an age of nuclear weaponry – that this set of priorities can be viewed as petty, selfish or submissive.

It is precisely this downgrading of 'personal' attachment in favour of 'national' interest – the abstraction from what we share with each other as human beings and highlighting by contrast of what is exclusive to us as members of a given nation state – that needs to be rethought as a condition of long-term peace. It is one of the great strengths of 'feminine' argument in the peace movement today that it has made explicit the manner in which traditional arguments against violence imply a fundamental critique of military values and priorities. In defending arguments against war that have typically been dismissed as 'petty' and 'womanly', feminist anti-militarism is also attacking the whole framework of nationalism invoked in justification of military aggression.

Its supposedly 'passive' resistance to war on the grounds of the suffering and bereavement it inflicts is grounded on principles that imply an 'active' onslaught on the macho-jingoist cast of mind with its callous dissociation from the pains and losses of the 'enemy'. In other words, a 'feminist' emphasis on the destruction of life and the personal agony caused by war is crucial to dismantling the militarism that flourishes on a refusal to acknowledge the humanity of the enemy.

It is, furthermore, of absolute importance in an age of nuclear armaments that the conception of the 'national interest' or 'public good', which has so often been invoked in justification of war in the past, should be discredited. For in a world where any recourse to arms threatens wholesale destruction of human life, there can be no genuine commitment to defence of 'national' or 'public' good that does not rest on a commitment to non-violent means of conflict resolution. In other words, the 'feminist' arguments against militarism, which have so often in the past been scorned for their failure to understand what is really at issue in matters of national defence, are the only ones that have not become anachronistic in an age of weapons of mass destruction.

For where the war at issue is nuclear war, not only does the distinction between 'military' and 'civilian' functions collapse, but so, too, does the traditional opposition between a supposedly feminine 'domestic and private' antipathy to war and a masculine patriotism and public spiritedness. So far has this mode of thinking become inappropriate in a nuclear world, that we now have a situation in which in the interests of species survival (and what is more public than that?), women have been deserting hearth and home to squat among the military.

Of course, there are certain situations – South Africa today is a case in point – where the argument for and against resort to violent means are by no means so clearcut. Nor, to my mind, can one endorse all the rhetoric invoked in support of the feminine perspective. The frequently heard injunction for women 'to take the toys from the boys' might be a case in point, for reliant as it is on the image of woman as natural childminder, it tends to perpetuate rather than confound current assumptions about the sexual division of labour and gender roles, and with its intimation that 'boys will be boys', even implies that nurturing is some special domain of activity for which men are incurably unfitted.

That said, there can be no denying, I think, that a general shift in cultural values of the kind demanded by the feminist critique of militarism will be essential to our long-term survival. The question then remains, what formulation we want to give to the alternative 'feminine' values, and in particular how far we are happy to allow their association with irrationalism.

My own position is that we should continue to insist on their rationality as an antidote to the irrationality of nuclear escalation

– and indeed to much that is done today in the name of science and human progress. But to press for this is, of course, to accept a 'neutral' conception of reason – a conception based on certain common standards of cognition, certain agreements about what a 'fact' or a 'knowledge' is, certain shared assumptions about the purposes of acquiring knowledge, and so on. And to accept that is to accept that there is a certain type of response (the 'Rainbow Dragon' type) to the irrationalism of the militarists that must itself be condemned as irrational.

In other words, in the name of ushering in an alternative, yes, if you like, more 'feminine' conception of rationality (at any rate a rationality that recognizes that child-rearing is not opposed as 'animal, non-cognitive' behaviour to the 'rational' activity of bomb-making) we eschew all such nonsense as the following:

> To many of us feminists aware of the Goddess within us, and in the universe, radical pagans, greens and general lovers of the Earth our Mother, the celebration of the ancient festivals is becoming increasingly important. The Wise Women (and men) – the wicce/ Witches – went to the stake rather than forsake the Goddess and her son, the Horned one, in their seasonal changes ...

But to reject this kind of mysticism is one thing. To formulate a critique of it reliant neither on the standard arguments used in support of 'masculine' instrumental rationality, nor reinforcing traditional conceptions of the 'masculine–feminine' divide is another.

This brings me to a final point. For while I certainly accept that the presumed superiority of masculine values is without justification (and also very dangerous), I would also argue that it will not do simply to reverse that evaluation in favour of those deemed 'feminine'. For in the last analysis, these remain the oppositional sets of values which conjointly have brought us to our present crisis, which is the crisis of our species existence as a whole, and which in that sense cannot be made the sole responsibility of one sex rather than another.

What is required, I believe, if we are to surmount this crisis is something more in the nature of a 'quantum-leap' transmutation of values and lifestyles, and this must put in question any current 'dialectic' of gender difference and affect all parties.

In other words, if it is acknowledged, as it surely must be, that the 'feminine' too has been at work in the creation of our current situation, then it must also surely be acknowledged that overcoming its alienations may depend not on a mere inversion of the oppositional gender values, but on their transcendence – a transcendence involving more than a one-sided critique of rationality.

This in turn requires us to reconsider separatist strategies from the means–ends point of view, which is to say, to question the wisdom of those strategies if the ends sought are those of human coexistence. Separatist peace activists might also do well to ponder the dilemma posed by the 'let there be womanly times' type of call: for if the aim is to develop nurturing capacities and feelings in men, then close relations and co-operation between the sexes are surely a precondition?

But at this point, of course, we are back with the question of futures, and what conceptions we have of the modes of existence we want to promote. My own position is that as part of their celebration of life values which constitutes the core of their anti-militarism feminists should be seeking to develop a more positive 'utopian' conception of relations between the sexes – to promote, in short, a less divisive gender politics. But that's an essay for another day.

8

The Qualities of Simone de Beauvoir

> For a long time I have hesitated to write a book on woman. The subject is irritating, especially to women; and it is not new. Enough ink has been spilled in quarrelling over feminism, and perhaps we should say no more about it.

Often quoted as they are, these opening sentences of *The Second Sex* can still amaze. Yet on reflection one can come to agree with their author in some sense, or at least to see what she meant. For the subterranean forces that were to erupt as modern feminism were still so far buried in 1949 that their rumblings were scarcely audible even to the more sensitive ear; and what Simone de Beauvoir then meant by 'feminism' was a surface discourse about a segment of reality supposedly so culturally marginal that 'to spill more ink on it' might well have seemed disproportionate – the mark of some intellectual obsession or lack of balance.

If today these words of apology seem anachronistic to the point of quaintness, then it is the work they preface which more than any other has been responsible. This is the measure of de Beauvoir's achievement for feminism. One cannot help feeling, moreover – and it is a further twist in the irony – that had she focused more narrowly on 'woman', or spilt her ink exclusively there, the enterprise of *The Second Sex* might not have meant so much to so many, nor occupied so founding a role in a movement she herself was only to join around her sixtieth year. For the intellectual appetite, wide learning and breadth of vision which went to make that work so uniquely influential in character are the same qualities which have always made her seek more registers than that of 'women's studies' alone.

Indeed, what one values in her work as much as any discussion of feminism is the record she provides of a life as it is lived: her capturing of the joys and miseries of living out her span in a world of infinite potential, but under the constraints of limited time and perishable flesh. At the same time, the sheer volume of her fiction and writings on topics other than gender is a reminder that the latter was never the sole – nor even always a central – thematic of her work.

Equivocations

It is this integration of more specifically feminist interests with other studies which has recommended her to many of her readers. Much the same might be said of the stance on feminism itself which she thereby embodies, equivocal as it is between two contrary but equally compelling assertions of identity: 'I am a woman' – 'I simply am'. But it is the sustained expression in her work of this 'woman – person' doublet which has also resulted in a compartmentalizing tendency in the commentary upon it. De Beauvoir's fiction, her existentialism, her politics and her writing on women have all received extensive treatment;[1] but her work as a whole has not hitherto been submitted to a distinctively feminist scrutiny. Of course, it is not just the multifaceted nature of de Beauvoir's contribution which is responsible for that, but the temporal anomaly of *The Second Sex* – its 'prehistoric' status, as it were, relative to the movement of modern feminism. The vexed issue of Sartre's influence has also made objective feminist assessment that much harder. As Michel Le Doeuff has suggested, it is one thing for Sartre to promise at the time of de Beauvoir's *aggregation*: 'From now on I will take you in hand', and another – and much more difficult to understand – for de Beauvoir to relate the episode years later without a hint of critical hindsight, even after writing *The Second Sex*.[2] These difficulties have to be faced. Only an ultra-feminism with no real grip on de Beauvoir would attempt to accommodate her 'Sartreanism' by pretending it did not exist. Equally to be resisted, however, is the converse attempt to circumvent her femininity – the route taken by those like Bieber who think they are complimenting de Beauvoir by 'forgetting' about her sex.[3]

The works under review here avoid both errors.[4] More importantly, they also make good the absence of any extended feminist critique. They are thus in refreshing contrast to academic recuperations of de Beauvoir, and attempts to restore her to 'honorific male' respectability. Mary Evans has written a timely and readable biography which for the first time discusses de Beauvoir's work in the light of the divergent currents of argument comprising contemporary feminism. Coming hard on its heels, Judith Okely's more personal assessment is less comprehensive but sets itself a similar critical task.

Both authors are sensitive to the difficulties of conducting this kind of 'retrospection' from within a continuing and complex debate upon so exceptional a figure as de Beauvoir, and both adopt distinctive strategies to accommodate them. On the whole the less embarrassed by the undertaking, Evans confronts the 'problem' de Beauvoir poses head on by questioning in what sense, if any at all, she can be reckoned a feminist. Neither in virtue of the fact that she wrote extensively *about* women, nor on grounds of her ambition and achievement, can she qualify, says Evans. For by both criteria many could be termed 'feminist' who have no particular concern for the social status of women or commitment to their emancipation. Moreover, even where de Beauvoir is explicitly addressing those issues which contemporary feminism has made its own, she is guilty, according to Evans, of imbuing her argument with the very patriarchal values and habits of mind that feminists would now question and condemn. 'Her uncritical belief in what she describes as rationality', argues Evans, 'her negation and denial of various forms of female experience, her tacit assumption that paid work and contraception are the two keys to the absolute freedom of womankind, all suggest a set of values that place a major importance on living like a childless, rather singular employed man.' Thus, though de Beauvoir accepts the essential thesis of the subordination of women, her message is confusing: 'reject subordination as a woman by rejecting traditional femininity and taking on male assumptions and values.'[5] For Evans, then, any assessment of de Beauvoir's contribution to feminism necessarily involves an attempt to define the nature and goals of the latter. This, however, she never really undertakes to do; but then, on the other hand, neither does she suspend judgement on de Beauvoir, but proceeds without much more ado to associate her with 'bourgeois feminism' (a position she briskly denounces as no more capable of offering a challenge to Western society than its antithesis in 'maternal thinking').[6] What is curiously absent from the discussion is any reference to de Beauvoir's own, rather straightforward definition of 'feminism' as 'fighting on specifically feminist issues independently of the class struggle'.[7] Consistently with that definition, de Beauvoir has argued that she has not been a 'feminist' for most of her life, and only became one through her association with the MLF in 1971.[8]

The Founding Figure of Feminism

In contrast, and less condescendingly perhaps, Judith Okely assumes de Beauvoir's entitlement to the feminist label from the start, and adopts a more evolutionary perspective; de Beauvoir is indeed the founding figure of feminism, but feminism has since moved on, and now calls in question much of its original message. Her strategy is that of a double 'then and now' reading in which she looks back upon a 'virginal' 1960s response to de Beauvoir's writings in the light of a later more critical 'experience'. This mapping of earlier and later selves proceeds at the cost of fluency and sometimes declines into mere juxtaposition of contrasting sentiments. But what it lacks in flow and organization, it makes up for in the richness of its evocations: in this generous and honest 'personal anthropology', Okely has excavated more than her own past, and provided a valuable archive of the experiences through which many women similarly placed to herself have passed in their initiation into feminism.

What she says of de Beauvoir's writing, in fact – that the reliance on autobiographical material which is responsible for its Eurocentric, ethnographic limitations, is also a source of its appeal in allowing many of her readers an immediate, intuitive identification with its author – could also be said of Okely's own case study given its likely readership. The difference, of course, is that Okely is aware of the very limited nature of her own experience, while charging de Beauvoir with 'ethnocentrism' precisely on account of her failure to question how far the experience of herself and her Parisian middle-class acquaintances could be treated as valid for women in general.[9]

One of the advantages of Okely's double reading is the reminder it provides of the nature of de Beauvoir's initial inspiration in offering an existentialistic alternative to the Hobson's choice of domestic conformity on the one hand or derided and ostracized spinsterhood on the other. Women, her example appeared to suggest, could lead diverse and autonomous lives freed of the normal constraints of marriage and motherhood without being doomed to loneliness or celibacy. What Okely does not sufficiently stress perhaps is the extent to which it was no more than appearance. Indeed, the appeal of the example lay as much in the escapist fantasy it offered as in any attractions it had as an image of life to which women might realistically aspire. The most – possibly the only really – infuriating aspect of de Beauvoir's writing is the way she manages to combine the most correct and upright socialist sentiment with almost total impercipience about the economic, moral and sexual pressures that make escape from conventional relations with men wellnigh impossible for the majority of women at the present time. Evans is absolutely correct to stress her deficiency in this respect and may even be right to query her sympathy with women in the light of it.

But while one can see exactly why de Beauvoir's stress on women's 'freedom' and 'choice' of action is so exasperatingly flawed politically in the eyes of a Marxist such as Evans, Evans herself detracts too far from what was (and still is) positive about de Beauvoir's nonconformism and fails to see the importance of a distinctively feminist 'individualist ethic' in generating a collective feminist politics. For even though the 'model' of emancipation de Beauvoir provided was either inappropriate or unrealizable for the majority of women (and even for a majority of her readers), the fact that it was provided did help to focus many of the demands on such key issues as abortion, birth control and civil rights, that were to provide the initial platforms of a specifically feminist politics. In any case, the 'bourgeois' label is somewhat misleading, as already suggested. It certainly does not fully capture what is actually a more complex – and shifting – political outlook, such that within an overall commitment to 'socialism', de Beauvoir first argued (at the time of *The Second Sex*) that 'revolution' would see to the liberation of women,[10] and now argues for the importance of separate, collective action by women precisely because 'overthrowing capitalism does not mean overturning the patriarchal tradition'.[11] Today, in fact, de Beauvoir appears to accept many of the arguments about feminist campaigning which Evans deploys in attacking her earlier championing of 'autonomy'.

Formative Influences

'Autonomy', it should be said, is not the easiest of concepts for feminism, and both Evans and Okely display ambivalence towards it. Thus, on the one hand de Beauvoir is accused of lending herself to the worst excesses of patriarchal ideology in her stress on independence; on the other, any instance of emotional reliance upon others tends to be presented as detracting from her claims to genuine emancipation. This is nowhere more true than in the lengthy and informative discussions which both books offer of parental and Sartrean influence (an influence, of course, which de Beauvoir herself cheerfully acknowledges on numerous occasions and which, particularly in Sartre's case, she is wholly glad to have enjoyed).

In her somewhat relentless pursuit of an explanation for every possible direction taken by de Beauvoir, Evans runs into a number of circular arguments (such that, for example, emotional dispositions towards personal autonomy and the acceptance of masculine values are supposedly both inculcated by her father and explain her preference for the model of rationality and independence that he held out to her). But Evans is surely right to emphasize the manner in which any emotional disposition towards the 'male world' must have been reinforced by certain structural features of her life – importantly, the requirement that she should support herself financially given the decline in the family fortunes, and the simple fact of her living in Paris in a country so academically and culturally centralized as France. Evans also offers a fairly sensitive account of the relationship with Sartre – a relationship which, as she says, 'raises fundamental questions about the ways in which men and women can live together in relations of honesty and trust, without imposing on either party bonds of oppressive or distorting constraint'.[12]

For many men and women the partnership to which Sartre and de Beauvoir pledged themselves – one that would allow for 'contingent' affairs with others while remaining itself 'essential' and based on absolute honesty – has seemed an attractive, if perhaps finally unworkable, option. For Evans and Okely it is shot through with problems deriving from the asymmetry attaching to formally egalitarian relations when pursued within patriarchal society. Citing evidence suggesting that Sartre never abided by the promise of honesty,[13] Evans goes on to argue convincingly that de Beauvoir was disadvantaged in the relationship on a number of scores: whereas Sartre's (not untypically male) tendency was to treat women as a generalized category and thus to enjoy their company in a more undifferentiated, hence inconsequential, fashion, for de Beauvoir men were always specific, her relations with them therefore more highly charged – and thus potentially more disruptive of her bond with Sartre. On the other hand, Evans makes the point that the weakness of de Beauvoir's position, or at any rate the aspect of the relationship that was to bring her unhappiness, was that she could not admit

her jealousies or her need for sexual exclusivity without abandoning her rationality and reneging on her pact. To compound
the problem, 'her powerful rational qualities may have concealed
from Sartre the true extent of her emotional torments and
needs'.[14]

Now it may be that in her role as biographer Evans is here too
reductive in her treatment of Sartre's attitudes towards women
(which after all encompassed some highly individualized
relations, beginning with that with de Beauvoir herself ...);
inversely, under her sociological hat, she may be too inclined to
allow asymmetries in the pain caused to individuals in this particular partnership to be generalized between the sexes (one
cannot help feeling that Sartre's lack of jealousy, for example, is
very untypical and betokens something quite specific about his
sexuality). For all that, credit must go to Evans for her deft
orchestration of the psychological and social factors which must
complicate attempts to dispense with sexual fidelity, even where
both parties have a will to do so. What is not discussed, on the
other hand, is the possibility that couples may choose to live
monogamously within relationships that are in other respects
unconventional (because homosexual, or based around shared
nurturing, or pursued within a community, etc.). What is also
not sufficiently acknowledged perhaps is the joy and satisfaction
Sartre and de Beauvoir gave each other, the very good quality of
their relationship in the long term.

Though sharing Evans's interest in questions of jealousy and
sexual loyalty, Okely adopts a more psychoanalytic perspective.
In particular, she fixes upon the crisis experienced by de Beauvoir over Sartre's relationship with Olga. Fictionalized in her
early novel *She Came to Stay* (in which Xavière, the rival, is finally
murdered by the jealous wife) this, claims Okely, should be seen
in terms of de Beauvoir's double and contradictory attitudes to
Olga: as 'daughter' whose entry threatened her unconsciously
incestuous relation with Sartre (the 'father' in whose affection she
had finally managed to replace her mother); and as a reminder
of her own guilty self, as young Simone, the daughter competing
with her mother for her father's love. What is more, Okely goes

on to argue that in turning her aggression against the 'other' woman rather than the unfaithful male, de Beauvoir illustrates the general pattern of female jealousy, a pattern attributable to the particular values invested in the father by the girl child at the oedipal stage: continuing to idealize the father, the woman 'forgives' his transgressions, while reenacting hostility towards the mother/rival. Thus, while viewed at the time of its writing as an existentialist exploration of the problem of individual existence when confronted with the other, what was overlooked about the novel was its gender-specific nature: the 'Other' is in fact 'the other woman', and de Beauvoir's resolution of a seemingly 'existential' dilemma conforms in fact to particular patterns of female behaviour deriving from the imbalance of power between the sexes.

But like all psychoanalytic explanations used in the context of defending feminism, this must present problems, since it refers us to a self-enslaving psychological mode of reaction that is supposedly common to all women. How, then, can it be overcome, except through the collapse of the patriarchal ordering responsible for its production? De Beauvoir's own more cautious approach to psychoanalysis must recommend itself in the light of this sort of difficulty. She does not reject Freudianism altogether. (Indeed, the interpretation of the Olga affair, in which she has suggested Sartre's role as 'father figure' and hinted at a psychoanalytical explanation,[15] is not as unentertained by her as Okely supposes.) But she does (like Sartre) voice considerable misgivings about its reductionism. Thus, she writes of those 'elementary psychoanalysts' who will assert that Sartre was a substitute father-figure and Olga the child she never had:

> In the eyes of such doctrinaires, adult relationships are non existent: they take no note of that dialectic process which from childhood to maturity – starting with roots the deep importance of which I am very far from misconceiving – works a slow transformation upon one's emotional ties with other people. It preserves them, but achieves this preservation through a bypassing process which encapsulates the object of one's feelings, and lets one reexamine it afresh.[16]

It is not clear how Okely would want to respond to such an argument, just as it is not clear how far she regards de Beauvoir's childhood experiences at the oedipal stage as finally determining upon her adult emotional life or political dispositions. But seemingly at odds with any strongly deterministic approach is the argument she brings against Evans's suggestion that de Beauvoir can be understood as a straightforward case of 'male identification' under the impulse of her petty-bourgeois family's emphasis on individual achievement. On the contrary, says Okely, the split between 'male' and 'female' identification is not as simple as generally made out by feminists: 'if de Beauvoir had aligned herself to many of the values conveyed by her mother and teachers, she would also in effect have been aligning herself with the hidden patriarch.' Given, moreover, that she grew up to dismiss almost all her father's political beliefs, his racism and his attitudes to women, one must grant that 'her intellectual training was turned round to subvert the content of her father's beliefs, not just those of her mother'.[17] All of which implies, counter to her psychoanalytic emphasis, that one *can* (given the will to do so?) throw off the 'hidden patriarch' – or at least correct one's childhood estimations of one's father.

Nature, Woman, Enlightenment

Both Evans and Okely lay stress on the importance of childhood influences in shaping de Beauvoir's attitudes to nature. Okely offers the more nuanced and systematic discussion around the theme of de Beauvoir's split view of nature as on the one hand a source of sensual freedom and erotic autonomy, and on the other a mysterious diversion dooming one to immanence and threatening eventual engulfment. The more negative of these attitudes undeniably played a major role in establishing the equivalences: woman = nature = emotion/man = culture = rationality which have provided the governing logic of de Beauvoir's writing. And it does indeed seem true that de Beauvoir encountered a particularly forceful instantiation of these associations in the oppositional personalities of her parents. But given the entrenchment of the 'Enlightenment' conception of Nature as a woman to be variously seduced, violated, mastered, cultivated or transcended by a 'masculine' Reason, it would have been surprising had either de Beauvoir (or her parents) escaped its conditioning. After all, it is still this conceptual framework which monopolizes feminist argument in determining the very categories in terms of which a feminine 'difference' can be defended.

Clearly, what is more specifically influential on de Beauvoir's attitudes to nature is her acceptance of existentialism; or, more precisely, of the particular processing of Enlightenment ideology to be found in Hegelian–Sartrean ontology. Okely astutely remarks that insofar as de Beauvoir accepted Sartre's theories, she then had to answer for their flaws. But what does not seem fully realized either by her or Evans is the particular relevance this has to the understanding of the 'impasse' they both discover in *The Second Sex*. They both claim that de Beauvoir fails to make out a satisfactory case for the 'Otherness' of women: though aware of the shortcomings of the biological, psychological or Marxist 'explanations' of this, she herself attributes it to the 'imperialism' of consciousness without explaining the masculinity of the dominating 'mind'. They both also argue, quite rightly, that de Beauvoir has mapped the Hegelian Master–Slave dialectic onto male–female relations but blocked its *dénouement*. Whereas, according to Hegel, the dialectic is completed in the disalienation of 'Slave' consciousness, de Beauvoir argues that woman's connivance in her Otherness appears to doom her to perpetual slave status. Thus, Evans complains that de Beauvoir is ascribing to woman a state 'of natural, almost innate bad faith'; Okely that 'if de Beauvoir's Hegelian theory is taken to be the major if not the sole message of *The Second Sex*, then it would seem that she is saying that women's subordinate state is fixed'.[18]

What is curiously missing here, however, is any recognition that it is not so much the influence of Hegel (who is acknowledged to allow the 'slave' to triumph in the end ...) but rather Sartre's reinterpretation of the Master–Slave dialectic which is in conflict with the explicit commitment to female emancipation and sexual reciprocity.[19] For according to Sartre, where Hegel went wrong was in supposing that consciousness can retain its subjecthood consistently with its presentation of itself in the eyes of the Other as object. To be a subject, according to Sartre, is necessarily to objectify the other, and vice versa. 'So long as consciousnesses exist', he writes in *Being and Nothingness*, 'the separation and conflict of consciousness will remain.'[20] Hence for Sartre 'Slave' consciousness is necessarily objectified in the Other's 'look', and thus incapable of transcending its immersion in life.

Given de Beauvoir's acceptance of this Sartrean metaphysics, it is difficult to see how *The Second Sex* can simultaneously demand any genuine reciprocity between the sexes. For even if women were to abandon their complicity with their 'objectification', it is not clear how the parity of status they would thereby attain could be anything other than parity in the eternal struggle for subjecthood. There is the additional problem that in accepting Sartre's existentialism, de Beauvoir has also accepted his conception of 'immanence' as inherently 'feminine', and even imbued the female body with something of those same repellent qualities of 'sliminess', 'viscosity', and the like which Sartre (uncritically incorporating his own neurosis into his ontology) attributes to it and associated with the 'in-itself'.[21]

Of course, it can be argued that what de Beauvoir is describing in her vaguely distasteful images of female flesh is only a cultural apperception.[22] Such an argument would be consistent with the anti-biologistic stance of *The Second Sex* and with its conviction that women too, *qua* being human, seek and can attain 'transcendence' – a conviction reflected in her remark that 'when we have to do with a being whose nature is transcendent action, we can never close the books ... woman is a becoming'.[23] But a fundamental difficulty still remains given that her argument as a whole relies on the acceptance of the Hegelian–Sartrean ideal of transcendence – and thus, by implication, of the 'femininity' of immanence.

It is because humanity calls itself in question in the matter of living – that is to say, values the reasons for living above mere life – that, confronting woman, man assumes mastery. Man's design is not to repeat himself in time: it is to take control of the instant and mould the future. It is male activity that in creating values has made existence a value; this activity has prevailed over the confused forces of life; it has subdued Nature and Woman.[24]

From this perspective, the very notion of a *feminine* transcendence would appear self-contradictory. The existentialism of *The Second Sex* mediates the gender determinism of the Enlightenment ideology, but in the last analysis offers no final means of escape from it.

It is these philosophical tensions which underlie the various oscillations in the argument of *The Second Sex* – where the injunction to women to realize their intrinsic freedom of choice is difficult to reconcile with the emphasis on the biological and social factors that conserve them in their 'Otherness', and where the denial of a 'feminine nature' is confounded by the seeming essentialism of the physiological and psychological commentary. Both Evans and Okely remark on this ambivalence while yet themselves reflecting it in their verdicts upon *The Second Sex*. This is particularly true of Evans, who charges de Beauvoir with biological essentialism only to complain later that she ignores differences in the morality and behaviour of women, and to argue that 'her emphasis on the cultural construction of femininity goes very far towards a denial of the female body'.[25] Okely, for her part, frowns upon the least hint of biological reductionism in the argument of *The Second Sex* while yet implying that de Beauvoir may be open to valid criticism from the standpoint of the anatomical determinism argued for by such feminists as Luce Irigaray and Julia Kristeva. As she points out, it would not so much be the traces of biologism that the latter would object to in *The Second Sex* but rather de Beauvoir's internalization of the negation of the female anatomy.

Yet this emphasis on 'biologism' may really be something of a red herring. To recognize that there are certain differences of genetic determination between the sexes is not to predetermine their social existence or finally to explain why they happen to fulfil any particular cultural role. That women possess 'maternal instincts' (if they do) no more justifies the oppressive division of labour to which they have been subjected than does a measure of innate aggression among men (if it exists) justify or in any way explain the overkill of the nuclear arsenal. And actually *The Second Sex* makes all these points reasonably well. The real trouble with the book is that it tends to betray its own argument. Thus the central, and basically correct thesis that women are 'made' not 'born' could have been so much more powerfully pressed home had de Beauvoir spent less time describing the symptoms of 'otherness' in the 'product' and more on analysis of the fundamental economic and social structures that have gone into its 'making'.

What de Beauvoir herself now criticizes about *The Second Sex* is its 'idealism' – which she claims she would today correct by grounding the argument not in the antagonism of consciousness but in the fact of 'scarcity'.[26] In this, of course, she has once again taken her cue from Sartre, who made precisely the same ontological shift in his *Critique of Dialectical Reason* – where it is only the 'contingency' of scarcity which introduces conflict into relations that could otherwise be those of reciprocity. Thus it would seem that any flaws in the argument of *The Second Sex* due to the influence of Sartre's early existentialism are to be rectified today by recourse to his later Marxism. Certainly, this would represent a definite advance in the sense that it would remove any ontological obstacle to the achievement of sexual parity. On the other hand, apart from the fact that Sartre is surely wrong to present inequality and exploitation as derivative from Nature's (supposedly temporary) insufficiencies, it is not at all clear how the appeal to scarcity helps to explain the exploitation specific to women. If, as de Beauvoir recognizes in her discussion of Engels, the antagonism of the sexes is not reducible to class conflict, then, *a fortiori*, it cannot be accommodated within Sartre's 'scarcity' theory of class conflict.

Socialism, Eco-feminism and the Politics of 'Difference'

Not surprisingly de Beauvoir has expressed very little sympathy for the recent trends in French feminism which she refers to as the 'new femininity', and which she clearly regards as a reactionary development. In an interview of 1982, she argues that these are hampering rather than enhancing the feminist cause and, in a clear reference to writers such as Irigaray and Hélène Cixous, speaks derisively of those who 'would even have women write with their wombs'.[27]

Certainly, any feminism of 'difference', if taken to its logical conclusions, would seem to make a nonsense of the demand for parity, integration and reconciliation advanced by de Beauvoir's style of feminist argument; indeed it would seem to rule out even the possibility of male–female dialogue. Thus, for the 'difference' feminists, the project of resistance to 'Otherness' ends, paradoxically, in a celebration of that 'Otherness' as such; the demand that women be given a voice becomes a denial of the possibility of her speaking in the tongue of 'man'; and what was once the scurrilous idea that women 'have nothing to say' is turned around to become a positive justification for an incapacity to communicate. And all this is indeed, as de Beauvoir says, reactionary – and not just because it is associated with an inflation of the 'maternal' body and function which then all too easily serves as an apologia for an existing sexual division of labour, but because it instantiates a 'linguistic' turn in theory whose typical effect is to screen out consideration of the material causes of oppression.

On the other hand, the materialist point of view – represented in much excellent socialist-feminist analysis – belongs to a tradition of Marxist argument which is itself cast within the 'Enlightenment' framework of values. The explicit commitment to sexual equality is thus arguably at odds with the underlying 'masculinist' bias of traditional Marxist attitudes to nature, industry, science and rationality. In this situation, it is not clear how the oppressive paternalism of the Enlightenment underpinning can be challenged other than via a deliberate positive assertion of the negated 'feminine' values. For example, whatever scruples we may have about the call for there to be 'womanly times', it is surely a demand which directs attention to qualities, functions and activities with whose absence or devaluation we have to associate the runaway militarization of society. Moreover, as science increasingly comes to serve precious little else except the advancement of military technologies, it is of vital importance that the critique of science implied in the charge of 'masculinity', together with the closely related question of the (allegedly negative) 'male' qualities of reason itself,[28] be placed more firmly on the agenda, not only of feminism, but of the left in general. Reluctant as one may be to take on the idea of a distinctively 'feminine' cognition, it is still important to understand why this idea is now so widely canvassed and to examine the extent to which it can furnish an adequate basis for a revaluation of scientific activity.

Nor is this simply an academic issue: the problem is not just to determine where, upon a spectrum running from 'green feminine' occultism at one end to 'masculine' scientism at the other, one can respectably set up intellectual camp. It is also, and more importantly, a political issue in the sense that any thinking about the nature of socialist alternatives – given that it must encompass the issues of peace, ecology, the Third World, the sustainable economy, the family and rearing of children, and the patterning of sexual relations – must now register and seriously engage with the tensions reflected in the traditional gender antitheses.

None of this, it has to be said, is recognized by de Beauvoir, who indeed (like most of her left-wing compatriots at the present time) seems disinclined to associate either socialism or feminism with the struggle for disarmament or the values of the green movement. On the other hand, it should also be said that neither Evans nor Okely is critical of her politics on these lines. In fact Evans attacks her rather for a too purely 'moral' political stance, a position she associates with a failure to adopt a properly necessitarian attitude to the coming of socialism. Thus she can cite approvingly Anne Whitmarsh's astonishing judgement in her recent study of de Beauvoir's politics that for de Beauvoir:

the disappearance of the proletariat as a class, which is imperative, is so in moral terms only, not because it is dictated as an inevitable historical process; it depends on those who are oppressed realizing this and doing something about it. They are free to submit or revolt: their future cannot be imposed from outside by, for instance, the Communist Party.[29]

But the mere fact that de Beauvoir does not think socialism is either guaranteed or 'imposable' by a party is hardly conclusive evidence that she cannot be counted a Marxist. Some indeed (including myself) would want to argue the contrary if anything. Where Evans goes wrong is in assuming that anyone arguing that socialism is not an inevitable destiny is committed to the (certainly mistaken) view that the working class has only to realize its lack of 'freedom' in order for it to bring about a socialist order. But the 'humanism' of the first of these positions by no means automatically commits one to the 'moralism' of the latter.

A further point of contention for Evans bears more directly on the specific issue of feminist strategy, and connects with her overall charge of 'individualism'. For she links this at a number of points to criticism of de Beauvoir for her 'heterosexism' and rejection of 'political lesbianism'. It is fairly clear, in fact, that when she argues for 'interdependence' rather than 'autonomy' as the goal of feminism, what she has in mind is not so much the promotion of greater solidarity between men and women, but rather the fostering of separatist collectivities. In other words her argument is implicitly directed at what she takes to be the anti-separatist implications of de Beauvoir's position. Now, it is quite true that de Beauvoir has consistently opposed any ghettoization of women. Her reasons for doing so, however, do not derive from any abhorrence of lesbianism as such (which, in fact, she has recently stated that she 'completely and utterly' accepts for herself 'on a theoretical level') but from a belief that relations between men and women do not have to be oppressive, and that to portray them as if they did is to alienate heterosexual women from the movement. 'I think it's a very good thing that some women are very radical', she wrote in 1972, 'but ... I find their mystique of the clitoris fatuous and irritating, as well as the sexual dogmas they try to impose.'[30] At the same time, it is reasonable to suppose that any opposition she has expressed in the past towards separatist tactics stems, at least in part, from a conviction that the political strategies to which one should lend support are those consistent with the aims one wants to achieve – in her case those of sexual parity and reconciliation.

It is a pity that neither Evans nor Okely chooses to pursue these lines of investigation, or to review their criticisms of de Beauvoir's failure of emotional empathy with women in the light of the objections she herself voiced against intolerance of heterosexuality – objections based in her sense that for many women, whatever their politics, homosexuality is simply ruled out because of the nature of their desire. It is a pity, too, that neither of the two authors – nor de Beauvoir either, it has to be said – has anything very positive to offer in the way of alternatives to conventional sexual and familial relations. The family is generally thought to be a bad thing, but very little is said about what to put in its place and there is scarcely any discussion at all of male nurturing or shared childcare. Indeed Evans seems almost to accept de Beauvoir's assumption that if women opt for motherhood they are automatically condemned to assume the major, if not exclusive, role in the upbringing of the children. One cannot help feeling however that this is an absence reflective of a more general gap in feminist argument – which, on the whole, has offered rather little in the way of imaginative projections of what relations between the sexes could be like in a post-patriarchal society. Yet without any 'utopianism' of that kind, or any clear sense of the goals to be achieved, it is not clear by what criteria the various strategies proposed by feminists are to be judged, or how progress in the advancement of feminism is to be measured.

It may well be that the development of more positive and constructive thinking about the family and heterosexuality is currently deterred by fear of the heresy of 'heterosexism' that a number of feminists today oppose to their own orthodoxy. But it is certainly a fear that should not be allowed to dominate feminist discussion, and to which de Beauvoir's particular sensibility offers a valuable antidote. It is difficult, at any rate, not to feel that some basic sense of balance is in jeopardy when one can read in an otherwise highly sensitive piece of feminist writing:

> Again, contemporary feminism must make us examine more critically the assumption that de Beauvoir and Sartre established a relationship different in its essential emotional and sexual assumptions from those of the conventional world: merely in terms of the services which they provided for each other, it is apparent that on many occasions de Beauvoir fulfilled the traditional female role of nurturing and assuming domestic responsibilities. During the Second World War it was she who scoured Paris for food, and cooked, and during the last ten years of Sartre's life – when he was terribly enfeebled and often ill – it was de Beauvoir who cared for him and tried to mitigate his suffering.[31]

Their relationship was, of course, 'conventional' in these ways, and there is no denying the importance of the struggle against the disparities in the respective positions of men and women responsible for that 'conventionality'. But it is important also to keep in mind that it is a *human* convention – or should be – to minister to a dying lifelong lover or companion. Any feminism that would sacrifice such a practice to its ideological purity would seem to hold out little promise of bliss to either sex.

Notes

1. General biographical studies in English include: Elaine Marks, *Simone de Beauvoir: Encounters with Death*, New Brunswick 1973; Robert D. Cottrell, *Simone de Beauvoir*, New York 1975; Carol Ascher, *Simone de Beauvoir: A Life of Freedom*, Boston 1981. Anne Whitmarsh offers a comprehensive survey of de Beauvoir's existentialist politics in her *Simone de Beauvoir and the Limits of Commitment*, Cambridge 1981. Studies of de Beauvoir concentrating on her literary contribution are to be found in Konrad Bieber, *Simone de Beauvoir*, Boston 1979, and in Terry Keefe, *Simone de Beauvoir – a Study of Her Writing*, London 1983 – whose stated aim is to correct the 'distorted' picture of de

Beauvoir as a writer resulting from concentration on her feminism or her association with Sartre.

2. Michèle Le Doeuff, 'Women and Philosophy', *Radical Philosophy* 17, Summer 1977, p. 8. De Beauvoir records this promise of Sartre's in volume one of her autobiography, *Memoirs of a Dutiful Daughter*, first published in 1958.

3. Bieber writes, for example, (*Simone de Beauvoir*, p. 17) that 'whatever qualms the male critic might have, Simone de Beauvoir puts his mind at rest: she speaks and writes in a way that one might forget about the sex of the novelist or the essayist.'

4. Mary Evans, *Simone de Beauvoir, A Feminist Mandarin*, London 1985; Judith Okely, *Simone de Beauvoir*, London 1986 (this is published in the Virago Pioneer series).

5. Evans, *A Feminist Mandarin*, pp. 56–7.

6. *Ibid.*, pp. xi–xv.

7. See *All Said and Done* (*Tout compte fait*, 1972), trans. Patrick O'Brian, Harmondsworth 1977, p. 491.

8. See 'I am a Feminist', translation of an article first published in *Le Nouvel Observateur*, 1972, included in *Simone de Beauvoir Today*, interview with Alice Schwarzer, London 1984.

9. At the same time, Okely quotes a number of testimonies from Third World readers to de Beauvoir's positive influence in allowing them to adopt more critical attitudes towards the West. In the words of one of the women cited: 'She became the idol, the ideal type, herself. But she also succeeded in relieving somewhat the contradiction of being anti-imperialist at the same time as being pro-"Western" for feminist reasons.' (*Simone de Beauvoir*, p. 4)

10. *The Second Sex* ends with the claim that 'when we abolish the slavery of half humanity, together with the whole system of hypocrisy that it implies, then the "division" of humanity will reveal its genuine significance and the human couple will find its true form' (see English translation, Harmondsworth 1953, p. 741. Much criticism has recently been voiced of H.M. Parshley's English version of *The Second Sex*). Okely follows Margaret Simons (see 'The Silencing of Simone de Beauvoir: Guess What's Missing from *The Second Sex*', *Women's Studies International Forum* 6, 5, pp. 559–64) in finding him guilty of mistranslation and distortion. Deirdre Bair replies to the charge in: 'In Summation: The Question of Conscious Feminism or Unconscious Mysogyny in The Second Sex', *Simone de Beauvoir Studies*, 1, 1, pp. 56–67.

11. *A Feminist Mandarin*, p. 40; cf. p. 32. Evans criticizes de Beauvoir for acceptance of the 'inverse' position (i.e. thinking that capitalism cannot survive the overthrow of patriarchy) and associates her in this with Michèle Barrett and Nancy Chodorow. Thus she writes: 'All three authors accept, and argue, that a transformation in gender relations and in the sexual division of labour would have a transforming effect on society as we now know it in the west'; and she herself rejects the argument on the grounds that the measures (shared

nurturing, etc.) advocated by Chodorow and Barrett could all be integrated into advanced capitalism without significant threat to the system (see pp. 125–6). It is not actually quite so clear where de Beauvoir herself stands on this. In her 'I am a Feminist' interview she claims not to know 'to what extent the destruction of patriarchal society by women would affect all aspects of capitalism and democracy'.

12. *A Feminist Mandarin*, p. 17.

13. *Ibid.*, p. 18. It is, it has to be said, fairly third-hand 'evidence' and differs from Sartre's testimony elsewhere (see, e.g., the interview 'We are not above Criticism', *Simone de Beauvoir Today*, p. 54).

14. *A Feminist Mandarin*, p. 22.

15. See *The Prime of Life* (*La Force de l'âge*, 1960), trans. Peter Green, Harmondsworth, 1962, p. 368, where she writes: 'Certainly my attachment to Sartre could, in one sense, be traced back to my childhood; but it was also a result of the sort of person *he* was.'

16. *Ibid.* Cf. Sartre's argument that the oedipal complex lacks 'dialectical irreducibility' in 'Itinerary of a Thought', in *Between Existentialism and Marxism*, London 1974, pp. 37f.

17. Okely, *Simone de Beauvoir*, pp. 43–4.

18. *A Feminist Mandarin*, p. 72; *Simone de Beauvoir*, p. 73.

19. On this, see Genevieve Lloyd's illuminating discussion, 'Masters, Slaves and Others' *Radical Philosophy* 34, Summer 1983, pp. 2–9 – now included in her book *The Man of Reason*, London 1984, pp. 86–102.

20. *Being and Nothingness*, London 1958, p. 242.

21. Cf. M. Collins and C. Pierce, 'Holes and Slime: Sexism in Sartre's Psychoanalysis', in C. Gould and M. Wartofsky (eds) *Women and Philosophy*, New York 1980, pp. 112–27 and Lloyd, 'Masters, Slaves and Others'. In *The Second Sex* de Beauvoir speaks of 'this quivering jelly which is elaborated in the womb', evoking too clearly the 'soft viscosity of carrion for him not to turn shuddering away'; of 'the slimy embryo' (p. 178); of woman's body as 'sunk in immanence' (p. 189); of the 'gloomy passion of a consciousness made flesh' (p. 196) – and the central idea of female corporeality as both yielding and engulfing is to be found *passim*.

22. Indeed she does argue this in so far as she claims that she uses the terms 'woman' and 'feminine' in *The Second Sex* not to refer to biological essences, but to conceptions, values and ideals. Cf. her remark that ' "weakness" is revealed as such only in the light of the ends man proposes, the instruments he has available and the laws he establishes. If he does not wish to seize the world, then the idea of a *grasp* on things has no sense' (p. 67).

23. *The Second Sex*, p. 66.

24. *Ibid*, p. 97; cf. Lloyd, *Man of Reason*, pp. 100–101.

25. *A Feminist Mandarin*, p. 127; cf. pp. 49, 57.

26. *All Said and Done*, p. 484.

27. *Simone de Beauvoir Today*, p. 103.

28. As raised by Brian Easlea, *Science and Sexual Oppression*, London 1981; *Fathering the Unthinkable*, London 1983 (which contains a bibliographical note on p. 222 on recent articles dealing with the issue of the masculinity of science). For works on the issues of rationality and gender, see the bibliographical essay in Lloyd, *Man of Reason*, and see note 5 to chapter 9 below.

29. Anne Whitmarsh, *Limits of Commitment*, p. 63, cited in *A Feminist Mandarin*, p. 49.

30. *Simone de Beauvoir Today*, p. 36.

31. *A Feminist Mandarin*, p. 13.

9

Feminism as Critique

The usual idea behind the collective anthology is that it should serve as a means for bringing together the thought of several different authors in debate upon a common theme. In practice this rarely happens, and it is all too common for volumes of this kind to be no more than aggregations of quite disparate pieces of writing. *Feminism as Critique* is an improvement on many collections in this respect.[1] It is by no means an entirely integrated whole, and some of the claims to unity made in the introduction are rather forced and not borne out in the articles themselves. Nevertheless, there is a definite community of purpose here which is manifest at the most general level in the concern of all the articles to move feminism beyond its initial phase of 'deconstructive' criticism towards a more positive work of theoretical 'reconstruction'. What is needed now, it is said, is not so much exposure of the gender bias or blindness of theory as a reworking of the theory itself in order to render it more adequate to female experience. This brings us to a second, somewhat more specific, unity claimed for this volume – namely, that its various authors are all in their differing ways engaged with strands of twentieth-century Marxism. The reworking of Marxist theory, which is viewed as an essential feature of feminist 'reconstruction', is held to consist centrally in a 'displacement of the paradigm of production', with the main assistance sought in Habermas.

At the same time there is a general agreement among all the

authors – and here we have a third thematic unity – that liberal theory, so far from providing any kind of resource for renewal, is rooted in conceptions of the individual and approaches to the social which have very little to offer feminism: several of the pieces are concerned with the implicit masculinism of the 'sovereign' and 'disencumbered' self appealed to in liberal theory, and with the ways in which liberal conceptions of the 'public' and 'private' serve to reinforce an existing gender division of labour and its associated devaluation of traditional female roles.

Such a critique of liberalism is of course by no means novel, but as Seyla Benhabib and Drusilla Cornell suggest in their introduction, it is distinguished from a good deal of recent communitarian writing by its keenness to avoid any collapse of personal identity into social role. Though a feminist critique must recognize, against liberalism, the 'situated' nature of the subject, it must do it in a way which also challenges conventional social roles and avoids any confirmation of the gender identities and persona behind which the real subjectivity of women has so frequently disappeared. This poses a dilemma that is addressed in several of the later essays: how can feminist theory base itself on the uniqueness of feminine experience without reifying a particular definition of femaleness as paradigmatic, and thus succumbing to essentialist discourse?

It is an extended and convoluted theoretical journey, and by the time we have arrived at Josephine Butler's existentialistic defence of the notion of 'gender choice' or Isaac Balbus's staged clash between the Foucauldians and the object-relations theorists, we may well wonder how far we are still addressing anything that could be called Marxist or seen as plausibly contributing to its feminist reconstruction. On the other hand, there is no doubt that the most interesting and original feature of this collection lies in the engagement of so many of its pieces – albeit sometimes quite indirectly and often critically – with a central body of Marxist work previously almost unconsidered by feminist writers: the Critical Theory of the Frankfurt School and in particular of its sole surviving representative, Jürgen Habermas.

This is in obvious contrast to the Lacanian and 'poststructuralist' preoccupations of a good deal of recent feminist theory, and allows one to mark out this volume as the site of a distinctive 'Habermasian' direction in feminist study.

The Turn to Habermas

In noting this turn to Habermas as one of the main (though not the only) interests of this book, one is bound to ask why it has come so late. For there would seem to be quite a number of factors predisposing towards it. In the first place, there is the distinctly 'Marxian' character of feminist criticism. By this I do not mean to imply that all feminists are Marxist – which would be wholly absurd – but only that feminist argument conforms with the theoretical exercise conducted by Marx under the name of 'critique' in fusing critical and substantive elements. The Marxist critique, in explaining the source in reality of the cognitive shortcomings of the theory under attack, called for changes in the reality itself. And it was to signal their commitment to this combined analytic and transformative project that the early theorists of the Frankfurt School gave such prominence to the notion of 'critique' in defining their own programme: critique was to function not merely as negative contestation or as Kantian constraint on the flights of speculative reason, but as argued justification for concrete, emancipatory practice. It is with a similar programmatic aim in view that feminist argument seeks to transform, as it exposes, the social reality of the sex/gender system responsible for the sexism and general opacity to feminine concerns of dominant cultural discourse and practice.

It is true that in some of the later writing of the Critical Theorists the negative criticism becomes so overshadowing that the emancipatory project dwindles to a flickering light against the general darkness of the historical nightmare. But it is never entirely extinguished; and in any case, as far as Habermas is concerned, his work has always been guided by an optimism which, he would insist, is not purely of the will but is grounded in the real possibilities of human communicative interaction. Contrasting his scientifically oriented critique with Adorno's more metaphysical leanings. Habermas has often stressed the aim of bringing social philosophy and the empirical social sciences into a mutually advantageous and corrective relationship, and suggested that it represents a return to the more collaborative and constructive spirit guiding the work of the Frankfurt School in the 1930s.[2]

Indeed, one might argue that it is the distinctive 'modernism' of its outlook that makes Habermasian theory more compatible with feminism. For both are opposed to 'postmodernist' subversion of the emancipatory project while resisting any 'antimodernist' nostalgic formulations of it.[3] Just as contemporary feminism, despite many other disagreements, would seem united in seeking liberation but refusing to find it in any erstwhile condition of women, so Habermas has disallowed the idea that renewal can be sought in traditional forms, insisting that 'cultural modernism' is the only resource of any historically enlightened consciousness, while at the same time avoiding all poststructuralist conclusions about the inevitability of domination.[4]

At the same time, the commitment to modernity and liberation has always gone together in his work with a 'Critical Theory' distaste for instrumental rationality and its technocratic values which chimes with many of the themes of feminist critique of science. Similarly, the resistance to 'truth-splitting' (especially in the work of Adorno, though it is present in more qualified form in Habermas too), and the polemic against the distortions introduced in the severing of propositional from aesthetic or moral truth, have a distinct family resemblance with the forms of opposition voiced in *Feminism as Critique*, as in other recent works, to mainstream ethics and epistemology.[5] Finally, Habermas's championing of non-adversarial dialogue – of the liberating potential of forms of communication which have been freed from the distorting and blinkering effects of conventional norms and modes of authority – must recommend itself to a movement which has itself placed such weight on the 'non-violent' strategies of discussion and consciousness-raising.[6]

Granted, then, that there are all these affinities of approach, why has it been only so belatedly that feminists have turned to Critical Theory? In part, no doubt, because of the all-male, monastical atmospherics of the Frankfurt School; in part, perhaps, because even in the School's engagement with obviously relevant issues (the family, the 'authoritarian personality') and despite a general condemnation of the oppression of women in bourgeois society, it offers no detailed and sustained investigation of the patriarchal formation and its repercussions. This lends a slight note of pathos to those essays in *Feminism as Critique* which engage most closely with Habermas's argument (notably Nancy Fraser's excellent exposure of the gender-blindness which, she argues, vitiates his otherwise potentially pro-feminist rewriting of historical materialism). For there is more than a suggestion here that the male theorist is being shown what his theory would have had to say about the subordination of women were he to have devoted more serious attention to it – a patience of theoretical disposition which has its echo in the suggestion here and there in the book that this or that bit of Marx or Habermas is 'not helpful' to feminism. (To avoid misunderstanding: I thoroughly applaud this kind of constructive engagement with non-gender-sensitive theories. I just wonder whether the theoretical ghettoization of feminism is not protracted by the modesty which allows such theories to be 'unhelpful' as opposed to seriously flawed.)

Economic Critique

Fraser's article is cued by Linda Nicholson's reproaches against the 'economic essentialism' of classical Marxism. Echoing much previous feminist criticism of Marx, Nicholson deplores the privileging of the labour of production (of food and objects) over that of 'reproduction' in which, from the standpoint of the philosophical anthropology of self-fulfilment through labour, she finds an abstraction from the whole issue of feminine self-realization. But she argues, in addition, that this implicit identification of economic activity with 'male' work is compounded by a projection on to Marx's cross-cultural theory of the distinctively capitalist severance between productive and reproductive spheres of action. Marx is thus viewed as guilty of a 'bourgeois' eternalization of the autonomy and ultimately determining nature of the economic – whose effect is to generalize the occlusion of child-rearing and domestic activity specific to market society. For it is only in this society, says Nicholson, that food and object production (the 'economy'), which unlike reproductive activities lends itself to commodification, comes to structure other human practices.[7]

Against this background, both Nicholson and Fraser endorse Habermas's down-playing of Marx's cross-cultural claims, and credit him with recognizing much more clearly than Marx that the splitting off of food and object production and its allocation to the 'official' realm of the 'economic' is specific to modern society. Fraser in particular approves his four-term model of 'private–public' relations as far more adequate to the complexities of capitalist society. Thus, Habermas's division between 'material' and 'symbolic' functions – between 'food and object production' and 'socialization of the young, group solidarity formation and cultural transmission' – theorizes a contrast between the 'public' work world and the 'private' domain of domestic reproduction. But at the same time, in the distinction between the 'systemic' integration accomplished by state and economy, and the 'social integration' characterizing the 'life-world', his theory incorporates a contrast *within* the 'life-world' itself between 'public' political participation and 'private' family concerns.[8] Nonetheless, it is argued that this categorial severance between 'material' and 'symbolic' and between 'systemic' and 'social' integration reproduces the same abstraction from gender division of which classical Marxism is guilty in its tendency to accommodate traditional female roles within 'symbolic' reproduction, thus obscuring the very material character of much child-rearing practice. Conversely, by treating such practice and familial relations as paradigms of 'social' rather than 'systemically' integrated action. Habermas also obscures the systemic aspects of family life – which is, says Fraser, 'thoroughly permeated with power and money.'[9]

Furthermore, Fraser claims that even as Habermas registers the ambivalence of welfare capitalism, and salutes the new social movements, including that of feminism, for contesting the 'erosion' of the 'life-world' by the systemic imperatives of power and money, he is deaf to the gender subtext of its dynamics. Habermas rightly sees that even as it enforces social rights which constrain the power of capital in the (paid) workplace and of the paterfamilias within the bourgeois family, the means employed in defence of such rights have tended to be bureaucratic, turning individuals into clients of the state system and preempting their capacity to interpret their own needs, experiences and life problems.[10] But, says Fraser, he fails to see that welfare systems are themselves dualized and gendered, reducing the woman's dependency on the individual male breadwinner but only at the cost of throwing her on the mercies of a patriarchal and androcentric state bureaucracy.

The problems, in short, of the encroachment of systemic-integration – which Habermas diagnoses and explores as typical of modern societies – are problems not only of overriding reification but also of 'rationalization' and 'modernization' of women's oppression. In his analysis of welfare capitalism. Habermas repeats the central error of his account of classical capitalism. By basing it in the same 'economy'/'life-world' and 'systemic'/'social' interaction divides, he allows the theoretic knife to 'cut for' patriarchal ordering rather than the overthrow of existing gender divisions of labour, social roles and values.[11] What is required instead, it is suggested, is a framework which does not put the male-headed nuclear family on the opposite side of the line from the state-regulated official economy, but is sensitive to the similarities between two institutions which, despite many other differences, conspire in enforcing women's subordination, 'appropriate our labour, short-circuit our participation in the interpretation of our needs and shield normatively secured need interpretations from political contestation'.[12]

System and Life-world

One of the interesting features of this critique is that it highlights, without resolving, the tension between on the one hand the ('feminist'?) values in the name of which one wants to resist the reification resulting from the advance of 'systemic' integration into the 'life-world'[13] and on the other hand the ('feminist'?) values in the name of which the life-world/system distinction is itself being challenged. It is true that Habermas's framework tends to legitimize the institutional separation of family and 'official' economy. Yet in contesting erosion of the 'symbolic' he is also defending that non-instrumental, socially interactive, affective modality of human relations which feminists themselves want to prioritize, and even claim as embodying a distinctively feminine ethic. Again it is true that in deploring the encroachment of systemic imperatives Habermas is relying on the idea that there are certain kinds of human activity (paradigmatically those of child-rearing and nursing) which *cannot* be commodified, because commodification proceeds only at the cost of their instrinsic qualities of personal and freely bestowed caring and loving. This might seem dangerously close to a rationalization of feminine domesticity, and such sentimentalism for the 'Symbolic' will not recommend itself to those women who have yearned for a bit more 'systemic' encroachment into their cherishing preserve in the form of proper public child care, not to mention wages for housework.[14] On the other hand, however, we might note that Nicholson explicitly appeals to the non-commodification of 'reproductive' work in establishing her case against Marxism; and neither she nor Fraser seems of a mind to deny the worth of 'symbolic' values. Indeed they and other writers in the book fear the loss of these feminine-associated values and forms of interaction even as they are critical of Habermas's failure to draw out the implications of his normative schema for feminist theory and practice. Much of the critique of the 'public'/'private' divide relies on a privileging of non-systemic activities which comes close at times to presenting these as essentially 'feminine'.

This means that any demand for a 'de-differentiation' of unpaid childrearing and waged work, or for a closing of the public/private divide, will need to be clearly differentiated from any mere call for wages for housework or for a Soviet-style acclamation of the 'national service' of mothering – moves which would serve not only to advance the deplored systemic integration of modern society but also to perpetuate the existing division of gender roles. Paying for childcare would no more guarantee its removal from the realm of 'women's work' than honouring housework as an act of citizenship on a par with soldiering would necessarily ensure that men took a share in it. The real question here is what is wanted: that women should retain their traditional tasks but freed of their subordinated and devalued aura; or that the gender division of tasks should itself be eroded? Similarly, in regard to the division between public and private: are we wanting an upgrading of the derided 'private' aims, values and activities, or an obliteration of the distinction: a 'utopia' without a 'public' realm of emulation, competition, fame and recognition, or a 'utopia' which held traditional 'male' activities of little account but esteemed everything 'womanly'?

Or shall we say, rather, that we are looking not so much for erosions or inversions of the existing divisions, as for a more radical redefinition of these spheres and values themselves – such that, for example, the 'public' would no longer designate the domain of national chauvinism and individual careerism, but become associated with the extension of political space for the renegotiation of 'public' interests, standards of success and existing divisions of labour? Just as such a redefinition would begin to reveal the narrowness of a 'public' life that down-played all other interests and attachments than those of work and career, so it would allow 'private' dimensions (one's existence as parent or spouse or domestic worker) to find some 'public' profile and political representation. It is this kind of extension of political space which I think Maria Markus has in mind in her interesting study of women's attitudes to success, when she draws attention to the importance of extending 'civil society' as a condition of the kind of institutional restructuring and revaluation of roles and relations that would take us beyond the existing conceptions of 'public' and 'private'.[15] Well aware that one is here talking as much about general human as about specifically feminist political concerns, she writes:

> Though such a civil society is voluntary-associative and pluralistic, it
> – at the same time – can express and promote critical concerns over
> general issues kept off the agenda or treated in an unsatisfactory
> way. That is, it can promote what may be called 'generalizable
> interests', putting them on the agenda of public discourse, and
> stimulating the appropriate changes.[16]

Ethical Critique

The separation of public and private is associated by several of the essays in this book, particularly those addressed specifically to the issue of a 'feminist ethic', with the divorce between 'reason' and 'desire': a divorce deemed to be a bad thing and in turn associated with the limited 'masculinism' of traditional moral and political philosophy. Here, too, Habermas figures as a recalcitrant ally who, on the one hand, is credited with 'developing a conception of normative reason that does not seek the unity of a transcendent impartiality and therefore does not oppose reason to desire', but, on the other, is charged with being too attached to an impartiality based on an abstraction from affectivity.[17] Iris Young, defending what she calls a 'dialogic' conception of normative reason against the 'monologism' of deontological ethics, would even claim that the very idea of an objective understanding of an issue arrived at through discussion aimed at consensus is an illusion directed upon an unrealizable and unwanted goal. More fundamentally, she contests Habermas's assumption that understanding rests on some common agreements about meanings – an assumption, she claims, which in invoking 'identitary logic' is guilty of the 'metaphysics of presence'.[18] But taken to its ultimate conclusion such an argument would make a nonsense of Young's own request for our comprehension and agreement, and rests on the undefended premise that language is exhausted in the *relationality* of terms. As Castoriadis (who in fact is one of the keener critics of the limitations of 'identitary logic') has pointed out:

> language is only able to function because, while on the one hand the significations which it conveys are nothing more than endless and indefinite referrals to *something other than* ... (what appeared to have been said directly), yet *at the same time* these referrals can only be referrals because they refer *from* one term *to* another, and can only exist because they are relations between terms posited as fixed.[19]

A more qualified, less Derridean, questioning of the value of impartiality is at work in Benhabib's critique of the supposedly universally substitutable subject of standard political and moral reasoning. Rooted as it is in the privileging of the 'wholly autonomous, male, narcissistic ego', such theory has, in Benhabib's view, perennially reproduced a divorce between autonomy and dependency, and hence between an 'ethic of justice' and an 'ethic of caring'. That this divide, whose effect is to relegate women to a timeless 'natural' sphere of nurture and domesticity, is still infecting contemporary moral theory is plainly visible, she argues, in its pervasive reliance on a 'general other' conceived in abstraction from all the differences of outlook, feeling and situation of actual, concrete persons. Indeed, it reaches a kind of apotheosis in the Rawlsian assumption that behind the 'veil of ignorance' one can plausibly talk of persons coming 'without prior moral ties': a form of talk which strictly speaking would mean that the traditional ethical principles of reversibility and universalizability could not be realized, since where there is no real, but only a formal plurality of persons, there is no coherent sense of the difference between self and others upon which such a principle could turn.

These points against Rawls's 'Cartesianism' are well taken, but they should not be seen as supporting the extreme moral 'particularism' advocated by Young, or at least not if one thinks that respect for justice and equality is fundamental to our very conception of ethics. For if one does not abstract from *some* differences between persons one removes the grounding for any moral demand that they be treated equally: why should they be, if they are not comparable in any respect at all? At the same time, one must surely resist the suggestion that in being 'impartial' one is abstracting from all differences of 'concrete' feeling and circumstance, since an ethics or legal system is only genuinely impartial precisely insofar as it takes account of certain differences and deems them relevant to decision and judgement. More sensitive than some to these problems, Banhabib herself advocates a 'communicative ethics of need' which combines recognition of the dignity of the 'generalized other' with acknowledgement of the moral identity of the 'concrete other'. This, she suggests, would allow all possible knowledge of the moral situation to come into play, including the affective constitution and specific history of the individual. The problem, however, with this attractive-sounding idea is that it would seem simply to shove the problem of moral agreement one step back. For how would the reconciliation of particular interests be practically achieved? One assumes through compromise and bargaining. But successful bargaining and compromise can only be conducted in the light of generally accepted moral principles.[20]

The issue of the compatibility of a 'feminist' ethics with respect for principles of justice and equality has been raised in acute form by Carol Gilligan's challenge to Lawrence Kohlberg's 'justice and rights' measurement of moral maturity (a measurement by reference to which women in his experiments persistently recorded lower 'scores' than men).[21] Benhabib makes extended reference to the Gilligan–Kohlberg dispute, which is of special interest in this context given Kohlberg's influence on Habermas, but which is also commanding a more general attention from feminists at the present time.[22] The issues raised by this controversy are too complex to be adequately treated in the space of this review, and I shall add here no more than one or two very general points.

The first concerns the arguably over-rigid and simple oppositions – for example, between reason and desire, cognition and feeling (the 'body'), justice/equality and caring/responsibility – around which the discussion revolves. In relying on these all too traditional philosophical polarities,[23] feminists reproduce the idea that 'male' reason and its 'public' forum and citizen modality do indeed represent a disembodied, affect-free zone, when nothing in fact could be further from the truth. Politics is all too much about conflicting desires, ambitions and dubious rationalizations of emotive forces; citizenship (from which Young claims the 'body' is excluded[24]) is all too obviously, in its central soldiering dimensions, organized around the butchering of bodies and esteem for physical prowess. And how can we collude in the idea that 'impartiality' falls on the side of a 'masculine' ethics when we know how famously impartial judges have shown themselves to be in their assessment of rape cases, to name but one example? This brings us to a second point: which is that the goals of 'impartiality' or justice can only be challenged at the cost of undermining the criticism which feminism has so frequently (and surely justifiably?) levelled at the gender-biased nature of a great deal of supposedly neutral social practice (including that of social science itself). Indeed, if one takes the position that the quest for impartiality is itself mistaken and opposed to feminine values, then the whole point of complaining that 'masculine' universalist appeals or supposedly 'neutral' claims are not what they appear, would seem to be lost. Catherine MacKinnon, for instance, protests that when the state 'is most ruthlessly neutral, it will be most male; when it is most sex blind, it will be most blind to the sex of the standard being applied.'[25] But does not the whole force of her argument rely on an implicit endorsement of the goal of objectivity and a demand that women should be treated to a genuinely 'sex-impartial' justice rather than placed at the mercy of a 'blind' subjectivity?[26]

Essentialism and Existentialism

One of the paradoxes of the 'particularist' critique of ethical universalism is that it can only be consistently sustained within the perspective of a 'difference' feminism at odds with any Marxian–Habermasian commitment to parity and transgender agreement. Equally, however, it is very difficult to defend the 'difference' perspective without falling into an essentialism of the feminine which all the authors in *Feminism as Critique* professedly wish to avoid. This tension is dominant in the later essays – most of which are much less Habermasian in outlook – and particularly affects those which draw on Carol Gilligan's defence of the feminine 'ethics of caring'. Gilligan herself grounds this defence on the account of gender-identity formation associated with the 'mothering' psychoanalysis of Chodorow and Dinnerstein[27] (which holds that 'mother-dominated' child-rearing lies at the source of patriarchy), and she has been accused for that reason of falling into an undesirable essentialism of the nurturant role. It has been argued, for example, that if it is only in virtue of their nurturing experience that women acquire this ethical outlook, then there would be a moral duty to confine them to the mothering role as a way of guaranteeing the presence in society of these 'female' caring capacities.[28]

Gilligan has been defended against this charge on the ground that the Chodorow–Dinnerstein thesis only supposes these capacities to be 'female' in the sense that they are culturally devalued and hence not developed by men at the present time.[29] This, however, rather misses the point, since the 'mothering' thesis, as Balbus makes clear in his eloquent defence of it against Foucault in *Feminism as Critique*, is precisely an attempt *to account for* this social devaluation of the feminine by rooting it in the male child's experience of the mother's separation. The resulting hatred of the mother is then transferred to 'all those who come to represent her, i.e. to women in general. And the exclusion of women from positions of authority outside the family reflects the terror of ever again experiencing the humiliating submission to the authority of the mother within it.'[30]

Certainly, however, there is no problem in defending the 'mothering' thesis against the charge of essentialism in any anatomical sense, since the repudiation of the feminine to which it appeals is not of the female *body* as such, but of the one who first satisfies, and then frustrates, the desire for identity – and though this has usually happened to be female (the mother) there is no necessity for this. Indeed the recommendation of the theory is precisely for coparenting as an alternative to this secular but allegedly contingent state of affairs. But in the light of this recommendation, it does, I think, become problematic to represent the 'particularist' ethic, or any 'ethic of caring' reliant on the 'mothering' thesis, as instantiating some distinctively 'feminine' set of attributes or mode of being in the world. For if it is supposed that men too will adopt this moral outlook insofar as they become nurturers, then its alleged femininity would seem to reside not in any gender difference as such but simply in its association with certain 'caring' functions (and indeed functions of a kind which many men are already involved in performing).

Moreover, even if the 'mothering' thesis avoids biological essentialism, it is arguably open to the charge of circularity in its reliance on ideas of selfhood and autonomy which could themselves be said to reflect patriarchal power relations. For it seems to suppose an inherent attitude of aggression to the (m)other's autonomy, in other words, to imply that the child can only establish his own selfhood through resistance to the (m)other's subjectivity. But it is precisely this ideal of 'disembodied' autonomy which is the explicit target of so much feminist attack, particularly of those defending an 'ethics of caring'.[31]

The value and interest, however, of the particular confrontation between Foucault and 'mothering' feminism which we are offered by Balbus in *Feminism as Critique* do not rely entirely on one's acceptance of that theory. For his suggestion that a Foucauldian feminism is a contradiction in terms would seem to hold good for *any* feminist argument laying claim to truth and transhistoric generality.[32] Balbus's main formal objections to Foucault, in fact, are that in rejecting the idea of continuous history, together with the pretensions to establish 'True Discourse' and uncover general historical meanings, Foucault has in effect ruled out any feminist claim to have discovered a truth or 'meaning' in the massive continuity of male preeminence. A discourse on patriarchy as a transhistoric formation would itself, from a Foucauldian point of view, figure as a flight into humanistic mystification. What is more, any feminist project, such as that of Chodorow and Dinnerstein, which seeks to reveal the sources of gendered subjectivity must be seen from this same perspective as simply lending itself to the constitution – hence 'subjectification' – of subjects. For Foucault, feminism's pretensions to reorganize the patriarchal 'totality' must present themselves as 'totalitarian'; for Balbus, this Foucauldian stance rules out as totalitarian the very awareness of domination.

Having argued Foucault into this theoretical corner, Balbus then obligingly offers him a way out by invoking a kind of Foucauldian epistemological 'better nature' which is always defying the ban on continuities, totalities and subjects. The logic of this rebellion, suggests Balbus, must in the end lead the Foucauldian to abandon the thesis of the authoritarian effects of *all* discourse in favour of a more discriminating position which would allow some true discourses to be libertarian in their effects. 'Mothering' psychoanalysis is, unsurprisingly, offered as the model of such a discourse, but again, in fact, Balbus's exposure of the inconsistencies of the Foucauldian argument and his detection of the possibilities of a more optimistic interpretation of its anti-totalitarian critique survive any scepticism about the truth of that particular exemplar.

The Origins of Gender Difference

I have suggested that the 'mothering' discourse survives the charge of biological essentialism,[33] but it certainly locates the origin of gender difference in the biological distinction of the sexes, and is thus firmly rooted in the binary opposition of male and female. It is this opposition itself which is challenged in the pieces by Butler and Cornell and Thurschwell.

In a scintillating mix of de Beauvoir, Monique Wittig and (the *bon à toutes causes*) Foucault, Butler questions the whole necessity of gender distinction, putting in its place a modified existentialist thesis of 'gender invention'. She cheerfully admits that this may look fantastical from the point of view of any Marxian or Freudian 'Reality Principle', but then wonders whether the 'Reality' observed through the Marxian–Freudian principle is the only one we'll ever have. Butler argues that despite occasionally appearing to embrace a view of autonomy modelled on the disembodied transcendence of consciousness, de Beauvoir's suggestion that woman is not born but 'becomes' her gender rests on an implicit rejection of the polarity between (masculine) transcendence and (feminine) immanence in favour of a view of the body as 'situation': as a locus of received, and subjectively reinterpreted, cultural interpretations. This dialectical conception of the body as a nexus of culture and choice means that the idea of a 'natural' sex becomes increasingly suspect: if gender is a way of existing one's body, and one's body is a situation, a field of cultural possibilities both received and interpreted, then both gender and sex seem to be thoroughly cultural affairs.

Butler goes on to suggest that Wittig, though espousing a separatism politically repugnant to de Beauvoir, makes this insight explicit in her argument that sexual demarcation follows from, rather than precedes, interpretation. This is so not in the idealist sense that discourse about sex creates the misnomer of anatomy, but in the sense that certain anatomical features are viewed as definitional not only of biological sex but also of sexual identity. (We want, for example, to know what sex a child is in order to discover what sexual identity (= 'social destiny') he or she will have.) And this view, Butler claims, is supported by Foucault's rejection of 'natural sex' and of all binary oppositions in favour of a 'proliferation' of roles and identities to the point where opposition itself loses all purchase.[34]

Butler, as we have seen, accepts that this vision of a 'non-sexed' world is open to all the usual charges brought against 'existentialist' theses: from the Marxist that it ignores the extent to which others constitute one's gender in spite of any 'choices' of one's own;[35] from the Freudian, that it represents a fantasized regression to pre-oedipal sexual ambiguity, rather than the grounding for any genuine emancipation. In defence, she does no more than suggest rather archly that 'we might do well to urge speculation on the dynamic relation between fantasy and the realization of new social relations.'[36] Agreed, we might – indeed without a little fantasizing about how things might be otherwise, it seems unlikely that the political energy needed to remake social relations would ever be summoned forth. But the imagining of other possibilities has hitherto never managed to surmount the 'obstacle' of physical realities in their natural properties and causal relations, and in the case in question we must test for the 'seriousness' of Butler's fantasy against the reality of biology. Butler suggests, for example, that motherhood is entirely a matter of choice.[37] This is true in the general sense that most women can choose whether or not to have children. But apart from the fact that the infertile do not have such a choice, it is not so clear that we can choose, whatever our policy on motherhood, not to be subject to maternal instincts. In a general sense, there would seem to be biological dimensions to sexual attraction and parenthood (some of a kind we might well choose not to be pulled by if we could ...) which structure the modes in which we are enabled (or disabled) in 'existing' our bodies. Unless the kind of culturalism espoused by Butler is prepared to evacuate anatomical sex of all involuntary aspects (which would make sexual functioning, for example, of a completely different order from respiration), then the Wittig aspiration to a desexualized utopia would indeed seem to be unrealistic. It is also arguably dystopian in implying that hetero-sexual sex (which would seem to be a condition of any human continuity for the forseeable future) is a mere norm. This problem connects with Wittig's implicit privileging of lesbianism and of female self-affection in her conception of the pleasures of the 'unsexed' world – and with her highly problematic sugges-tion that the 'lesbian' is 'not a woman' but stands outside the gender binary system. But even if we allow that 'the lesbian' is definable other than by reference to the male–female distinction, why is male homosexuality excluded from this transcendence?

The fundamental question raised by Butler's account is why one can advocate a more 'polysexual' or 'sexually confused' future only from the standpoint of a 'culturist' account of gender formation which denies any necessary link between biological sex and genderization. Can we not, after all, acknowledge what seems very plausible: that there is an objective link (otherwise, why the gender grid at all?) which is massively overdetermined in the way it is lived, both by the specificity of genetic constitution and by the play of cultural power relations; and that the link between sex and gender should not therefore be accorded any great importance as such in our assessment of the possibilities of future sexual arrangements and desires?

This same question is raised, but left unanswered, in Cornell and Thurschwell's less 'unilateralist' (but rather dauntingly theoretical) advocacy of a gender reconciliation beyond any rigid male–female binary opposition. Actual sexuality, they imply, is always more blurred than our cultural symbolism would have it be, the feminine never wholly female, the male never wholly masculine. Emancipatory strategy should therefore be directed at a restitution, in consciousness as in social practice, of this more vague and nuanced, but never entirely undifferentiated eros. Their proposed forum is essentially Habermasian in character: psychoanalytic insight into the mediating role of language should make it possible to establish an 'ideal communication situation' freed of the rigid categories of structuralist feminisms such as Kristeva's (who, it is suggested, is compromised even in her opposition to Lacan's anti-feminism, by her reliance on his notion of Woman as otherness – as ineffable negation of male culture-discourse). For such structuralist essentialism of gender relations 'defeats the subversive power of the negative, and would cast women outside the masculine society they would disrupt.'[38]

From the standpoint, however, of an intersubjective linguistic constitution of gender – which reintroduces the duality of world and language – we can begin to perceive that gender differentiation is not exhaustive of actual human subjectivity, which is always more than, or 'in excess of', the strait-jacketing binary system of language. Or, in Adornian terms: 'the concept of gender can never be fully adequate to its masculine subject or feminine object.'[39] Thus, though supporting the psychoanalytic interpretation of the feminine as the 'negative' or escaped 'otherness', we might say that it is conceived not as the polar opposite of the 'masculine', but as a constantly disrupting 'otherness' which gives the lie to the supposedly univocal self-identity of a 'masculine' totality. The whole is not masculine, and feminine negativity surfaces as the immanent refusal and critique of this supposed 'truth'.[40]

Now, this is a perspective which seems to allow us to prise male domination away from gender differentiation, and hence frees us of the idea that a de-differentiated world is essential to the overthrow of patriarchy. On the other hand, when Cornell and Thurschwell proceed to denounce gender difference as itself an evil, and aspire to Butler's 'non-sexed' world, they seem to be accepting similar culturist assumptions – that only by denying any biological base for gender distinction can we plausibly call for a less rigidly demarcated sexual universe. Their own account of gender difference would seem to suffer from some of the explanatory void that we have noted before. For I am not at all sure that they *do* show (as Cornell and Benhabib claim in their editorial introduction) that the gender divide is constituted only as an 'effect of multi-gendered, intersubjective relations that leave traces in everyone'. Does this not simply beg the question of why an inept binary grid was imposed upon an originary pluralism? Their appeal to a Hegelian account of the subjective constitution of identity would not seem to solve this problem, since it presupposes the 'mirror' of gender difference as that through which men and women have hitherto always had to establish an identity (even if the identity is arrived at only through a rejection of image).

Equally, however, it is questionable whether Cornell and Thurschwell are to be placed together with those (Fraser, Young and Butler) who are said in the introduction to see no utopian traces 'of a future mode of otherness' within the present forms of gender constitution. It is true that Cornell and Thurschwell join these other authors in offering a critique of the identity logic of binary oppositions; and in their final invocation of the Derridean dream of a place beyond all sexuality and its discriminating codes,[41] they certainly seem to aspire to the transcendence of all currently constituted modalities of sexual difference. On the other hand, their 'Adornian' critique of Lacanian feminism is rooted in respect for an *immanent* critique – in respect, that is, for the possibilities of another ordering latent in the existing actuality. The logic of their argument against structuralism would thus seem to require that they problematize any notion of feminist transcendence.

The tension which Benhabib and Cornell rightly detect in the various arguments of *Feminism as Critique* – between those who see the desirable forms of gender relations already adumbrated in the present psychosexual arrangements, and those who aspire to a radical surpassing of the logic of binary oppositions altogether, and who see the current frozen grid of gender difference as offering no utopian escape routes whatsoever – this is a tension to be found actually *within* the arguments of Cornell and Thurschwell. Indeed, it is there within the pieces of Fraser, Young and Butler as well, insofar as they fail in the end to give content to their own 'utopian' categories. In the absence of any clearer sense of what is entertained under the notions of the 'multigendered' society, or the society of 'proliferating gender' or 'bodies and pleasures', one inevitably tends to conceive these as designating either a melange or blurring of existing sexual distinctions – which they therefore do not transcend – or else an alternative so devoid of specificity that it can hardly qualify even as fantasy.

Feminism, Modernism and Beyond

Despite these reservations, the consistently high level of theoretical self-awareness, and of alertness to the political implications of the distinctions within the spectrum of feminist theory, makes this book a valuable contribution which takes us a move beyond existing divisions and tensions within contemporary feminism. In particular, one must welcome the insight it sheds on the relations between Marxism and Marxist-oriented argument, postmodernism and feminist theory.

Dissatisfaction with orthodox Marxism's gender-blindness and theoretical one-dimensionality has led many feminists over to the camp of structuralism and poststructuralism: to a deeper engagement with the seemingly more fruitful offerings of Lacanian psychoanalysis, Lévi-Strauss's kinship theory, or Foucauldian and Derridean 'culturalism'. But such moves are made only at the risk of being drawn into anti-emancipatory positions: either towards the necessitarian framework of structuralism's untranscendable binary oppositions for which culture and discourse must remain unremittingly phallocratic; or else towards a Foucauldian–Lyotardian scepticism, from whose standpoint the 'grand narratives' of transhistoric feminine oppression and patriarchal ordering, together with the aspiration to an 'end of oppression', manifest an erroneous (and inherently totalizing totalitarian) commitment insofar as they must rest on a consensual claim to truth about what is wrong, and what needs to be done to correct it.[42] In this context, the recourse to a body of theory which is both unapologetically revisionist from any Marxist perspective, but nonetheless emphatically anti-capitalist, oriented towards 'progressive' social transformation,[43] and committed to the discovery of a 'truth' (and a 'community' to replace the mere aggregations of people in systemically 'integrated' societies) must have obvious attractions for femininism. A gender-sensitized Habermasian theory of the kind sketched in several of the articles of *Feminism as Critique* must be thought to provide a promising alternative to the Hobson's choice between unreconstructed Marxism, and structuralism/post structuralist fatalism and nihilism.

On the other hand, those who complain of Habermas's 'impartiality' and presumption of objective truth, and see in this not merely a gender-blindness but a structural incapacity of his categorial framework and epistemological disposition to accommodate a 'feminist' ethics, will inevitably be drawn to postmodernist discourses of 'proliferation' and 'pluralism'. In other words, those like Balbus, Markus and Benhabib who feel bound to seek for liberation in potentials immanent in existing society, will follow the bias of Critical Theory in using the values and tools of Enlightenment to criticize, subvert and transform the various irrationalities and oppressions perpetrated in its name – including, not least, the age-long subordination of women and devaluation of the 'feminine'. Those, on the other hand, who regard gender difference as infecting the very values of Enlightenment, such that justice, reason, freedom and objectivity can be seen as at the source of that subordination itself, will direct their sights to that ever enticing yet ineffable utopia unmeasurable by all previous yardsticks. There is always the danger, however, that in contesting 'truth' in the name of progress one finds that one has 'proceeded' only back into oppression. It is worth recalling that when Lyotard, in his 'thinly veiled' attack on Habermas,[44] contests the idea of 'consensus' as an 'outmoded and suspect value',[45] it is in the name of an 'agonistics' of speech whose presumption that in speaking we are always sparring with our adversary in a game of 'one-upmanship' is deeply antipathetic to feminism. Indeed, is it not the case that when we strip away the ludic affectations of this language-gaming, we are seeing a celebration of those old-fashioned, pompous, male adversarial modes which Virginia Woolf saw straight through back in the 1930s?

This is not to deny the importance of feminist questioning of the gender bias of traditional epistemological, metaphysical and moral categories, or the contribution in this respect of *Feminism as Critique* to a growing body of work which has taken 'feminist philosophy' well beyond its former preoccupation with revealing the all too predictable sexism of Plato, Hegel *et alii*. Nor do I want to suggest that a certain wit and playful antagonism do not have a role in any amicable resolution around these matters. (Chaucer's Wife of Bath understood this well enough when she advised that 'Since a man's more reasonable, he should be the patient one.')[46] I am suggesting only that we should be cautious lest the feminist critique of reason leaves us with no neutral space for either serious disagreement or ironic assent.

The issue here is not simply the incoherence of a feminist discourse which seeks our agreement to the idea that agreement is impossible, or which tries to reason us out of a commitment to reason. The point, rather, is that if one is going to challenge notions of 'impartiality', 'objectivity', 'justice', 'equality' and 'rationality' as incompatible with the 'particularist' and 'caring and nurturing' priorities of a feminist ethic, one should be quite clear about the epistemological and moral and political implications. Epistemologically, the challenge implies the elision of reality and appearance, an outright subjectivism, an equivalence of all 'biases' and 'partialities'. This is surely not what most feminists want since it would make their viewpoint but one among many of equal validity (or futility). Instead, it has to be recognized that one cannot seriously engage with gender 'bias' or offer grounds for defending the call for it to be corrected, except on the assumption of an impartial and objective model of relating. Politically and morally, this in turn implies a commitment to the principle of justice as that which grounds the demand for an end to discrimination, not only against women but against any marginalized or oppressed grouping. Liberal theory has obviously thought justice is detachable from equality in the sense that it regards any society as just which respects the rights of each individual to his or her property, freedom and protection before the law. In practice, such a conception of the just society serves to reinforce the vast disparities of property and freedom of the market society, and feminists are right to denounce the 'abstract' (but implicitly middle-class, male, property-owning individual) who is posited as the representative of humanity at large by such rights-based theories of justice.

But one must be careful, all the same, to distinguish between the exposure of this kind of abstraction from differences of gender, status, race, etc., and denunciation of all ethical abstractions altogether as inherently and undesirably 'masculinist': for that would mean depriving the feminist ethic of the grounds for calling for any kind of social norms, moral codes or legal rulings at all. If it is being suggested that we fall into a dubiously 'male', authoritarian and instrumental form of reasoning the moment we abstract from the specifically situated and unique position of the individual, the moment, in other words, we overlook difference, then obviously no comparisons between us can be made of the kind essential to legislation or to a more equal social distribution of goods, resources and opportunities. In short, this kind of 'difference' feminism, if taken to its ultimate conclusion, must condone an anarchist and wholly deregulated economic and social policy: and again we must ask whether this – with its obvious neo-rightist overtones – is what feminists are wanting.

For all these reasons, those who argue, like Benhabib and Markus, that the core of present conceptions of justice and equality needs to be retained as the condition of future emancipation, seem to me to have the interests of the vast majority of women more closely at heart than those holding out the promise of a utopia of multiplying difference.

Finally, in this connection let me note two related reservations I have about much of the theory offered in *Feminism as Critique*. In the first place, there is the problem of its own relative abstraction and difficulty. Just as it has been asked of Habermas's theory for whom it is intended and who is conceived as the agent of its 'communicative' revolution, so of this feminist critique one can ask: who will read and understand it and how does it relate to the practical changes needed to implement quite minor improvements in the lives of the most severely economically and socially oppressed women? (The same question, I accept, can be addressed to this review.)

It is true, of course, that theory is important, and if there was ever an area where it might be claimed that change in the modes of thinking and talking had issued in material rearrangements, it is that of sexual politics, and the initial theorists of the feminist movement must take much of the credit for this. But as feminist argument becomes more complex and metatheoretical (because more alert to the conceptual difficulties unearthed by its earlier critiques), so it will need also to be more sensitive to the risk of losing sight of the original goals.

This brings me to a second difficulty: that of the under-theorized relationship between feminist theory and empirical social science. One comes away from *Feminism as Critique* feeling quite positive about its undogmatic stance and readily admitted ambivalences about future directions; but also feeling that rather little other than one's own subjectivity (including perhaps one's own desire and sexual situation) are considered relevant in helping to decide the issue. One key problem, in short, which is raised through the feminist critique of science and its standard philosophical underpinnings is how far feminist discourses are aspiring to any scientific status (in the sense of seeing themselves as open to empirical controls and seeking their validation); how far they are happy to settle for a poststructuralist perspectivism. Towards the conclusion of her article in *Feminism as Critique*, Josephine Butler asks: 'When the essential feminine is finally articulated, and what we have been calling "women" cannot see themselves in its terms, what then are we to conclude? That these are deluded, or that they are not women at all?'[47] The point is well taken: one does not want an arbitrary essentialism to foreclose what women can be. But equally one does not want to lend oneself to the kind of anti-naturalism and anti-objectivity which removes all grounds for discriminating between what can truly or falsely be said of women. Or at least I do not. Let me conclude, then, by revamping Butler's question: if one does not see oneself entirely through the gaze of feminist self-affection; if one's intuition is that objectivity and truth must be preserved against deconstruction; if one even follows Habermas in his 'stubbornly Kantian' desire to 'preserve a sense that questions of truth can be isolated and a discourse kept open where it is not mixed with questions of justice and taste' – what than?[48] Is one deluded, or not properly feminist? Or, more happily, but perhaps still not good enough, is one tolerated but only as one of many equally valid voices?

Notes

1. *Feminism as Critique*, edited and introduced by Seyla Benhabib and Drusilla Cornell. Oxford 1987.

2. See Peter Dews (ed.) *Habermas, Autonomy and Solidarity*, London 1986, p. 108. Elsewhere, however, in the same collection of interviews, Habermas acknowledges that Adorno's critique of reason 'never darkens to a renunciation

of ... Enlightenment', and that in contrast to the 'poststructuralists' Adorno 'does not merely bale out of the *counter* discourse which has inhabited modernity ever since the beginning' (see pp. 155-8).

3. To describe contemporary feminism as 'anti-postmodernist' may seem a trifle bizarre given the extensive reliance of many of its leading exponents on poststructuralist argument. I have tried below to give some sense of the tensions this makes for between analytic and evaluative aspects of feminist theory. But to my knowledge no one has yet produced a professedly feminist argument which explicitly shares in the postmodernist nihilism.

4. See *Habermas*, pp. 106-7.

5. See, for example, Sandra Harding, *The Science Question in Feminism*, Milton Keynes 1986; Ruth Bleier, *Science and Gender: A Critique of Biology and Its Theories on Women*, New York 1984; Carol Gilligan, *In A Different Voice: Psychological Theory and Women's Development*, Cambridge, Mass. 1982; Sandra Harding and Merill Hintikka (eds) *Discovering Reality: Feminist Perspectives on Epistemology, Metaphysics, Methodology and Philosophy of Science*, Dordrecht 1983; Evelyn Fox Keller, *Reflections on Gender and Science*, New Haven, Conn. 1984; Janet Sayers, *Biological Politics: Feminist and Anti-Feminist Perspectives*, London 1982; Lorraine Code, Sheila Mullett and Christine Overall (eds) *Feminist Perspectives: Philosophical Essays on Method and Morals*, London 1988; Morwenna Griffiths and Margaret Whitford (eds) *Feminist Perspectives in Philosophy*, London 1988.

6. The pluralism of Habermas's ideal of communication does, however, tend to conflict with the impulse of separatist feminisms.

7. Nicholson further argues that this essentialism of the economic is embedded in Marx's concept of class, which in giving priority to changes and conflicts in the sphere of commodity production, tends either to negate the role of biological reproduction, and to treat its activities as unchanging and asocial; or else to regard its changes as purely superstructural. Not only does this obscure the integration of 'productive' and 'reproductive' labour in precapitalist societies; it in effect preempts analysis of the distinctive character of the gender division of labour within relatively integrated kinship and feudal societies – thus leaving out of account the class-like features of gender division in the very different standing of the sexes in regard to the means and relations of social reproduction as a whole. Marxism, in short, despite its value in granting feminists insight into the historic character of the separation of family, state and economy, stands in the way of a proper history of the forms of integration and disintegration of 'productive' and 'reproductive' spheres, and thus in the way of any proper accommodation of gender relations (see *Feminism as Critique*, pp. 23-7). One might note that a problem which receives no discussion by Nicholson is that of the occurrence in existing socialist societies of the divorce between 'productive' and 'reproductive' activity which she regards as specific to the market economy.

8. Fraser also welcomes Habermas's distinction between 'normatively secured' and 'communicatively achieved' contexts – that is, between contexts where relations are what they are in virtue of unquestioned conventions, hierarchies, norms of power and possession – the male-dominated family, for example, and contexts based on an explicit consensus achieved through uncoerced discussion – Habermas's 'ideal communication situation'. See *Feminism as Critique*, p. 38, and cf. Jürgen Habermas, *Theory of Communicative Action*, vol. 1, Cambridge, 1984, pp. 85–6, 88–90, 101, 104–105.

9. *Feminism as Critique*, p. 37 ('Systemic' integration is, according to Habermas, essentially steered by the media of power and money.) One might note that David Held has laid similar charges against the overly formal quality of Habermas's systemic/symbolic distinction, though not from a specifically feminist point of view. See his *Introduction to Critical Theory*, Berkeley 1980, pp. 390–92.

10. *Feminism as Critique*, pp. 47f.

11. This mistake, says Fraser, is in turn based on and reproduces three errors: that of thinking there is a 'natural' division between symbolic and material reproduction with child-rearing falling to the former; that of thinking the domestic sphere has hitherto been virginally preserved from the penetration of power and money; and that of thinking that the basic vector of motion of late capitalist society is from state-regulated economy to life-world and not vice versa (since in fact gender norms and meaning continue to channel the influence of the life-world into the 'systems' both of the economy – the continuation of the 'male' workplace, modes of division of labour, norms of pay, etc. – and of government administration – gender-divided welfare schemes, treatment of single-parent households as 'defective' families, etc.).

12. *Feminism as Critique*, p. 56.

13. Whether it be that of the state or of money (as is increasingly the case with the ascendancy of the monetarist policy and the neo-conservative erosion of welfare provision).

14. The more cynical may even detect a note of nostalgia for the loss of 'family values' despite Habermas's own emphasis on 'cultural modernism'. Why, it might be asked, has Habermas only begun to get really panicky about systemic invasion at the point where it threatens to come right into hearth and home?

15. *Feminism as Critique*, p. 108.

16. *Ibid.*

17. *Ibid.*, pp. 68–9.

18. *Ibid.*, p. 70.

19. Cornelius Castoriadis, *Crossroads in the Labyrinth*, Brighton 1978, p. 213. Young associates Habermas's reliance on 'identitary logic' with his tendency to ignore non-verbal and non-literal aspects of communication – which, she suggests, reflects his failure to see that communication is moved not only by

desire for agreement but by desire to love and be loved. This elision of charges, however, seems rather dubious. Habermas has himself suggested that he has abstracted from gesture and bodily communication in the interests of concentrating initially on speech but that their analysis remains part of his project (see Held, *Critical Theory*, p. 332). More plausibly perhaps, it may be objected that he has mistakenly treated irony, metaphor, illusion and paradox as either derivative or deceptive versions of 'genuine' speech.

20. Habermas himself, of course, stresses the role of compromise and bargaining in reconciling particular interests. But given his commitment to a universal moral intuition as the ground for principles guiding decision-making, this would seem to present less of an obstacle to his theory, at least in principle. This is not to deny, however, that the theory may be open to other charges of circularity – for example, the definition of truth as the consensus reached in an ideal speech situation whose 'truth' itself, as such a situation, would seem to have no prior guarantee. See Dews, *Habermas*, pp. 163–4.

21. Cf. Carol Gilligan, *In a Different Voice*, and 'Moral Development in Late Adolescence and Adulthood: A Critique and Reconstruction of Kohlberg's Theory', *Human Development* 23, 1980. Lawrence Kohlberg's most recent reply to Gilligan is in L. Kohlberg, C. Levine and A. Hewar, *Essays on Moral Development* vol. 21 San Francisco 1984.

22. See Sandra Harding, *Science Question*, and discussions by Lorraine Code and Barbara Houston in *Feminist Perspectives*.

23. Polarities which, after all, are part of the baggage of the patriarchal conceptual schema – cf. the suggestion from both Rousseau and Hegel that women should be excluded from the public domain because they are the caretakers of affectivity, desire and the body – as if there were no bodies, desires, or affects roaming loose in the public domain.

24. *Feminism as Critique*, p. 66.

25. Catherine MacKinnon, 'Feminism, Marxism, Method and the State: an Agenda for Theory', *Signs* 7, 1982, p. 658. Cf. Marsha P. Hanen's discussion of legal theory and feminist critiques of scientific objectivity in *Feminist Perspectives*, pp, 29–45.

26. Note that what is at issue here is not so much the feminist attack on the hypocrisies of the supposed neutrality of 'masculine' science but the feminist critique of the value of neutrality itself.

27. See Dorothy Dinnerstein, *The Mermaid and the Minotaur: Sexual Arrangements and Human Malaise*, New York 1976; Nancy Chodorow, *The Reproduction of Mothering: Psychoanalysis and the Sociology of Gender*, Berkeley 1978; Jane Flax, 'Political Philosophy and the Patriarchal Unconscious: A Psychoanalytic Perspective on Epistemology and Metaphysics', in S. Harding and M. Hintikka (eds) *Discovering Reality*; Isaac Balbus, *Marxism and Domination*, Princeton 1982. Defending and expounding the 'mothering' or 'object-relations' theory, Balbus writes: 'The heretofore culturally universal pheno-

menon of patriarchy is rooted in and reproduced by the equally universal fact of virtually exclusive female responsibility for early child-care. In all cultures it is a woman ... who is both the source of satisfaction and the frustration of the imperious needs of the infant; she is at once the being with whom the child is initially indistinguishably identified and the one who enforces the (never more than partial) dissolution of this identification. Thus it is the mother who becomes the recipient of the unconscious hostility that accumulates in children of both sexes as the result of this inescapably painful separation. The mother who is loved is also the mother who is hated.' *Feminism as Critique*, p. 112.

28. James Walker, 'In a Different Voice: Crypto-separatist Analysis of Female Moral Development', *Social Research* 50, 3, October 1983.

29. Cf. Barbara Houston, *Feminist Perspectives*, pp. 178–9. Without this devaluation, claims Houston, 'we would have more boys identified with their mothers for longer periods in a non-traumatic fashion, who could then learn the relational capacities we think have a moral importance.'

30. *Feminism as Critique*, p. 113.

31. Why should the child react to the necessary separation from the mother figure with 'hatred' unless there is an underlying presupposition that the separation of the Other from the Self will be perceived as a threat to subjectivity?

32. Balbus writes: 'From a Foucauldian perspective the discourse of the mother looks like a paradigm case of a "disciplinary" True Discourse, while from a feminist psychoanalytic standpoint the Foucauldian deconstruction of True Discourse betrays assumptions that can only be characterized as a classically male flight from maternal foundations. If feminism necessarily embraces these foundations, then a Foucauldian feminism is a contradiction in terms.' *Feminism as Critique*, p. 110.

33. Or it does unless it is assumed that the theory implicitly rests on the idea that it follows from the nature of the female body or psychic disposition that the nurturing of the species should hitherto have fallen almost exclusively to women.

34. Though Foucault of course differs from Wittig in also rejecting any Marcusian liberated 'eros' of the kind to which she aspires. For Foucault, the 'liberated eros' is always structured culturally and therefore saturated with the dynamics of a manipulative power. Cf. *Feminism as Critique*, p. 137.

35. We might add, too, as part of the 'Marxist' objection, that it is not simply the objectifying 'gaze' of the other which limits 'choice' of gender; there are some very material economic and social factors which make any meaningful 'flexibility' in this matter well nigh impossible still for the majority of women.

36. *Feminism as Critique*, p. 140.

37. *Ibid.*, p. 132.

38. *Ibid.*, p. 152. It is admitted that Kristeva is alert both to the risk of 'reification' ensuing from any Lacanian essentialism of the negative in the form

of the feminine, and to the 'terrorism' of blanket negations of the actual to which it can lead both in theory and in political practice. But Cornell and Thurschwell argue that neither of her more 'positive' theoretical moves suffices to overcome these problems. Her appeal to the 'positive' immanent in the actual forms of motherhood and maternal modes of relating can proceed only at the cost of a conflation of 'Woman' with 'women' (and indeed with the particular empirical group of them who choose to be mothers) – and hence implies a political separatism. Her idea, on the other hand, of a 'semiotic' restoration of the 'She' which resides in all of us, is blocked by the Lacanian framework in which it is entertained. For insofar as this 'feminine' power is conceived as unassignable to any sex – as a power which 'no one represents and not women either' – it also falls outside the Symbolic order, and hence cannot be restored discursively. Once again, then, in language, symbolically, Woman does not exist, and there is no place for her to 'be' other than in the fantasy of pre-oedipal relations. Woman as a mature, non-regressive, non-fantastical principle of social life, is literally excluded from the very possibility of cultural presence by anyone, Kristeva included, who has recourse to the structuralist account of psychoanalysis.

39. *Ibid.*, p. 159.

40. All this, of course, complies with Adorno's recommendation that 'Totality is to be opposed by convicting it of non-identity with itself – of the non-identity it denies according to its concept' (*Negative Dialectics*, London 1973, p. 147). But even Adorno relies too much, they suggest, on identity-thought's own version of itself, that is, on the distinction it posits between self and alien, and is thus insufficiently alert to 'self-differentiation' of the subject. It is thus to Derrida that they finally refer themselves.

41. *Feminism as Critique*, p. 162.

42. It should be stressed, however, that in contrast to Foucault's pessimism about the inevitable cycle of domination, Lyotard explicitly aspires to a politics which 'would respect both the desire for justice and the desire for the unknown.' *The Postmodern Condition*, Manchester 1986, p. 67.

43. Though Habermas recognizes the difficulties around the notion of 'progress' and has argued in particular that it cannot be identified with the overcoming of the 'alienation' of labour. See Dews *Habermas*, pp. 28f.

44. So described by Fredric Jameson in his introduction to *The Postmodern Condition*, p. vii.

45. Lyotard, *Ibid.*, p. 66, cf. pp. 10–16; 25; 57–9; 63–5.

46. 'Oon of us two moste bowen, doutelees; And sith a man is more resonable/ Than womman is, ye moste been suffrable.' 'The Wife of Bath Prologue', *The Canterbury Tales* (in Modern English trans. Nevill Coghill, Penguin edn, 1951, p. 288).

47. *Feminism as Critique*, p. 142.

48. Dews, *Habermas*, p. 127.

10

Feminism, Humanism, Postmodernism

I shall not begin, as I probably should, by offering to define my terms. Instead I shall acknowledge that I have brought together three concepts admitted on all sides to be wellnigh indefinable. Or if they are definable, they are so only by reference to a particular thinker's usage (Lyotard's or Huyssen's or Baudrillard's of 'postmodernism'; Heidegger's or Wolf's or Foucault's of 'humanism'; de Beauvoir's or Kristeva's or Wittig's of 'feminism', etc. – and this is to speak only in the French or German of the last fifty years. Yet we know too, even as we recognize our reliance on this more specific anchorage of terms, that the concepts of 'postmodernism', 'humanism' and 'feminism' also embrace the sum of these more particular discourses – and that a large part of their usefulness lies in this generality of reference. So I shall not begin with further definitions, but with an appeal to intuition: an appeal to that vague sense which I am assuming anyone at all interested in reading a piece such as this will already have of these terms.

For the point of their conjunction, really, is to signal a problem, and a problem which I *shall* here attempt to make as explicit as possible. Postmodernist argument (or the argument of 'modernity' as others have wanted to call it)[1] has issued a number of challenges: to the idea that we can continue to think, write and speak of our culture as representing a continuous development and progress; to the idea that humanity is proceeding towards a telos of 'emancipation' and 'self-realization'; to the idea that we can invoke any universal subjectivity in speaking about the human condition. Lyotard has argued, for example, that neither of the two major forms of *grands récits* ('grand narratives') by which in the past we have legitimated the quest for knowledge can any longer perform that function. Neither the instrumental narrative of emancipation which justifies science and technology by reference to the poverty and injustice they must eventually eliminate, nor the purist defence of knowledge accumulation as something inherently beneficial, can any longer command the belief essential to warding off scepticism about the purpose and value of the technosciences. With this scepticism has gone a loss of confidence in the whole idea of human 'progress' viewed as a process more or less contemporaneous with Western-style 'civilization', and a calling into question of the emancipatory themes so central to the liberal, scientific and Marxist/socialist discourses of the nineteenth century.

This loss of credulity is in turn associated with the collapse of 'humanism'. There are two aspects to the collapse, both of them registered in much of the writing, theoretical and literary, of recent times. Firstly (though this aspect of the critique of humanism was launched by the humanist Karl Marx, and continued within a tradition of socialist-humanist thinking), there is an acknowledgement of the partial and excluding quality of the supposedly universal 'we' of much humanist discourse. Secondly, and partly as a consequence of this exposure of liberal hypocrisies and the ethnocentricity of Western humanism, there has been a refusal of the 'we' which lurks in the unifying discourse of the dialectic: a rejection of all attempts to find a sameness in otherness. Instead, we have been witness to a theoretical celebration of difference, a resistance to all synthesizing discourse, an assertion of an indefinite and multiplying plurality of particulars and specificities.

Insistence on the specificity of 'woman' or the 'feminine' has by no means been confined to the latter wave of criticism. An initial feminist 'deconstruction' of the humanist subject was made as long ago as 1792 by Mary Wollstonecraft in her demand for women to be included within the entitlements claimed by the 'Rights of Man'. But it is only in comparatively recent times that feminists have gone beyond an exposure of the maleness of the supposedly universal subject invoked by humanist rhetoric, to denounce the 'masculinism' of humanism as such. Whereas in the past, the call of feminist critiques of liberal humanism was for women to be recognized as 'equal' subjects of that discourse, equally entitled to the 'rights' which were claimed for 'all men',[2] what is more at issue today is the maleness of the subject place to which these earlier feminists were staking their claim. Today there is a whole body of feminist writing which would shy away from an 'equality' which welcomed women (at last) as human subjects on a par with men. For this 'human' subject, it is argued, must always bear the traces of the patriarchal ordering which has been more or less coextensive with the 'human' condition as such: a patriarchal culture in the light of whose biased and supposedly 'masculine' values (of rationality, symbolic capacity, control over nature) the 'human' is at the 'beginning' of 'culture' defined in opposition to the 'animal', and the discourse of 'humanism' itself first given currency. As so conceived, 'feminism' and 'humanism' would appear to aspire to incompatible goals, for 'feminism' is the quest for the registration and realization (though quite in what language and cultural modes it is difficult to say ...) of feminine 'difference': of that ineffable 'otherness' or negation of human culture and its symbolic order (and gender system), *which is not the human* as this human is spoken to in humanism. Humanism, inversely, according to this way of thinking is the discourse which believes or wishes or pretends that there is no such difference.

But humanism is also, we might note in passing, the discourse which likes to think it can take back into the fold of the human all those who conceive of themselves as excluded. Or perhaps it would be better to describe it as the discourse which would say to all those who feel themselves excluded, or who prefer to exempt themselves from its sentimentality, that even in their exclusion or exemption they are within the fold; for resistance or indignation, they too are human, and humanism can embrace all opposition, difference and disdain for it. To say this is only to point out that there are *many* humanist discourses contesting each other's collectivities and claiming that theirs alone is truly universal. Thus it is in the name of a more universal humanism that Sartre delivers his 'anti-humanist' fulminations against bourgeois humanism. And thus it is, more generally, that religious conflicts, political battles, as between liberals and socialists, even the philosophical oppositions between dialectic and anti-dialectic, can be viewed as 'humanist' sparrings for the right to represent the human race, its meaning and its destiny.

I shall return to these points at a later stage, particularly as they affect the ultimate incompatibility of a feminist and a humanist outlook. Here, for the time being, let us stay with the arguments of the so-called 'difference' feminists: with those who, in varying ways, have questioned any ultimate compatibility. Two of the more prominent voices here are those of Hélène Cixous and Luce Irigaray. To these one might very tentatively add the name of Julia Kristeva: very tentatively because she herself has forcefully criticized 'difference' feminisms, and is opposed to all theoretical moves which tend to an essentialism, of 'femininity', and hence to a 'denegation of the symbolic' and removal of the 'feminine' from the order of language.[3] On the other hand, her own position is very equivocal. For insofar as she is concerned to forestall any discourse on femininity which implies the 'ineffability' of the 'feminine' at the level of the Symbolic, and to remind us that if the 'feminine' exists it only does so within the order of meaning and signification, she is herself implicitly invoking a feminine 'otherness'. The anxiety to check this 'silencing' of the 'feminine' is itself premised on a notion of the latter as a transgression and disrupting element within the prevailing code of the Symbolic. The 'existential crisis' of the 'feminine' as so conceived lies in the fact that it can only be spoken to within the existing order of language but is also that whose existence is denied or occluded by the very terms of that language. In other words, insofar as Kristeva relies on a Lacanian framework her argument is constantly pulled towards acceptance of an equivalence between the 'masculine' and the Symbolic, whose effect, willy-nilly, is to cast the 'feminine' in the role of 'otherness' or 'difference' to the cultural order.

The resulting tensions have if anything been made more acute by recent developments in Kristeva's arguments wherein she has associated this feminine 'negativity' with a more positively accented prelinguistic sensuality which she refers to as the 'semiotic', and that in turn with the 'maternal'. It is true that this 'semiotic' is not theorized literally as 'outside language' or inevitably deprived of cultural expression. For Kristeva finds it manifest not only in women's writing, but in the works of Joyce, Lautréamont, Mallarmé and a number of other male modernist writers. (Indeed she has suggested that modernism should be viewed as a cultural movement of restitution or realization of the feminine semiotic, though this is certainly a controversial interpretation.)[4] But the association of the feminine semiotic with a pre-oedipal eroticism characteristic of the mother–infant relationship; and the suggestion that the maternal activities of gestation and nurturance break with conceptions of self and other, subject and object, which are of the essence of masculine logic: this surely does come dangerously close to a differentiation of the feminine in terms of maternal function – precisely the essentialism which Kristeva has warned feminism against espousing and professes herself to wish to avoid.[5]

Irigaray and Cixous, on the other hand, have rejected the Lacanian eternalization of the cultural 'negativity' of women; but their challenge, nonetheless, to the supposed inevitability of masculine preeminence relies on an invocation of feminine difference which would seem to offer no better guarantee of outlet from a phallocentric universe. For the difference in question refers us to the difference in the female body and body experience in a manner which arguably reintroduces the masculine Symbolic identification of sexuality with genitality,[6] and essentializes the maternal function (particularly so in the case of Cixous's inflated celebrations of the plenitude, richness and fecundity of the feminine body). As has been pointed out in respect of Kristeva's appeal to the maternal,[7] this tends to an elision of symbolic and empirical features which is theoretically confusing: after all, if feminine difference is being defined in terms of maternal function, then many actual, empirical, women are going to find themselves cast out from femininity insofar as they are not mothers nor intending to become so. At the same time, the association of the feminine with the maternal or with the feminine body is deeply problematic for many feminists who see in this precisely the male cultural signification which they are attempting to contest, and which, they would argue, has been the justification for a quite unreasonable and unfair domestication of women and a very damaging social and economic division of labour from the point of view of female self-fulfilment and self-expression.

In a more general way, we must surely also contest the reductionism of the argument found in different forms in both Irigaray's and Cixous's theories of the feminine (in Irigaray's advocacy of '*parler femme*' and Cixous's notion of *écriture féminine* as speaking to a kind of feminine unconscious) that language, whether spoken or written, directly mirrors physical morphology. It is a radical misunderstanding of the nature of signs to suppose that the two lips of the vulva or breast milk or menstrual blood are 'represented' in contiguous statements or in the unencodable libidinal gushings of a feminine prose *in any but a purely metaphorical sense*. But if we treat the supposed representation as purely metaphorical, then 'feminine writing' is being defined in terms of a certain image or metaphor of itself, and we end up with a purely tautological argument.

Again, the whole association within the writings of Cixous and Irigaray of feminine subjectivity with the prelinguistic and preconceptual: with that which has no meaning and cannot be spoken in (male) culture, comes very close to reproducing the male–female dichotomies of traditional epistemology and moral argument, for which woman is 'intuitive', 'natural', 'immanent' – and 'silent'; and man is 'rational', 'cultural', 'transcendent' – and 'vocal'. The only difference is that the supposedly feminine characteristics will have been accorded a positive charge – and given the recurrent romanticization and idolization of the feminine within the masculine cultural order itself, even that may not prove a very major shift.

At any rate, the important point would seem to be that where the appeal to difference is made, it tends to an essentialism of the female physique and function which reproduces rather than surpasses the traditional male–female divide and leaves 'woman' once again reduced to her body – and to silence – rather than figuring as a culturally shaped, culturally complex, evolving, rational, engaged and noisy opposition. The total disengagement of the feminine in the position of Cixous and Irigaray,[8] the complete severence of any masculine–feminine cultural intercourse, removes this opposition to the point where one might say there was no longer any feminist critique of patriarchy but only a self-absorption in the feminine.

On the other hand, if difference is not given this kind of anchorage in the feminine body and function, it is not clear why there is any reason, once set on the path of difference, for feminism to call a halt. In other words, if one disallows the feminine universal of a common bodily essence, then the commitment to difference ought to move one into a deconstruction of feminine difference itself. Having exposed the 'masculinity' of humanism in the name of feminine difference, one must surely go on, by the same logic, to expose the generalizing and abstract (and quasi-humanist) appeal to feminine difference in the name of the plurality of concrete differences between women (in their nationality, race, class, age, occupation, sexuality, parenthood status, health, and so on ...) For on this argument 'woman' can no more be allowed to stand in for all women than can 'man' be allowed to stand for all members of the human species. The way, then, of course, lies open to an extreme particularism in which all pretensions to speak (quasi-humanistically) in general for this or that grouping, or to offer an abstract and representative discourse on behalf of such putative groups, must give way to a hyper-individualism.[9] From this standpoint any appeal to a collectivity would appear to be illegitimate – yet another case of 'logocentric imperialism', to use the inflated rhetoric of poststructuralism.

But at this point one is bound to feel that feminism as theory has pulled the rug from under feminism as politics. For politics is essentially a group affair, based on the idea of making 'common cause', and feminism, like any other politics, has always implied a banding together, a movement based on the solidarity and sisterhood of women, who are linked by perhaps very little else than their *sameness* and 'common cause' as women. If this sameness itself is challenged on the grounds that there is no 'presence' of womanhood, nothing that the term 'woman' immediately expresses, and nothing instantiated concretely except particular women in particular situations, then the idea of a political community built around women – the central aspiration of the early feminist movement – collapses. I say the 'idea', for women do still come together in all sorts of groups for feminist purposes, and will doubtless continue to do so for a good while to come even if their doing so transgresses some Derridean conceptual rulings. But *theoretically* the logic of difference tends to subvert the concept of a feminine political community of 'women' as it does of the more traditional political communities of class, Party, Trade Union, etc. And theory does, of course, in the end get into practice, and maybe has already begun to do so: one already senses that feminism as a campaigning movement is yielding to feminism as discourse (and to discourse of an increasingly heterogeneous kind).

In the face of this dispersion, with its return from solidarity to individualism, it is difficult not to feel that feminism itself has lost its hold, or at any rate that much of contemporary theory of the feminine is returning us full circle to those many isolated, and 'silent' women, from which it started – and for whom it came to represent, precisely, a 'common voice'. It is a *renversement*, moreover, which leaves feminism exposed to the temptations of what are arguably deeply nostalgic and conservative currents of postmodernist thinking. It would seem quite complicit, for example, with the distaste for anything smacking of a militant feminist politics implicit in Baudrillard's suggestion that it is our very resistance to reactivating traditional feminine charms which is preempting cultural renewal. 'Only by the power of seduction does woman master the symbolic universe', he tell us, in a piece of rhetorical blandishment redolent with nostalgia for the good old days when men ruled and women cajoled.[10] It is true that it is not officially as an ideologue of patriarchal culture that Baudrillard offers this Rousseauean advice. On the contrary, he would seduce us back into seduction with the altogether more respectable end, so he claims, of taking us beyond all sociality, sentimentality and sexuality.[11] But it is interesting, all the same, that it remains out of place for woman directly to contest the father's authority, and that our cultural duty requires us still to have recourse to the subtler arts of cajolery: to beguile the phallus round. By such means, so Baudrillard tempts us to think, woman will readily contrive to wrap the symbolic order around her charming little finger.[12]

This kind of sophistry, in truth, is not very tempting and probably unimportant. But I think in a general way it is fair to claim that the same logic of 'difference' which ends up subverting the project of feminine emancipation by denying the validity of any political community in whose name it could be pursued also deprives feminist argument of recourse against such retrograde poststructuralist idealism.

In introducing the term 'emancipation' one opens the way to consideration of another aspect of the problem of the relations between feminism, humanism and postmodernism. For if the building of political collectivities becomes problematic in the light of anti-humanist critique, this also reflects a reluctance of these critiques 'to speak on behalf of' others: to say, in short, what others – in this case women – want. In other words, the observance of the logic of difference has also made feminist theorists reluctant utopians.

This caution in speaking for others' desires is understandable against a background of so much claimed knowledge of the 'alienation' and 'true needs' of others (especially of that notorious 'universal subject' of humanity, the proletariat). It is a needed corrective to the enforced collectivizations of interests and needs which have been given theoretical legitimation in the past. But again, the thinking which motivated this healthy resistance to glib pronouncements of solidarity and struggle has also in recent argument developed a momentum which begins to undermine the possibility of speaking of any kind of political collective and agreement at all. Foucault, for example, has denounced any totalizing attempt in theory (any attempt, that is, to offer general diagnoses and general remedies for the ills of society) as 'totalitarian'. Even Habermas, who is hardly a Stalinist in theory, and who argues no more than that people should be allowed to discover the truth of their interests in the free discussions of his 'ideal communication situation' has been denounced by Lyotard for aspiring to a consensus.[13]

In other words, the drift of such arguments would seem to rule out any holistic analysis of societies (any analysis of a kind that allows us to define them as 'capitalist' or 'patriarchal' or 'totalitarian'), together with the radically transformative projects which such analyses tend to recommend. Indeed, as Isaac Balbus has argued in his defence of object-relations feminism against Foucauldian logic, if we accept the claim that any continuous history or *longue durée* accounting is posturing as 'True' (and therefore dominating) discourse, then feminism itself becomes a form of totalitarianism. The very idea of a centuries-old subordination of women explicable by reference to transhistorical patriarchal structures becomes deeply problematic from the standpoint of the 'postmodernist' rejection of truth and scientific knowledge and of the continuities they posit. If all that we once called knowledge or theory is now mythopoeic 'narrative', then the narrative of male oppression is itself but one more myth of Knowledge generated in response to a 'Will to Power'. And by the same token, 'progress' out of oppression becomes a meaningless aspiration.[14]

My primary aim in this survey has been to diagnose a problem rather then prescribe its remedy. It is true, however, that insofar as I have presented both the 'maternal' feminism of Kristeva, Irigaray and Cixous, and the more radical deconstruction of the 'feminine' invited by the logic of difference, as 'problematic' for the project of female emancipation, I have implied the need for some alternative course. Indeed at times I have gone much further, suggesting that both positions are inherently conservative: either difference is essentialized in a way which simply celebrates the 'feminine' other of dominant culture without disturbing the hold of the latter; or the critique is taken to a point where the 'feminine' and its political and cultural agents in the women's movement and feminist art and literature no longer exist in the sense of having any recognizable common content and set of aspirations. These implications of my argument, however, stand in need of more elaboration than I have given them and admit of certain qualifications which I have not yet considered. In conclusion, then, I would pursue the charge of political conservatism a little further, offering some arguments both in defence but also in mitigation of it.

I have already indicated my main reason for thinking that 'maternal' feminism and *écriture féminine* are open to this charge. But my objection is not only to the fact that the emphasis on the distinctness of the female body and its reproductive and erotic experience comes so close to reinforcing patriarchal conceptions of gender difference. I would also argue that despite its avant-gardist pretensions, the style in which this feminism is couched is disquietingly confirming of traditional assumptions about the 'nature' of feminine thought and writing. The dearth of irony; the fulsome self-congratulation; the resistance to objectivity; the sentimentalization of love and friendship and the tendency always to reduce these relations to their sexual aspect; the focus on the 'erotic' conceived as an amorphous, all-engulfing, tactile, radically unintellectual form of experience; the overblown poetics and arbitrary recourse to metaphor (which so often lack the hardness of crystalline meaning as if exactitude itself must be avoided as inherently 'male' . . .): all this, which is offered in the name of allowing 'woman' to discover her 'voice', itself voices those very conceptions of female selfhood and self-affection which I believe are obstacles to cultural liberation. And the reason I find them obstacles is not simply because they so directly lend themselves to a patriarchically constructed ideology of femininity and its modes of self-expression, but because the ideology is, like all ideologies, at best partial in its representation and therefore illegitimately generalizing of a certain specific form of understanding. Moreover, when this understanding relates so directly to images of selfhood and subjectivity, it is peculiarly offensive and arrogant – to the point, in fact, of operating a kind of theft of subjectivity or betrayal of all those who fail to recognize themselves in the mirror it offers. At the same time, because ideologies of their nature are always fractured reflections of society, exploded in the very moment which reveals their ideo- logical status, those who cling to them and reinforce their decaying hold are also always marginalizing their own discourse; ensuring that it cannot be taken seriously in the world at large.

In response to this it will be said, perhaps, that the neutrality of my own presentation of the issue is misleading since 'the world at large' is essentially a 'male' world, and for women to reject eulogies of the 'feminine' on the grounds that this guarantees a shrugging off of their importance, is itself to be complicit with a culture which has consistently treated reproduction and nurturing activities as of secondary importance to traditional 'male' pursuits. If to be 'taken seriously' women must speak and act 'like men' are not those who do so lending themselves to these standard cultural norms and thus equally open to the charge of quietism?

The premise of all such objections, however, is a simplistic acceptance of the equation between masculinity and culture (or the 'Symbolic'); and this premise is itself conservative because it rules out the identification of 'masculine' with 'maternal' activity which I would argue must be an important part of the aspiration of all those wanting a revaluation of cultural norms. To put the point crudely, and more empirically, it is only when men are enabled to identify themselves as (among other things) nurturers and women as other things (as well as nurturers) that nurturing will cease to be signified as 'feminine'. But it is precisely this transformability of cultural codings and norms which is ruled out by a theory premised upon the permanence of their existing meanings. What is wrong with 'maternal' feminism is not that it celebrates a hitherto derided femininity, but that it seems to rule out aforehand as 'masculinst recuperation' any general cultural revaluation of it.

Associated with this preempting of any confusion of traditional cultural gender codings is an overly rigid and stereotypic conception of what it is to act and speak 'like a man'. For in the last analysis, it is only if we assume that 'acting like a man' is of its nature to act in a conservative and self-defensive manner that the admonition not to do so retains its critical force. But the self-defeating nature of this assumption is revealed rather clearly if we consider that the very designation of the 'cultural' or 'symbolic' as patriarchal implicitly admits that subversion, disruption, the continual challenging of received wisdoms (for that is what culture is, or at any rate includes) is the outcome of 'male' speech and action. In other words, if everything that is 'cultural' is 'masculine' then 'masculinity' itself ceases to retain any distinctive meaning, and we are deprived of any means of discriminating between cultural modes which serve the maintenance of patriarchy and cultural modes which tend to subvert it.

These points bear on the lesser confidence I feel in pressing the charge of 'conservatism' against the other direction of post-structuralist feminism: against the position which would pursue the logic of difference to its ultimate conclusion in the dispersion of any essential conception of the 'feminine'. For it might seem to follow from them that we should welcome this collapse of 'femininity' as a progressive rather than retrograde development. Ought we not to approve it as a break with feminist theories and strategies which, in focusing always on feminine gender and the distinctive experiences of women, have helped to reconfirm the binary system? Such a feminism, if it can be called such, would be directed towards the realization of the 'in-difference' advocated by Derrida, who has been suggesting that feminists should give up 'feminine difference' as the first strategic move in the dissolution of the 'phallologocentric'.

This definitely seems a more attractive and progressive policy. But it, too, is not without its problems and particular tendencies to conservatism. In the first place, Derrida's recommendation to give up describing the specifically female subject in favour of 'in-differentiation' is inherently self-subverting since it must invoke the gender difference it invites us to ignore. In this sense, as Linda Kintz has argued, it is 'posed from the very terrain of the binary oppositions he warns against'.[15] The injunction, in other words, for women to be 'in-different': neither to speak 'as a woman' nor to speak 'like a man' (for both in their differing ways reinforce phallocracy, or at any rate do not disturb it) can arguably only be offered from a male subject place since it depends on presenting woman as 'other': it depends on the assumption, for example, that woman is 'imitating' even if she speaks 'like a man'. You have not to be a man in order to do it, just as in nineteenth-century India you had not to be English in order to be Anglicized.[16] The issues here are complex and I shall not pursue them further here. Suffice it to say that there is indeed a distinction to be drawn between gender-blind and gender in-different positions, and that Derrida's advice may be delivered from a position which has not sufficiently discriminated between the two. (I acknowledge, however, that a 'Derridean' response to these kinds of objection might simply be to point out that any 'Derridean' strategy will of its nature contain these elements of self-subversion.)

In any case, a more important difficulty with the strategy of 'in-difference' is that it recommends changes at the level of discourse and consciousness rather than at the level of material – economic and social – circumstance, and like all such recommendations is open to the charge that it is politically conservative because it is too little dialectical. Because it refuses to discriminate between 'world' and 'text', between the 'material' and the 'discursive' it follows that it has no theoretical purchase on the interdependency and mutual conditioning between the two. Of course, these arguments themselves can have no purchase on a position which eschews the metaphysical vocabulary of materialism and idealism. There is simply here no common discourse and all that one can do is to charge poststructuralist 'idealism' with lacking the conceptual apparatus for marking important distinctions between different areas or modalities of social life. Adopting this critical position, however, I would argue that there are many material circumstances firmly in place which tend to the disadvantaging of women and whose correction is not obviously going to be achieved simply by a revaluation of theory on the part of a poststructuralizing feminist elite. In fact there are some concrete and universal dimensions of women's lives which seem relatively unaffected by the transformation of consciousness already achieved by the women's movement. To give one example: despite the indisputable gains of feminist theory and action, the fact remains that women live in fear of men and men do not live in fear of women. When I say 'live in fear' of men, I do not mean that we live our lives in a continual and conscious anxiety, or that we think an attack on our persons is very likely (it isn't statistically and we are rational enough to accept it). I mean that women live in a kind of alertness to the possibility of attack and must to some degree organize their lives in order to minimize its threat. In particular, I think, this has constraints – from which men are free – on our capacity to enjoy solitude. As a woman, one's reaction to the sight of a male stranger approaching on a lonely road or country walk is utterly different from one's reaction to the approach of a female stranger. In the former case there is a frisson of anxiety quite absent in the latter. This anxiety, of course, is almost always confounded by the man's perfectly friendly behaviour, but the damage to the relations between the sexes has already been done – and done not by the individual man and woman – but by their culture. This female fear and the constraints it places on what women can do – particularly in the way of spending time on their own – has, of course, its negative consequences for men too, most of whom doubtless deplore its impact on their own capacities for spontaneous relations with women. (Thus, for example, the male stranger has to think twice about smiling at the passing woman/ exchanging the time of day with her, etc. for fear he will either alarm her or be misinterpreted in his intentions ...) But the situation all the same is not symmetrical: resentment or regret is not as disabling as fear; and importantly it does not affect the man's capacity to go about on his own.

This, then, is one example of the kind of thing I have in mind in speaking of 'material circumstances' which have been relatively unaffected by changes at a discursive and 'Symbolic' level. They are circumstances which relate to conditions which are

experienced by both sexes, and in the most general sense are therefore culturally universal. But they are conditions which are differently experienced simply in virtue of which sex you happen to be,
and in that sense they are universally differentiated between the
sexes: *all* men and *all* women are subject to them *differently*. It is
this sex-specific but universal quality of certain conditions of
general experience which justifies and gives meaning to collective gender categories. To put the point in specifically feminist
terms: there are conditions of existence common to all women
which the policy of in-difference – with its recommendation not
to focus on *female* experience – is resistant to registering in theory
and therefore unlikely to correct in practice.

The implication of these rather open-ended remarks, I think,
is that feminism should proceed on two rather contrary lines: it
should be constantly moving towards 'in-difference' in its
critique of essentializing and ghettoizing modes of feminist
argument; but at the same time it should also insist on retaining
the gender-specific but universal categories of 'woman' or
'female experience' on the grounds that this is essential to
identifying and transforming all those circumstances of women's
lives which the pervasion of a more feminist consciousness has
left relatively unaffected. In short, feminism should be both
'humanist' and 'feminist' – for the paradox of the poststructuralist
collapse of the 'feminine' and the move to 'in-difference' is that it
reintroduces – though in the disguised form of an aspiration to
no-gender – something not entirely dissimilar from the old
humanistic goal of sexual parity and reconciliation. And while
one can welcome the reintroduction of the goal, it may still require
some of the scepticism which inspired its original deconstruction.

Notes

1. Thus Alice Jardine, *Gynesis: Configurations of Women and Modernity*, Ithaca
and London 1985, see especially pp. 22–24; cf. Barbara Creed, 'From Here to
Modernity: Feminism and Postmodernism', *Screen* 28, 2, Spring 1987.
2. Although there was a definite class bias in much of the early liberal

discussion of such rights: 'all men' being conceived often enough as having practical extension only to all males in possession of a certain property and concomitant social status.

3. See J. Kristeva, 'Women's Time' (first published as *'Le Temps des Femmes'* in *Cahiers de recherche de sciences des textes et documents* 5, Winter 1979), in Toril Moi (ed.) *The Kristeva Reader*, Oxford 1986, pp. 187–213; cf. *'Il n'y a pas de maitre à langage'*, *Nouvelle Revue de Psychanalyse* 1979, cited in *Kristeva Reader*, p. 11.

4. See the discussion by Andreas Huyssen, *After the Great Divide: Modernism, Mass Culture and Postmodernism*, London 1986, pp. 44–62.

5. For a sense of this development in Kristeva's thinking, see the excerpts from *About Chinese Women* (1974); 'Stabat Mater' (1977); 'The True-Real' (1979); and 'Women's Time' (1979) included in Toril Moi, *Kristeva Reader*. Cf. also the discussions of Kristeva in Toril Moi, *Sexual/Textual Politics*, London 1985; and in Jacqueline Rose, *Sexuality in the Field of Vision*, London 1986. For a critique of Kristeva's 'ethic' of feminine negativity, see Drusilla Cornell and Adam Thurschwell, 'Feminism, Negativity, Subjectivity' in Drusilla Cornell and Seyla Benhabib, *Feminism as Critique*, Oxford 1987, pp. 151–6.

6. Irigaray, for example, has treated *parler femme* as an analogue of female genitalia, in which the contiguous, non-adversarial and elliptical quality of the statements of feminine writing is a reflection of the two lips of the vulva.

7. Drusilla Cornell and Adam Thurschwell, *Feminism as Critique*, pp. 150–1.

8. A disengagement reflected in Kristeva's Lacanian presentation of the feminine as semiotic 'other' of the Symbolic even as it is criticized by Kristeva herself.

9. Recent feminist self-criticism regarding the 'white middle-class' outlook of feminist politics reflects this anxiety about conceptual conflations, even if it does not collapse into the extreme particularism which would seem to be its ultimate logic.

10. Jean Baudrillard, *De La séduction*, Paris 1979, p. 208; see also his *Cool Memories*, London 1990. Cf. Jardine, *Gynesis*, p. 67.

11. Jean Baudrillard, interview in *Marxism Today*, January 1989, p. 54.

12. There will be some, no doubt, who will come to Baudrillard's defence. They may argue, perhaps, that he is in fact repaying the debt of patriarchy with a clear and self-confessed vagina envy. Or they may point out that Baudrillard is simply saying that the means must match the end, and that for women to use 'male' methods is to give themselves over to the masculine forms of power they wish to contest. Very well, then, let him for his part, show his good faith by yielding up the language of 'female sacrifice' and 'female seduction'. And let him ask men, too, to put a hand to the churn of cultural revolution. Or is the subversion of the Symbolic to be wholly women's work?

13. François Lyotard, *The Postmodern Condition*, Manchester 1986, p. 66, cf. pp. 10–16; 25; 57–9; 63–5.

14. Isaac Balbus, 'Disciplining Women', in *Feminism as Critique*, pp. 110–127.

15. Linda Kintz, 'In-Different Criticism', in Jeffner Allen, and Iris Marion Young, *The Thinking Muse: Feminism and Modern French Philosophy*, Indiana 1989, p. 113.

16. *Ibid.*, pp. 130–33.

11

Stephen Heroine

They passed from behind Mr Bloom along the curbstone. Beard and bicycle. Young woman.

And there he is too. Now that's really a coincidence: second-time. Coming events cast their shadows before. With the approval of the eminent poet Mr Geo Russell. That might be Lizzie Twigg with him. A.E.: what does that mean? Initials perhaps. Albert Edward, Arthur Edmund, Alphonsus Eb Ed El, Esquire. What was he saying? The ends of the world with a Scotch accent. Tentacles: octopus. Something occult: symbolism. Holding forth. She's taking it all in. Not saying a word. To aid gentleman in literary work.

James Joyce, Ulysses

– *Sonnez*!
Smack. She let free sudden in rebound her nipped elastic garter smackwarm against her smackable woman's warmhosed thigh.
– *La cloche*! cried gleeful Lenehan. Trained by owner. No sawdust there!

James Joyce, Ulysses

But *sonnez la cloche* on Lizzie's Twigg's warm, silk-hosed, smackable ...? Not likely. Her stockings are loose over her ankles. Bloom, observing, finds it 'detestable' and 'tasteless'.[1]

Bloom, of course, is not with Lenehan and Blazes Boylan at the bar of the Ormond watching as Miss Douce, the barmaid, snaps her garter. (He is in the dining room eating liver and bacon.) His observation of Lizzie Twigg and her poet-mentor

'A.E.' comes over a hundred pages earlier. The two incidents are quite discrete and separate. Why then juxtapose them? Because they belong to a shared perception on women, and, as it were, respectively stake out its limits. This is only a shared perception in a very general sense, not an identity of responses. Bloom will later relish Gerty McDowell's self-display. Earlier he has cursed a tramcar for denying him the flashed 'rich stockings white'[2] of another woman as she mounts her carriage, and it has put him in mind of the girl he had 'gaped' at a few days before in the Eustace Street hallway 'settling her garter'.[3] But his sensibilities would not have allowed him to do what Lenehan and Boylan do: boldly to ask for it in a public bar; gleefully to cry '*La cloche!*' Equally, it is doubtful whether a Boylan or a Lenehan would even have noticed a Lizzie Twigg.

But all the same, there is an extensive 'eye-to-eyeness' here, a single perspective which links Bloom's response to Lizzie Twigg with Lenehan's towards Lydia Douce, and ties them, like two ends of a chain into a common universe. It is a universe, moreover, shared to a significant degree by all the characters of *Ulysses* despite their vast differences of disposition – by Stephen and Molly, Buck Mulligan and Lynch, as well as by Blazes Boylan, Leopold Bloom and Lenehan. Sensing this closure, which I do most forcefully in those moments when, for example, reading about Lydia Douce's hose I remember Lizzie Twigg's baggy stockings and juxtapose them mentally across the text, I sense also my own exclusion, and am suddenly brought back with a jolt to the reality of myself.

Between Lizzie Twigg's earnest, blue-stocking, bedraggled ankle and Miss Douce's plumped, bronzewarm, scented, all-woman's thigh, there is a moment of recoil. Maybe it is personal to me, or maybe shared by other women readers, or maybe it could even be called a 'feminist' recoil experienced by male and female readers alike. At any rate, I am suddenly smacked back into place. A bell has sounded to recall me to my all too fulsome, overspilling presence, which amounts, really, to a reminder of my absence: a reminder that I have no place in the universe of *Ulysses*.

A woman is a Lizzie Twigg or a Lydia Douce, but an amalgam never. She is either savant or siren, literary sycophant ('She's taking it all in. Not saying a word'[4]) or supercilious servant ('Wept! aren't men!' murmurs Lydia Douce to herself, pondering the antics of the male of the species.[5]). More generally within the symbolic orbit of *Ulysses*, she is either death or eros, 'ghostcandled', 'all-wombing tomb'[6] or 'tumbled beauty',[7] 'sweets of sin'.[8] Either maternal–eternal, handmaid of the moon,[9] or shefiend, female sloth of the underworld, rancid rags.[10] Either tea and jam breathed, sweet-kissing, yum-yum,[11] or pus-mouthed, *dents jaunes*, fang of lasciviousness.[12] Madonna or whore. Helen or hag.

This feels familiar. ('Wept!, aren't male authors!' sighs the feminist literary critic).

But this, in fact, is not my own sigh, nor does it capture the exclusion I feel. For I am not particularly troubled by the standard imagings of women in *Ulysses*, or at least not primarily or simply in themselves. A feminist reading of Joyce's writing which simply sighed over his sexual stereotypes would, from the perspective of my own reading, be a stereotype itself – as one-dimensional as Lydia Douce's view of men. What is involved here, rather, is a kind of empathy which, open as it no doubt is to the charge of ideological compromise, is also always erecting its moral and intellectual barriers against this type of objectivity. If I am troubled, it is by something more obscure and dubious than is allowed within that feminist gaze.

To speak of empathy is to speak of identification, the primary concept, so it seems to me, in any explanation of the particular 'pain' of my moment of recoil. For what hurts here is the slap delivered to my snugly Bloom-enfolded, Dedalus-identifying, Joyce-enjoying self-forgetfulness. In the moment of recoil I am dragged away from a previously calm, uncomplicated reading – a 'reverie' form of reading in which I am submersed in *his* (Joyce's–Stephen's–Bloom's) perspective to the point of being indifferent to its sexuality. Inside the charmed circle of this form of reading, I forget I have a sex. Aware as I am of the gendered world of the text, I am without gender as a reader until some image, or association of images, intrudes too grossly for me to continue in this ignorance, and I am suddenly brought up against the fact that it does after all matter somewhat that I happen in the real world to be a woman. Within the same moment, I am made aware that I cannot really share the textual world. Exiled from it, I experience the kind of 'feminist indignation' which Joyce himself found so unsexy and distasteful, and tended always to portray unsympathetically: a mode of Lizzie-Twiggness.

It is impossible not to feel this rude awakening and its moment of rancour. But it is equally impossible for me not to 'side' against myself in my reaction to this reaction. The self who is reading *with* Joyce nods ironically to the self who is resenting what she reads, but nonetheless refuses to disown her. Identifying as I do with the key subject places of *Ulysses*, and in particular with the figure to whom Joyce himself seems often closest, namely Stephen, I am enfolded within a perspective on women from which I also sense my exile.

This 'bi-location' is by no means confined to my reading of Joyce. Proust has something of the same effect, so too Beckett to a lesser degree. Indeed, it is something I tend to experience in response to any writing which offers an extensive space for soliloquy and self-examination to a central male figure. Since this is a feature of a good deal of modernist writing, one might say that the response in question has a fairly specific character: it is that of a contemporary 'feminist' consciousness to a particular modernist mode of 'masculine' self-awareness. But earlier writing can elicit it (*Hamlet* is an obvious example, but also Donne, Herbert, Marvell, and a good deal of romantic poetry).

Moreover, given that the schism involved here reflects the tension between the 'feminist' and the 'gender-unselfconscious' reader, it is likely to be a feature today of one's reading response to a great deal of literature whether of male or female authorship. For writing which is 'gender-blind', in the sense of deploying the classic conceptions of sexuality, is necessarily 'blind' to any feminist critique of that classic perspective, and therefore provides no space wherein it can be registered. It is writing, therefore, which denies or occludes the 'feminist' reading self.

But writing of a more self-consciously feminist approach can provide this space only by a deliberate incorporation of a 'feminine' outlook or subjectivity: a move whose very deliberateness tends to deny one that unreflective reading self which lies outside the space of gender apperception. If we can speak, in other words, of a 'masculine' privilege in writing or culture, then it resides precisely in an unselfconsciousness of gender which every attempted 'feminist' reclamation tends paradoxically to reaffirm.

Such points would obviously need to be elaborated in regard to particular texts in order to function as any serious critical appraisal. But they do bear on my isolation of Joyce as the subject of this particular discussion. For if I select him, it is in virtue of the particularly acute experience of 'bi-location' he arouses, which is in turn owing to the strength and scope of the identification he offers me. A Dickens or a George Eliot novel may in their differing ways exclude or register my 'feminist' self, but if they do not elicit the same sense of conflict it is because they do not offer any very sustained mirror of my own subjectivity.

Women are always 'out there' relative to the consciousness and sensibility from which the universe of *Ulysses* unfolds. They are disallowed its subject place and exist only within the space circumscribed by rather standard imagings of the female. But as a reader I feel closer to this consciousness and sensibility than to those of many an expressly 'feminist' work. More specifically, there is no female character in modernist fiction with whom I feel the empathy I do with Stephen. I am walking on the strand with Stephen–Hamlet–Shakespeare not with Ann Hathaway–Ophelia–Mary Dedalus.[13] I watch with him under the upswelling tide as the writhing weeds 'hise up their petticoats'.[14] I am lying with him in mulberrycoloured vomit beneath the lifted skirts of the daughters of Erin, wittily parrying the malevolent Mulligan's jibes about my drunkenness ('the most innocent son of Erin for whom they ever lifted them').[15] With Stephen, I recall how it was when, safe from myself, the snares of womanly charms, the 'mind's darkness' and 'dragon temptress shifting her scaly folds', I was quietly reading Aristotle in the serene light of the library of Saint Genevieve.[16] (And indeed why should I not be with him? I, too, in my youth read Aristotle on the form of forms at midnight in the chaste quiet of my college library ...)[17]

If I state the identification here with some violence it is to emphasize the conflict within it, and to contrast the tension of my own reading to the relative composure of a more objective, more properly literary critical feminist assessment of Joyce. I have already indicated my distance from any criticism which dwells only on the 'masculinity' of the Joycean world, citing this as evidence of some misogynist disposition or anti-feminism. For what that leaves out of account is everything which for a lover of Joyce (whether male or female) is confirming in his sensibility. But there is also a much more serious and sophisticated feminist approach to Joyce from which I am also stating my distance in this rather naive and violent talk of 'empathy' and 'identification'. For this approach, too, offers a kind of resting place, an objective critical composure into which I cannot slip myself.

This is a reading which would tax those who see Joyce as some kind of misogynist with failure to appreciate the androgynous motivations of his work, and the extent to which it is constantly, subversively, interrupted by the 'feminine'. From the perspective of this more sympathetic approach, Stephen and Bloom in the *Portrait* and in *Ulysses* are viewed as relative outsiders to their 'masculine' environment, as representing a disruptive 'feminine' sensibility. It has been suggested, for example, that in Stephen's various personal and cultural resistances (to Church and politics, to father and mother, to the literary canon and literary establishment, etc.) we should see evidence of a kind of feminist sympathy and mode of rebellion; and that through Bloom, too (as revealed to us in his pacifism, his Jewish 'otherness', his respect for women, his embarrassed relation to the all-male Dublin bar-room culture, etc.), Joyce should be seen as registering an empathy with the condition of women and with their particular outlook – an empathy continued and reinforced in the sexual autonomy granted to Molly.[18]

All this has its element of truth. Joyce certainly does through his main protagonists in *Ulysses* (Stephen, Bloom, Molly) deliver a challenge to various authorities of distinctly patriarchal cast, and to stereotypical conceptions of male–female relations and their standard depiction in fiction. The Nausicaa chapter ends in masturbation not marriage, Bloom is uxorious towards an adulterous wife, Molly is the living antithesis to the iconic 'virtuous' heroine. And there are many less central episodes, narratives and meditations in the book which one might cite to similar effect. From this perspective, moreover, it could be argued that any special affinity I feel with Stephen is precisely accountable to his own 'femininity', to his being the mouthpiece, as it were, of a certain 'womanly' sensitivity and sympathy in Joyce himself.

But the reason I cannot share in the composure of this reading is that it relies on my accepting the very distinction of 'masculine' and 'feminine' sensibilities to which I find myself so resistant in the text of *Ulysses* itself. Presupposing as it does, that we have always known in what the 'feminine' consists, it then reads the text through the a priori binary grid of that assumption. A gender essentialism which the text itself reproduces (the 'feminine' is 'cosmic', symbolized in 'fluidity', the 'maternal', etc.) is uncritically accepted by the 'feminist' critic, who then symptomatically peruses the text for its sympathetic responses to these supposedly 'feminine' attributes.

Equally problematic from the standpoint of my own reading is the assumption running through this approach that one can detect a 'feminine' responsiveness in any rebellious or anti-establishment sentiment which is given its expression in the text. For I find it both naive and imperializing to define a 'feminine' consciousness in such a way as to discover it in a critical sensibility as such: naive because it would tend to make almost all major works of art 'feminist'; imperializing because it comes close to denying the autonomy and heterogeneity of masculine authorship. After all, a great deal of what comprises the 'male dominated' literary and artistic canon was decidedly nonconformist and engaged in polemical struggle with its times. In this sense what is 'typically' masculine in culture is typically critical, controversial, and highly self-aware. None of this means, however, that it is not also typically androcentric. It means rather that there is a considerable range of sensibility or critical response to the world which it is mistaken to categorize in gender terms. In this sense, I would say that in my 'identification' with Stephen I am not responding to a Joyce–Stephen 'feminine' understanding, but to a Joyce–Stephen morality, irony, self-doubt, anti-authoritarianism, self-love, religious ambivalence, and so on. And that the identification is both gratifying *and* discomfiting precisely because the universe of *Ulysses* wherein it comes so naturally remains itself so spontaneously or naturally androcentric: a world, indeed, in which women are viewed from within the conventional frame from which the (male) ego senses its distance and alienation.

The tension this causes can be expressed more formally in terms of a difference in modes of identification, of which I shall here distinguish three: the 'direct', the 'blind' and the 'indirect'. The mode of 'direct' identification is pretence or make-believe, and involves the fantasy that one actually is the (fictional or historical) personage with whom one is identifying. It is always intentional and usually based on unabashed admiration for the role model offered in the character. It is the identification of 'childish' reading – which is not to suppose that it is not something which adult authors and readers indulge in to a significant degree. The 'blind' identification, by contrast, is not based on any conscious attachment to a particular character, but is that of which one is unaware: it is the identification of an unthinking acceptance of the general authorial perspective. It is an unconscious sharing of the implicit worldview of the text. The author writes naturally from within it and unwittingly projects it. The reader reads unjarred by its perspective and without questioning its conventions.

The 'indirect' identification lies somewhere between these poles. In contrast to the blind identification, it is conscious and focused on a particular character, but the character in question is not someone one wants or pretends to be, but a figure whom one picks out as most reflecting one's own sense of self. Its mode is not 'pretence' but 'representation': it is the identification of one's actual self with another who represents it. Very often, though not always, it is with the figure whom the author intends you to recognize as being most cognizant of the universe of the text: it is the figure, to use a phrase of Joyce himself, whom one cannot 'walk round'.

Viewed in these terms, my tension as a reader of *Ulysses* arises out of the clash between my failure of 'blind' identification and the strength of my 'indirect' identification. Absorbed within the text through my indirect identification, I am at the same time excluded from it in being conscious of (i.e. not blindly identifying with) its overall androcentrism, and the moment of 'recoil' is the recognition of this form of exclusion within inclusion. It is a kind of 'coming to' of the self in the discovery of one's absence. Engrossed in one's indirect identification one reads from the masculine perspective (Joyce's/Stephen's/Bloom's) from which the work unfolds. Hence there is a loss of gendered self, which is not to say one loses a sense of gender. The gender distinction and its symbolisms saturate most fiction and Joyce's perhaps more than any. But there is loss in the sense of abstraction from the self as gendered. This is the level at which one (he or she) is simply reader. Its pleasures are various. But insofar as they have to do with identification with the author/protagonist, they have the form of self-recognition. So the absorption or non gender-reflective consciousness is in its particular way a self-discovery. The reader finds him or herself in finding the authorial viewpoint confirming of his or her own, and the difference between author and reader is not so much to do with a difference of selfhood or experience as to do with the expressive powers of the former. Only the author is able to render what the reader feels is common between them. (This was the sense of Virginia Woolf's tribute to Proust as awakening ideas previously sleeping on the walls of the mind: the reader has had the same ideas, but only recognizes this in the form of a restored memory of them which the writing suddenly arouses and illuminates.)

For example, abstracting for a moment from my own perhaps rather idiosyncratic empathy with Stephen in *Ulysses*, I would say that it is this intimacy with the 'authorial' sensibility which most readers of the *Portrait* experience in respect of Stephen's ordeal with Father Dolan and his pandy-bat, and its sequel in his discovery from his father that the Rector of Clongowes (to whom he had complained about his beating) and Father Dolan had shared a 'hearty laugh' about the whole episode.[19] Few of us (and no women) have been subjected to the particular cruelties and diplomacies of the Jesuit college education, but most of us recognize the cadential quality of the childhood experience which runs from original humiliation at the hands of an adult, through vindication and restoration of self-esteem, back, via the shock of seeing one's self-righteous indignation the object of adult amusement, to a renewed, if wiser, form of humiliation. I would say, moreover, that experience of that kind has no gender specificity but is common to us all.

But this gender-'indifferent' intimacy can persist even when the content of the protagonist's experiences and soliloquies is much more explicitly sexual. For example, one sides with Hamlet's indecision as reflecting a kindred moral sensibility even though it 'victimizes' Gertrude and Ophelia in ways that many a feminist will want to 'reread'; one sides with him in the egoism of his sexuality, its self-irony and existentialist modes of distance and transcendence, however vulnerable these may be to feminist deconstruction; one even sides – to put it at its bluntest – with Hamlet's edge rather than Ophelia's groaning.[20] Likewise, one identifies with Stephen (Shakespeare) and his discomfiture in the National Library even as he offers his most phallocentric, patriarchal ruminations: shares in his struggles against the church-mother and her sickliness; is with him in his 'transcendence' of brothel 'immanence', etc. Or again, one is with Bloom caressing his 'opulent curves', in his underwear fetish, his sense of hypocrisy at his own forms of puritanism, even maybe with him hoping that Gerty McDowell will …

But always superimposed upon this unreflexive level of identification, or rather, rumbling along subversively beneath it, half

---

consciously kept at bay lest it disturb too severely the gender indifference of one's read, there is the other awareness. This is the awareness which is the failure of blind identification – the quiet knowledge that it is indeed all received, reorganized and handed on as if one were male. As if the world one is within were always a world in which to be a woman is to be a member of the opposite sex.

And then something on top of all this goes snap: the moment of recoil. One cannot, without strain, remain in that universe. But nor can one retreat from it, for to do so would be to sacrifice too much of one's subjectivity, too much of what one had found of oneself within it. Conversely, to retreat into 'feminist' objectivity would be to gain an otherness one does not want: to settle for an 'identity' of 'feminist' reading resistance which is not where one is either.

Joyce himself knew very well the *form* of this form of pain, and expresses it better than anyone. It is captured for me in Stephen's reflections on the Elizabethans in the *Portrait*:

> His mind, in the vesture of a doubting monk, stood often in shadow under the windows of that age, to hear the grave and mocking music of the lutenists or the frank laughter of waistcoateers until a laugh too low, a phrase tarnished by time, of chambering and false honour stung his monkish pride and drove him on from his lurking place. (p. 176)

What he is here sensitive to is obviously not my own moment of 'feminist' recoil. If anything, the content here (a monkish puritanism offended by the ribaldry of the bedchamber) embodies typical modes of masculine dissociation from which I myself might feel repulsed. But it is certainly an expression of the mode or form of 'feminist' withdrawal which his own work at times induces. There is 'formal' recognition here of what is at issue. Lurking under the windows of his Dublin and its 'age', I might speak of myself as driven on eventually by some 'tarnished phrases' in his own writing 'stinging my womanly pride'.

But it is above all in regard to his Irishness that Joyce registers most forcefully this form of exclusion within inclusion. A little later in the *Portrait* Stephen finds himself offended by the English dean's overemphatic interest in the (supposedly) Irish word 'tundish':

> He felt with a smart of dejection that the man to whom he was speaking was a countryman of Ben Jonson. He thought:
> The language in which we are speaking is his before it is mine. How different are the words *home, Christ, ale, master* on his lips and on mine! I cannot speak or write these words without unrest of spirit. His language, so familiar and so foreign, will always be for me an acquired speech. I have not made or accepted its words. My voice holds them at bay. My soul frets in the shadow of his language. (p. 189)

Joyce–Stephen feels 'unrest' with the foistedness of the English language, but it is also the language which is his, and which he will insist on staying within, claiming it as the instrument for 'forging' the 'uncreated conscience of his race'.[21] The 'unrest' here has to do with a refusal to accept an exclusion from a language in which he also knows he is never quite at home. But to accept this Irish 'otherness' to the cultural dominance of the English 'Symbolic' is not Joyce's mode either. There is no way in which he will resolve this tension by recourse to Gaelic or a celebration of the 'difference' of 'Irishness'. To stay speaking is to stay speaking in English. But this is an option to persist in the tension-ridden experience of making 'one's own' a language from which one also finds oneself 'disowned'.

Again, there is nothing in the content here which reflects my feminine 'unrest', but something of the form of it is apprehended here. I, too, insist on my identity within, or identification with, the symbolic universe of Joyce's writing, and reject any escape from it. I cannot opt to be in the place to which it relegates women, the place of the male viewpoint, and simply assert that 'otherness' as a form of cultural exclusion within which I can finally discover and express my feminine identity. My 'consciousness' is not to be forged in the semiotic of a feminine difference, but only within the communality of a culture whose 'authorial' outlook is decidedly masculine. But there will be 'unrest', and my soul will 'fret in the shadow' of that language. *Home, Christ, ale, master*: I know how they sound on Stephen's lips, and know that they also sound a little differently on mine. Or, to put the point more forcefully, such words as *stocking, drawers, foetus, naughty, flower, light*: these are his words, familiar words, but foreign too, words which my own voice both shares and holds at bay.

These words are familiar because I am intimately aware of, and subscribe to, the power they have for Joyce. Words like *stocking* or *drawers* are no more neutral for me than they are for him. As a reader sharing a common world of language and meaning they come to me already imbued with the eroticism which Joyce so potently re-evokes, presenting it in a kind of bas-relief. But they are foreign too, or my mind 'frets in their shadow' insofar as the eroticism with which they are saturated and which Joyce distils for us derives from masculine desire and its view-point. *Stockings* and *drawers* are what 'he' observes, is enticed by the flash of, senses the invitation within, and there is no way in which these words as meaningful for me can be detached from the responses they summon up in 'him'. But these words are also for a woman the name of her garments, the items of clothing she puts on and wears, and only sees herself within as if from a distance through the imagined – and hence indirect – gaze of the male. Insofar, then, as their meaning is inseparable from their erotic charge, such words present themselves to the woman as the terms of an acquired language, or of a language which is 'his before it is hers'. They gain their resonance from the perspective of a gender subject whom I can no more be than Joyce can be English. The word *perfume* comes to me in Joyce's prose heavy with the odours which *women* exude; the *foetus* is a dark, unformed, oxymoronic image of *his* potency latent in *her* womb; *naughty* is what *girls* are, and what Bloom, to titillate his *feminine* masochism, want women to accuse him of being; *flower* is *her* sexual freshness and lightheartedness, a saying 'and yes ... yes I will Yes' on Howth head;[22] *light* is the cool serenity of the mind untroubled by thoughts of the carnal delights to which *she* tempts him, and so on.

It is not that one resents these meanings. Or at any rate I do not. To speak of resentment here would be as absurd as to speak of Joyce 'resenting' Shakespeare or Ben Jonson. As Joyce relishes and identifies with the voice of these poets, so I relish and identify with the voice of his own writing. But the affinity here is with a voice which is always erotically looking the other way, in regard to which my desire is permanently wrong-footed. I can seriously identify with this voice only to the extent that I abstract from myself as a full member of my species. The moment of recoil is the moment in which one is brought back to the reality of this schism.

At its most general and fundamental, this schism – which I have already suggested is by no means experienced simply in reaction to Joyce – can be related to the absence from our language of a feminine 'erotic', by which I mean the absence of any feminine equivalent to the world of sexual love as viewed from the standpoint of male desire: the absence of a romanticism and erotic charge which would be equally 'classic', as firmly lodged in language, as much a part of a common cultural heritage, but which derived from the place of the female subject. The absence is not that aspired to in a 'lesbian' or 'different' feminism. What is absent is a feminine heterosexual equivalent whose ineffability would seem to defy the *écriture féminine* or *parler femme* of Cixous or Irigaray. Nor is it the space of Kristeva's pre-oedipal 'semiotic' or Wittig's separatist sensualism. What is culturally 'missing' is not the antithesis to heterosexuality (which in fact has always found its marginal expression) nor a feminine 'other' rediscoverable within it, but a feminine counterweight to its symbolic asymmetry. The feminine (heterosexual) erotic is neither opposed to, nor the inversion of, nor residual within the 'phallo-erotic' since it is merely the hypothetical alternative to that cultural predominance. If it had been, it would have been on a par with it, and therefore cannot now be its difference. It is essentially, therefore, a meaningless notion, or at any rate futile in its aspiration. For a genuine alternative to masculine pre-eminence and the sexual asymmetry of its erotic perspective, must already have enjoyed the prevalence or 'majority' status of the culture and language to which it opposes its 'minority' claims. One can neither restore what has no preexistence nor forge a tradition in breaking with the past. In other words, to pursue the idea of a 'feminine erotic' is to pursue a will-o-the wisp, a history as 'fabled by the daughters of memory'.[23]

How then can one charge any writing with failure to 'speak' what is unsayable? One cannot. But one may charge writing with closure to the 'unrest' its unsayability occasions. And certainly at the level of its characterization and overt symbolization of women one can charge *Ulysses* with being closed to the 'feminine erotic': closed to the subject place where woman is not 'walkroundably' in the world, but before it, backed up against it. No one perhaps quite captures as Joyce does the mesmeric and sexually arresting quality of language, its 'heart-quopping'[24] powers. But the condition of his doing so is that the reader remains in a kind of complacent suspense, tacitly at one with its masculine gaze. Sensitive though he is to his 'Irish' exclusion from 'English' and to the asymmetry between the two (the one cannot be opposed to the other as an equally valid and cosmopolitan tongue) he nowhere in *Ulysses* shows himself sensitive to the schismatic position of women within this gaze or to the asymmetry which must dog every attempt to escape or transcend it.

One is speaking here of the surface discourse of the work, and of *Ulysses* in particular, which is quite surprisingly removed from all aspects of the 'woman question' and no less surprisingly devoid of the sympathy Joyce brings to his portrayal of women in his earlier work, and perhaps most particularly in the *Dubliners*. The women of the *Dubliners* are a good deal more complex, enigmatic, emotionally vital, intellectually competent creatures than the women of *Ulysses*. Molly Ivors in *The Dead*, for example, is a portrait of a woman with Nationalist leanings against the wind of Joyce's, and an 'education' which we are asked (through the perception of the sensitive Gabriel Conroy) to view as detracting from her 'humanity'. But though she is shown as jarring and 'difficult' she is never dismissed, her fullness as a person never flattened out into a 'Lizzie Twigg' caricature. She offends Gabriel Conroy, but she also remains a subject for him, a disturbing and in some way compelling, even attractive, personality. Unlike Molly Bloom, one senses her as both sexually vital *and* informed of the meaning of 'metempsychosis'. Other women in the *Dubliners* – Mrs Sinico in *A Painful Case*, Gabriel's wife Gretta in *The Dead* – are equally, though in differing ways, transcendent people with histories, ghosts, memories, mental worlds of their own which are much more akin in their open-endedness to those which Joyce grants to Stephen and Bloom in *Ulysses*. They are not simply wives, or widows, or prostitutes, nor can we ever quite 'walk round' or see through them: an element of enigma, of their own privacy persists which is of the essence of the fictional depiction of character as person, as a fully formed subjectivity.

In *Ulysses*, by contrast, the women are presented entirely within the objective mode, which is to say that we are asked to view them only as they appear to men or as they appear in their own eyes to men. In this respect – to take issue now with an objection which may have been gathering force in the reader's mind – Molly Bloom is no exception to the absence of the consciousness of the 'feminine erotic' in *Ulysses* but rather the culminating confirmation of a presiding masculinity.

This may seem a perverse and somewhat heretical claim to some readers of *Ulysses*. It will be objected that Joyce gives to 'woman', through Molly, the final subjectivity, i.e. the final power to 'objectify' others. It is true that all the male protagonists of the book, and many of its more minor characters are here viewed from her viewpoint, passed under her gaze, and in the process exposed to a feminine scrutiny which in its combined candour and humanity is unmatched elsewhere in fiction. It is true, too, that in Molly we are offered an image of a woman who is no longer yoked in service to a romantic ideal. She is neither rapacious nor chaste, neither pure nor defiled, neither dutiful wife nor tormented adulteress. She is a cynic and a sentimentalist, a hedonist and a worker. Moreover, placed as it is at the end of the book and in the form of a monologic sequel to the very dialogic Ithaca chapter, Molly's solitary meditation seems to assume an almost monumental authority. The ongoing, un-resolved dialectic of Stephen-as-experienced-by-Bloom, Bloom-as-experienced-by-Stephen is finally put to rest (Stephen and Bloom both sleep), and Molly stands forth alone, awake and very voluble. This is woman having the last say, what more should one ask?

But the woman who has this final word is herself along the same spectrum which runs from Lizzie Twigg to Lydia Douce and her world circumscribed by the same perspective. Molly experiences herself as a woman experienced from that viewpoint. Very little happens to her, or very little of emotional importance, which is not refracted through the male gaze and orchestrated around the sexual desire of the men in her life. She is almost incapable of seeing herself as other than a sexual partner, and an inordinate proportion of her soliloquy is taken up with reminis-cences relating to herself as sexual being: either with fucking itself, or with the style she will adopt for Boylan, or Bloom or Stephen, etc., or with the clothes she will buy or wear for amorous encounters. Moreover, while Stephen and Bloom have just been presented as doing a good deal of mutual observation and consideration of how the other figures in the world, neither of them is portrayed as devoting much attention to how the other appears to women. We may contrast this with Molly's mono-logue wherein she scarcely thinks of another woman without thinking of her as how she appears to men. In other words, the Molly chapter exemplifies to the full the 'asymmetry' of an erotic perspective in which men experience (look at, desire, etc.) women, and women experience women as being experienced by men. Molly is not simply the object of Bloom's, Boylan's, Ben Dollard's, etc. 'look'. She is very much a subject, too. But her subjectivity is engrossed in looking at the look, and this takes up a far larger share of her experience of the world than is the case with Bloom, Boylan, Dollard, etc.

Now there are two different lines of objection which might be pressed against this. It might be said, on the one hand, that all this is beside the point, since in *Ulysses* Joyce is no longer engaged (as in the *Dubliners*) with a descriptive 'phenomenology' of life but with an exercise of a more Freudian character. In *Ulysses*, it may be said, Joyce is not presenting 'lived experience' but its sexual underbelly. The aim is to unsettle all that piety and cultural nicety which had the emotions seated in the heart rather than located somewhat lower. If the world from the perspective of *Ulysses* looks sexually obsessed and sexually reductive, this cannot constitute a legitimate complaint against it for its lack of 'realism', its stereotyping or one-dimensionality, since a significant part of the design was to reveal the crude, sexually fixated, unfortunately stereotypical quality of the fantasy world lurking within the complex etiquette of 'real' relations. The suggestion here would be that privately our hearts revolve around our genitals, privately we confound and betray our best-held ideological beliefs, privately in fantasy we enact the roles of the most standard pornographies, privately we continually desecrate what we dignify and respect in our more open and explicit relations with other people – and that Joyce has junked the superficies and gone rooting out this 'private'.

Joyce certainly (despite his dislike of Freudianism) seems to have been inclined to view the world as more reducible to its sexuality than it liked to believe, and some of the surreal character of *Ulysses* can be seen as serving his interest in this form of exposure. It may even perhaps be possible to claim that in the rather limited and standard women of *Ulysses* we should detect a Joycean dissent from romantic myths of ethereal love and the 'marriage of true minds'. But the debunking of any such pieties is nonetheless always conducted in a mode which preserves conventional ideas of the role and significance of women in the lives of men. This remains true even of Molly's ridicule in that it relegates men so firmly to the position of an 'opposite' sex and relates to them essentially only as carnal beings with whom she can share rather little other than sexual congress. In other words, in that is it confined to the follies of men in their sexual behaviour, Molly's irreverence reinforces the idea of women as the 'sexual' sex: that part of humanity which represents it in its sexual dimension. Allowed so little identification with men in anything but their erotic fascination with women, Molly indulges the notion of their cultural transcendence even as she mocks their sexual dependency.

We might note, moreover, that whatever subversion of masculine pretensions we may read into *Ulysses*, Stephen is allowed very largely to escape the clutches of its profanity, and to retain his spiritual autonomy. In other words, even if we view the book as offering (alongside much else) an ironic commentary on 'typical' male attitudes and obsessions, Stephen – and Bloom, too, to a significant degree – are precisely not so typical: they evade typicality in a way denied to the women in the book. They are accorded that existential distance from cultural norms which is enviously claimed for women in the moment of 'feminist indignation'.

On the other hand, it may be said – to address now the second line of possible objection – that it is mistaken to treat Molly as any kind of symbolic representation of women and female sexuality. Molly is simply a realist portrait of a particular woman. Now, at one level this is true, and if we approach her only at that level, we can have no quarrel with what she represents: for she is 'representative' only in the perfectly acceptable sense that we recognize there to be many women like her. There is no disputing the existence of her 'type', nor would she strike us in fact as so 'realistic' were she not so 'representative' in this respect. But to read only at this level is to abstract from another level of representation at which she is precisely not specific, but mythic and general. For there can be little doubt that Joyce did also view her as a kind of universal, and that in this universality she conforms to a symbolization of the 'feminine' in *Ulysses* as cosmic, eternal, nature-bound and amoral. She configures the 'feminine' within the prevailing sexual mythology of the work.

In *Ulysses*, all the abrasive elements of gender, its political and social 'difficulty' are subdued, distanced and dehistoricized by a kind of sexual fatalism. Sounded in the 'high' mode of the Homeric or biblical epic, the solemn message is of a sexual difference which cannot be otherwise. Both sexes are caught up in destinies of desire and corporeality which forever ensnare men in their lusts and consign women to a maternal long-sufferance.

Sex is as old as the hills, as recurrent and irreversible as the tides. Men and women do the coupler's will, act out a continuous cycle of concupiscence and parturition. In this serial repetition, the role of the woman is that of a fundamentally affirmative and stabilizing force. She is the one who says 'yes' to the caprice and contingency of sexual promptings, and through whom sex is restored to the necessity and equilibrium of its natural, reproductive function. She is the species in its ahistorical sameness of biological continuity, the one through whose maternal labours the navel cords of all 'link back', united in the 'stradentwining cable of all flesh'.[25]

Particular and even in some ways idiosyncratic 'character' that she is, Molly is also symbol of the 'womanly' as conceived from this cyclical perspective. Writing to his friend, Frank Budgen, Joyce says of Molly's monologue that it

> turns slowly, evenly, though with variations, capriciously, but surely like the huge earthball itself round and round spinning. Its four cardinal points are the female breasts, arse, womb and sex expressed in the words *because, bottom* (in all senses bottom, button, bottom of the class, bottom of the sea, bottom of the heart, *woman, yes*).[26]

Or again, that Molly is:

> sane, full amoral fertilisable untrustworthy engaging limited prudent indifferent Weib. '*Ich bin das Fleische das stets bejaht!*'[27]

But this universal, all-affirming, eternally revolving cosmic woman encompasses only that space in which she is 'out there', essentialized through this sexual mythology as a specific dimension or component of the earth. The one thing she is not is the whole of the earth. The world is culture, industry, journalism, invention, sport, politics, etc. – *and* woman. There is this world, on the one hand, and woman on the other, as one element contained within it.

What, then, the Molly universal does not encompass in her all inclusive femininity is the 'feminine' which is the consciousness of this exclusion; the 'woman' who has her back up against the wall of the novel; who is not one item in the furniture of the world but the maker of its inventory. What Molly's 'sanity' will not tolerate is the maddened woman, the woman of conscience, the woman stricken by remorse and eaten by ambition. What her 'fullness' denies is the woman who experiences the world in its density, the woman, in other words, who will not accept the vacuity of her 'cosmic' identity. What her 'amorality' has no conscience about is the 'Agenbite of Inwit' in every woman. What Molly's yesness says no to is the woman who is Stephen, the Stephen Heroine.

Notes

1. *Ulysses*, pp. 210, 343, 210 respectively. (References are to The Bodley Head 1960 edition as being the one with which I am most familiar. Since the authenticity of the later Penguin 1986 edition is still in dispute, this seemed to me to be a warranted enough practice.)

2. *Ibid.*, p. 90.

3. *Ibid.*

4. *Ibid.*, p. 210.

5. *Ibid.*, p. 343.

6. *Ibid.*, p. 60; cf. p. 46.

7. *Ibid.*, p. 53.

8. *Ibid.*, p. 304; p. 351.

9. *Ibid.*, p. 60.

10. *Ibid.*, p. 30; pp. 51–59.

11. *Ibid.*, p. 29; p. 353.

12. *Ibid.*, p. 53.

13. Stephen, identifying with Hamlet, 'proves' that Shakespeare is the ghost of Hamlet's father, thus casting Ann Hathaway in the role of the guilty queen (p. 241), who in turn is associated with Stephen's mother, Mary Dedalus (p. 243).

14. *Ibid.*, p. 62.

15. *Ibid.*, p. 279.

16. *Ibid.*, p. 30.

17. I do not, of course, claim that my experience was typical. But, then, neither was Stephen's.

18. This is a theme of Bonne Kime Scott's discussion of *Ulysses* in her feminist study of Joyce, *James Joyce*, Brighton 1987. See in particular her chapter on Joyce's (Stephen's) 'Challenges to Male-Centred Literature and

Stephen Heroine

History' and on 'Gender, Discourse and Culture'.

19. *Portrait of the Artist as a Young Man*, Harmondsworth 1916, pp. 48–59; 72–3.

20. *Oph.* You are keen, my lord, you are keen.
Ham. It would cost you a groaning to take off mine edge.

Hamlet, Act III, scene ii

21. *Portrait*, p. 253. In contrast to my own comparison between feminist and Joycean 'unrest', Bonnie Kime Scott discovers 'tantalizing parallels between Ireland's efforts to recover a lost literature and the feminist gynocritic's efforts to reclaim a muted female literary tradition' (*James Joyce*, p. 34). She regards Joyce as 'patriarchal' insofar as he remained aloof from the Irish revival (p. 35), and implies that we should approve instead his championing of Irish writers like James Clarence Mangan – in whom Joyce claimed to detect a 'female' imagination.

22. *Ulysses*, p. 933.

23. Cf. Stephen's challenge to Blake's view of history: 'But can those have been possible seeing that they never were? Or was that only possible which came to pass? Weave, weaver of the wind' (*Ulysses*, p. 30). Cf. also Richard Ellmann, *Ulysses on the Liffey*, London 1974, pp. 20–23.

One cannot stress too much that the 'impossible' history which would have been the 'feminine erotic' is not the antithesis to the 'masculine erotic' but the correction to its asymmetry. There is not one world as experienced from a masculine viewpoint, and then an 'equal' and antithetical one as experienced from a feminine perspective. There is only one world, common to both sexes, but in which the experience of the one sex is largely overlapped by the experience of the other. It is a world in which the woman, alongside her own more unshared experience, experiences herself continually as she is experienced by men: includes his experience of her as part of her own. The asymmetry here relates to the way in which in this common world of experience, male experience typically includes a good deal less of being experienced than is typical for women. When a man sees himself through a women's eyes he does something which typically requires a certain reflective effort, which is not part of a spontaneous, unthinking experience of self in the way that it typically is for the woman.

24. Joyce of Bloom's heart on sighting Blazes Boylan (p. 234):

Mr Bloom came to Kildare St. First I must library.
Straw hat in sunlight. Tan shoes. Turnedup trousers. It is. It is.
His heart quopped softly. To the right. Museum. Goddesses. He swerved to the right.

25. *Ulysses*, p. 46. Cf. 'Wombed in the sin darkness I was too, made not begotten. By them, the man with my voice and my eyes and a ghostwoman with

ashes on her breath. They clasped and sundered, did the coupler's will. From
before the age He willed me and now may not will me away or ever' (pp. 46–7);
'Day by day: night by night: lifted, flooded and let fall. Lord, they are weary;
and, whispered to, they sigh. Saint Ambrose heard it, sigh of leaves and waves,
waiting, awaiting the fullness of their times, *diebus ac noctibus patiens ingemiscit.*
To no end gathered: vainly then released, forth flowing, wending back: loom of
the moon. Weary too in sight of lovers, lascivious men, a naked woman shining
in her courts, she draws a toil of waters' (pp. 62–3).

26. Frank Budgen, *James Joyce and the Making of Ulysses*, Oxford 1972, p. 29.

Bonnie Kime Scott is happy to speak of the 'flow and recirculation we have
been associating with the female' (*James Joyce*, p. 118) and herself sees
connections between the 'cosmic imagery' of Molly's description at the end of
the Ithaca chapter, and Stephen's 'unspeeched' motherly semiotic in the
Proteus chapter: 'Most interesting in relation to the creation of language is the
play with language which escapes the word of the world, a rite that immediately
precedes Stephen's scribbling words. He lips and mouths a kiss to his departed
mother "mouth to her moomb. Oomb, alwombing tomb". The soft alliterative
sounds and repetitive rhythms suggest pre-speech associated by Kristeva with
the mother. He is at first "unspeeched", his noises resembling an interplanetary
and primal roar; planets "globed" as he was in the womb. It is cosmic imagery
that Joyce will repeat in the descriptions of Molly at the end of "Ithaca".' (*Ibid.*,
p. 117)

27. Frank Budgen, *Making of Ulysses*, p. 272.

PART FOUR

Elke's Testimony

Excess, *the novel from which this extract is drawn, is loosely based on the story of Erysichthon, the 'Earth-tearer', whose story is told in a poem of Callimachus, and summarized by Robert Graves in his* The Greek Myths *(Penguin 1955, vol. 1, p. 89):*

Demeter herself has a gentle soul, and Erysichthon, son of Tropias, was one of the few men with whom she ever dealt harshly. At the head of twenty companions, Erysichthon dared invade a grove which the Pelasgians had planted for her at Dotium, and began cutting down the sacred trees, to provide timber for his new banqueting hall. Demeter assumed the form of Nicippe, priestess of the grove, and mildly ordered Erysichthon to desist. It was only when he threatened her with his axe that she revealed herself in her splendour and condemned him to suffer perpetual hunger, however much he might eat.

The idea of recasting the myth as a modern fable first came to me when I was writing 'A Difference of Needs', where I refer to it in discussing Ignatieff's suggestion that insatiability is indissociable from modernity (see p. 81).

Erysichthon becomes self-made billionaire Eric Sicton, who has amassed a fortune from exploitation of the Brazilian rain forest, and heads the vast and ramified E–Enterprises corporation, a conglomerate which owes part of its success to an integrated commodity range marketed in the name of a total 'E' philosophy of life.

At the acme of his career, Sicton is 'cursed' with insatiability by the

'Demeter' of the novel, an Indian woman who is driven to recourse to magic by despair over the death of her son, killed in the course of a protest against the logging operations of one of the E–Enterprises subsidiary companies. Thereafter, he becomes seized by various increasingly bizarre and obsessional appetites, and is finally gripped by a ravening hunger which knows no satisfaction and plunges him into extreme and ultimately suicidal forms of degradation.

In the extract here, his former personal assistant recalls certain episodes to which she was party at an earlier stage of Sicton's degeneration, when he is consumed not by hunger itself but by manic compulsion to pollute and waste a luxurious abundance of food in painful contrast to the squalor of the modes of satisfying his craving to which he is later reduced.

At first, it was all quite fun. Later it ran out of control. But to begin with, it seemed fairly harmless, and – well – a bit of a laugh, I suppose. And Eric, particularly in the early stages, he seemed so – so alive. It was as if he only really came to life on those occasions. His eyes would shine, he would grow quite talkative, start quipping and sometimes speaking in that incredibly nervy way he has at times, and flicking his hair back all the time ... It was sort of sexy, in a way. Or at any rate, a bit of a high. And after all, as I say, it didn't seem to be doing much harm. It wasn't like taking drugs or anything.

The idea first came to Eric after there'd been a little squabble at Balders, where we'd gone for a Smörgasbord. Although Eric owns the place he hardly ever eats there on the grounds that the lighting gives him a headache. Nevertheless, he likes to drop in unexpectedly and incognito on all his restaurants every so often, just to keep them on their toes, and it happened to be the turn of Balders. Part of the fun of these little expeditions was that we could both dress up in disguise. I wore a dark wig to conceal my normally honey-blond hair, and Eric had on shades and a false moustache and had temporarily dyed his hair. I have to say I didn't go for this disguise terribly, which I thought made him look quite a lot older than his true years, and even a bit old-fashioned. The place had been put under new management since Eric had last paid a visit, and it was clear to us as we took our seats at a table for two in one of the pine-panelled alcoves that we had not been recognized.

The sales figures for the last two months of the UK E–Burger chain, which he had received that day, had not been as high as he had expected, and Eric was not in the best of moods. He kept going on about 'turnip-heads' and 'bean-farters' who were going off meat and how they were taking the place over, and putting everyone out of a job, and he would have to go in for the veggie-burger. Of course, Eric wouldn't have touched one of his own E–Burgers with a bargepole, but I could understand him feeling it was a bit of a let-down to have to go in for that kind of feeding, which he associates with the 'whingers', and which E–Enterprises have held out against much longer than other burger outfits.

For a long time he just sat at the table morosely toying with a glass of Evian and mumbling that he was going to give it all up and retire to Mustique. Eventually, however, I persuaded him to let me select a few delicacies for him from the Smörgasbord table. I myself was dying for a bite as no solid food had passed through my system for the last sixteen hours, and I was quite famished.

The table at Balders is probably better than the Stockholm *Olaf Sköttkonung* and nearly as good as the *Viking International* in Copenhagen. Though Eric's diet strictly speaking doesn't allow for pork products, over the summer he had started to indulge occasionally in non–E titbits, and on this occasion he had agreed to a slice or two of smoked ham and some marinated herring. There was also a rather delicious caviar dip with sour cream which I thought he might like to try, and of which I knew I could eat two portions if he refused. So I took him some of this together with two or three slices of rye and aniseed crispbread.

I have to say I had not noticed it myself, but Eric immediately announced that the crispbread was stale. The waiter declined to sample it, but said that if Eric thought it was stale he would instantly fetch some more. But Eric's reply to this was, 'Oh, no thanks, once bitten twice shy', and he began slowly drawing on his black kid gloves and making as if we were about to leave. At this point the waiter, who was blond like Eric but slightly taller, and except for the pallor would have been quite a good looker, started protesting that they had never had any complaints before. The bread, he said, was always kept hermetically sealed until it was put on the table, so he was very puzzled as to how it could have come to be in a less than perfect state.

Eric muttered something about how the waiter might find himself in a less than perfect state if he didn't let up on the excuses, and then turning to me said in a louder voice, 'Come on then, Elke, let's hit the road'. This was not really what I wanted to hear, as I had hardly started on my caviar dip, and had a bowl of crawfish tails and a dish of cold roast reindeer shoulder with cranberry jelly and assorted salads still untouched. However, in the circumstances, I had no choice but to support Eric in his decision.

To our astonishment, however, as we collected together our belongings, which in my case included my second-best sable, and made for the door, the waiter came after us waving a bill at us and clearly expecting us to pay. He was obviously trying to be discreet and keep his voice down, as the other guests had already shown some interest in the goings-on and he was anxious to avoid a scene. However, when Eric realised the waiter was coming after us for our money, he turned round on him and asked in a loud voice how long the man had been working at Balders. The waiter replied quite evenly that he'd been there for nearly three months.

'And are you aware,' says Eric, 'for whom you have been slaving away these last twelve weeks?' So the waiter then tells him that the manager is a Mr Fox.

'Oh, is he indeed,' said Eric, 'and who owns Mr Fox?'

The waiter looked a bit confused at this question, and said something about not understanding what Eric meant but that it might be better if he were to speak directly to Mr Fox himself. I could tell that he still felt he was in the right, and that we ought to pay up without any further ado. But when Eric said to him that he agreed that a confrontation with Mr Fox might well be more profitable, he scowled but almost immediately went off to fetch the manager. He must have realized from the sable alone that it wouldn't do to mess with us.

Eventually, Mr Fox arrives and invites us to come and sit down again in the alcove we'd just vacated. He then has the audacity to ask whether there's anything he can do to help! He is overweight and not at all Scandinavian looking. In fact, if it hadn't been for the BBC English, I would have said he was Spanish. His skin hung around his cheeks and jaw like pieces of uncooked pastry, and the flesh below had been poured into a blue double-breasted with a pin-stripe at six-inch intervals. God knows where he managed to acquire it, or the self-confidence to sit wearing it in Eric's presence, rubbing his hands and asking if there's anything he could do to help.

But Eric put him in his place. No, said Eric, it was nice of him to offer, but the assistance was on him today. Thereupon, he reached into his briefcase and withdrew his Waterford crystal E–shaped bottle of Essence, which is the most exclusive of the perfumes in the male toiletries range, and drawing out the stopper asked if we didn't agree that the atmosphere was a little close and that the best help he might offer was to freshen it up a little.

'In fact,' he said, 'not to put too fine a point on it, this place stinks.' As he was saying this, he pushed back his chair and strode over to the Smörgasbord table, which ran nearly the full length of the restaurant. He still had the open bottle of Essence with him, and slowly began to walk round the table pouring a little dribble of perfume over everything, as if it were brandy on a plum pudding. In fact, the last drops did land in the chafing stove, causing a small fire in the frying-pan, and one of the waiters had to rush over to extinguish the blaze.

The speed with which Eric had acted had left Mr Fox and the tall, blond waiter absolutely stunned, and it was only as he returned to the table where we were sitting that they moved to grab hold of him. Mr Fox started to say something about not tolerating customers just walking in and contaminating the food, and that he would have to call the police.

275

'To arrest whom?' asks Eric.

'Why you', says Mr Fox.

'And for doing what?' said Eric.

'For damage to the restaurant's property', said Mr Fox.

'To my own property, then', said Eric, drawing out one of his personal cards and depositing it on the pine table. 'Big deal,' he went on, 'very nasty. One can get a criminal record for that kind of thing.'

He hadn't removed his shades but you could tell he was mocking them from behind the dusky glass. His kid gloves, too, he had kept on throughout and he now stood with the long black fingers laced together at a little distance from his chest rhythmically feeling the pressure of his knuckles as he continued to stare at them. Then he said, 'Let's go! Let's get the hell out of this property,' and grabbing me by the arm he more or less frogmarched me towards the plate-glass door.

It was only when we were sitting together in the taxi a few minutes later, and Eric temporarily removed his glasses, allowing me to see the glint of excitement in his eyes, that I realized quite what pleasure he had taken in this incident. He was trembling slightly, as if in a state of sexual arousal. Just as I was about to ask him whether he was all right, he grabbed my hand squeezing it so tightly that it hurt, and with a rather strange shrill little laugh, like a girl's giggle but even higher pitched, said, 'I could do that again!'

And in the ensuing weeks it became a kind of passion with him to contaminate the Smörgasbord. He would descend without warning, storm up to the table, empty the contents of his bottle of Essence over it, and then stride off through the revolving plate-glass doors and disappear into his waiting taxi as quickly as he had arrived. Later, he started to do something similar in other restaurants he owns. It became obvious that if he was going to be able to carry on indulging this particular whim, it would have to be, as it were, by previous arrangement. So I set this thing up at the office that whenever Eric felt one of his frenzies coming over him, I would phone through and the office in turn would organize with one of his restaurants for it to close that evening, cover each table with the choicest items from the menu, and wait for Eric's arrival.

The manager of *Entertaining Out* in Belsize Park told me that Eric had ruined over £1,000 of food when he had descended upon him, and that if he had not had the foresight to lock the kitchens he felt sure that Eric would have charged in there too and spoiled everything edible he found.

You might think that we should have made more effort to restrain Eric, and no doubt lots of people would have regarded this behaviour as completely insane. But in fact the curious thing was that Eric seemed to infect everyone around him during this period with his own, almost boyish, delight in these antics, and a lot of the entourage and even some of the restaurant staff seemed to get quite a kick out of watching the destruction. Also, I felt personally that it was all probably quite good for him – a needed form of relaxation. It's a well-known fact that lots of key figures in business suffer from anything from mild to very severe stress, and that if they don't want to shorten their lives, it's important for them to find some way of defusing this. I think fouling the food was just Eric's way of doing that. It allowed him to get back in touch with his childhood, and in that way to throw off the burdens of the adult world. One could say it was simply his grown up way of throwing jelly around at a kid's party.

Unfortunately, however, this urge came over him more and more frequently as time went on, till by the end of the year he was going on a wasting binge two or even three times a week. It was beginning to leak out to the media. For although all the restaurant staff involved were always strictly vetted, and under pain of instant dismissal if they exposed Eric's disguise or dared breathe a word of his funny doings, it was inevitable that one or two rumours got about. They never found their way into the quality press, whose financial pages in fact were full of Eric's recent successes. In particular, there was news of his takeover bid for the Fleetair international airways company, and of the success of his new venture Exodus, which specializes in warfare simulation equipment. He was included in a Sunday colour supplement article featuring the 'financial wizards' of the decade, and there was quite a lot of informal talk about his coming in for a knighthood in the New Year honours. But the tabloids were a different matter, and by late autumn there were several rumours circulating to the effect that Eric had gone off his rocker or was suffering from some mysterious metabolic disorder which the doctors didn't know how to treat, or else had become completely crazed from drug-taking.

In fact there were any number of stories going around. One of the first of these, which had quite a catastrophic effect on share prices, was that Eric was planning to close down his entire restaurant chain. Then there was a story about Eric having overdosed on some Latin American aphrodisiac compound – although some of the papers claimed it wasn't an aphrodisiac but a herbal preparation which was supposed to delay the ageing process. More plausible – in fact Eric himself believed it for a while – was the story that was going the rounds about the time of Hubert Delaware's resignation from the Pan–E–Cea (Brazil) Board that one of Delaware's supporters on the Board had secretly administered some kind of hallucinogen. Later there was the absurd thing about the witch in South Croydon who was supposed to have put a spell on him after she'd used the Enlitenment slimming pill and hadn't experienced any weight loss.

Of course, you'd have to be pretty stupid to take that kind of idea very seriously but it was strange, all the same, that in the odd moments (and they were very infrequent) when Eric himself seemed aware of something having gone wrong, he muttered about spells and witchcraft and some woman in the Amazon. I didn't at the time pay much attention to any of this, and I don't really think Eric ever believed any of it himself either.

The main problem, so it seemed to me at least in the beginning, was not so much to do with what Eric was getting up to, which after all was entirely his own affair, but how to keep him out of the glare of publicity. This wasn't easy and it seemed to me eventually that the one way of protecting Eric's reputation in the long run would be to arrange for his binges to be conducted as secretly as possible. This in effect meant that his staff would have to organize for him to indulge in them only in the privacy of the Chelsea apartment or at Estancia, and preferably only at the latter where security is tighter and the press could not come barging in quite so easily.

To this end, I suggested to him one weekend when we happened to be down at Estancia that it might be better in view of the adverse publicity if we organized for his little parties to be held on the estate. It was the word 'parties' which did it: one, innocent little word which, had I only known what it was to lead to, I would certainly never have let pass my lips! His eyes lit up when he heard it in the same odd manner they had on the first occasion of my coming to Estancia when Eric had been explaining about the sperm teeming in the queen bee.

He immediately wanted to organize a party. He said I should go down to the kitchen there and then and order what he called a 'banquet' for the following Saturday. He also insisted that if it was going to be a proper party there would have to be some guests. I wasn't nearly so happy with that idea, which I thought would be bound to defeat the purpose of the more discreet approach we had decided to adopt. Even if we invited only the closest intimates it was inevitable, I felt, that the news would leak out. I tried to explain all this to Eric, but he simply flew into a rage and shouted at me that he supposed that was a typical piece of female logic to try to argue him out of the party idea when it had been me who had put it into his head in the first place.

I should add that there was something about Eric's manner during this period which made it very difficult to reason with him. He changed moods so fast that dealing with his psyche was like trying to catch a fish with your bare hands. Every time you thought he was going in one direction he would suddenly flip over and push off in another. And so it was on this occasion. No sooner had he started bawling at me about my crappy mental faculties than he changed tack and coming over to where I was sitting, which happened to be in one of the Venturi armchairs on the mezzanine overlooking the main lawn, plunged both his hands into my bodice so as to cup a breast in each, and started whispering fiercely in my ear that the whole point of having a party was to allow others to share in the fun: and we were all going to have a lot of fun, a lot of very, very wasteful self-indulgence. As he spoke the words 'very, very' he squeezed each nipple between his thumb and finger causing a quite pleasurable rush. A curious tremor passed through me, and I felt at that moment as if he had passed on to me some of his own compulsion: all of a sudden, I became quite excited at the idea of the party, and every time I thought about it over the following week, which was quite often, it was with a little thrill of anticipation. It wasn't that I didn't fear the consequences. In fact I rather dreaded them, but the dread always came together with a kind of perverse pleasure at the thought of getting others in on the act and risking public exposure. In the end I found that the only way I could control the rather funny feelings I was getting was by engrossing myself completely in the party preparations.

We decided on a fairly intimate gathering: just a few of the closest equites and their women, myself and Virginia. For an hour or so, after Eric had first insisted on Virginia being one of the guests I'd felt all the usual jealousies and the pleasure of the event had suddenly drained out of it. Of course, I never said anything to Eric about my resentment of Virginia for fear it would belittle me in his eyes: Eric himself always seemed incapable of those kinds of feelings and could not, I'm sure, understand them in others. But for a while I had a hard struggle to contain myself, and thought that the whole thing had been ruined for me by this insistence of Eric's on Virginia being there. Later, however, I became more or less reconciled to the idea, and as the day drew nearer even began to think that it might be quite fun to be one of the harem for the evening. I took some comfort, too, from the fact that Eric's bodyguard Roddy wouldn't be coming. I felt certain that Eric would have wanted him, too, to be included among the guests had he been available, but fortunately he had disappeared off somewhere and hadn't been around for some months. Every so often Eric had muttered something about tracking him down, but most of the time he either seemed to have forgotten about him altogether or else to be under the impression that he himself had told Roddy to get lost. Personally, it seemed to me that Roddy's doing a bunk at the first hint of adverse publicity was exactly what you would have expected of the fair-weather friend that I'd always sensed him to be. So his disappearance during this slightly difficult period for Eric didn't surprise me in the least.

Eric concerned himself a great deal over the edible side of things, and spent several hours going through the menu for the party. He was very keen on what he called the aesthetics of the meal. He said he wanted the table to be a 'work of art' and even hired some food-design consultant to spend a day with the head chef at Estancia going through the 'presentation'.

I have to say – and I say it with the pride of one who made her small contribution – that the results of these efforts were quite spectacular. Eric had wanted mainly cold food so as it could all be laid out together, and when it was finished nearly every inch of the long polished oak table in the Estancia dining hall was covered with one dish or another, all of them most exquisitely arranged in the latest Japanese or fin-de-siècle modes. The centrepiece was a cold roast spiced boar coated in a dark glaze and inlaid with a mosaic of orange, kiwi and pineapple, cherries and lychees, all of them variously shaped to form a very attractive pattern rather like some of the curtain material and matching wallpaper they sell in *Arty-Crafty*. Eric, however, said it was by someone called Morris. The boar was, as it were, beached on a raised island of endive, parsley, asparagus and other salads, but surrounding it was a 'sea' of fine-cut pale green and ultramarine turbot-flavoured jelly, and in this various types of fish were sporting: a perfectly skinned salmon with a gold leaf and cucumber motif, scallops, oysters, several colourful red mullet, a shoal of crayfish, a lobster mayonnaise and a cold lobster Thermidor, a turbot à la grecque, and so forth. Bordering this were dishes of every possible description: of pesto, hollandaise, re-moulade and other cold sauces, of asparagus and aubergines, mushrooms, pepperonata, salade à la Russe, a sformato of spinach, ham and truffle, cold partridges on nests of quails eggs, raised pies of game and veal and ham, a variety of quiches, a duck à l'orange, a cold Vichyssoise ... The desert was laid out on the smaller side tables and consisted, at Eric's request, of a number of very rich gateaux of the kind he never normally touches. There were also dishes of various fruits in salad, pyramids of profiteroles, several Milanaise soufflés, crème brulée, meringues, ice-creams, granita and sorbet of many different flavours, laid out in cut-crystal self-chilling goblets, baskets of florentines, petit fours, brandy-snaps and other choice biscuits, shells of handmade chocolates, mints and turkish delight, and of course fruits of every variety spilling out of a number of large, fluted china horns.

The guests were received in the rouge-et-noir anteroom, which is an octagon with a red and gilt domed ceiling and latticed paned windows running from floor to ceiling on three of the walls, with the rest gilded and lined with black Chinese silk. We plied everyone liberally with champagne and any other alcoholic beverage which took their fancy. Eric had told me beforehand that if possible all our guests should be inebriated before the start of proceedings since this would assist the release of inhibition.

We were an even smaller gathering than Eric and I had intended since several of the guests had been unable to come at such short notice and we had been reluctant to replace them with others less suitable. There was Eric, myself, Dan Sparrow, Eric's UK DIY Chief, and his new wife Lizzie, who is an ex-model like myself and was formerly married to the fashion photographer Bob Byron. She used to be always throwing scenes but has mellowed quite a bit since giving up modelling and putting on some weight. Dan Sparrow, her new husband, is big and broad and looks like one of those ex-footballers turned manager. He is very easy going and acquiring a bit of a beer gut these days, and his jokes get filthier every time we meet up. There was also Mercutio Donleavy, the editor of *Emporium*, who is thin and dark and a very flash dresser. For the party, he had gone in for a punkish outfit, involving quite a lot of black leather and a shocking-pink frilled shirt slashed open to the waist. He is one of those types who likes having it all handed to him on a plate. The other day I bumped into some regular girl of his and she was complaining that he expected her to fuck him while he was watching television. Then there was Virginia, of course, who surprised everyone by turning up in the garden outside in some fancy underwear and a white fur coat, and mounted on a horse which kept rearing up at the window of the rouge-et-noir. Why on earth Virginia is so keen on displaying her everything to all and sundry I cannot imagine, but at least she had the decency to put on some rather nasty apple-green silk pyjamas before joining us for drinks.

I don't know why, thinking about it, that I hadn't realised earlier what Eric had in mind. I suppose I'd been thinking he wanted some fairly ordinary kind of orgy, and I guess that's what the others had been expecting. Certainly, I don't think any of us had been prepared for the kind of excesses into which we were subsequently drawn. I had imagined that at some point in the evening Eric would want to go wasting – preferably, I was hoping, after we had all eaten our fill – but I'd never thought he'd want the rest of us to join in.

It was with some surprise, then, when after about an hour of fairly steady drinking, I heard Eric clap his hands briefly and announce to the assembled company that they had been specially chosen to share with him in a very pleasurable primal experience, which he suspected they had not really allowed themselves to indulge in since early infancy. Then he threw open the double doors leading into the dining-room, standing aside to allow us to pass in, before entering himself and locking the doors behind him. Our guests, of course, were overwhelmed by the feast which lay spread out before them and cried out with delight and surprise.

The room was carpeted from wall to wall in a cameo-beige of a very thick pile, and was panelled on three sides from floor to ceiling. The fourth wall was entirely plate glass, beyond which lay the white marble terrace leading by a short flight of steps into the Elizabethan rose garden. The curtains had been left open, and the lights of the several crystal chandeliers and wall lamps which illuminated the room could be seen quite brightly reflected out on the terrace above a duller reflection of the dining table. Through the window I even caught the gleam of the mirrored meat glaze on the boar's flanks before Eric moved across to the electronic panel, and in response to a touch of one of the buttons the heavy olive-green drapes began to move smoothly and steadily across the plate glass until nothing was left of the scene outside. Then in response to another touch the light in the chandeliers and wall-brackets dimmed from 'dayglo' to 'romantic' and the whole room was suffused in a soft pink glow.

Dan had uncorked several more bottles of champagne and wine while this was going on, and was pouring out drinks for everyone when Eric moved towards the table saying he would open proceedings in the traditional manner. He thereupon withdrew his bottle of Essence and poured its contents into the tureen of Vichyssoise, laughing as he did so in that curious, high-pitched staccato manner he had when very excited. He then picked up the tureen of contaminated soup, sprinkled a little of it about the room, and tipped the remainder into a bowl of Comice pears in burgundy. It so happened that a plate of meringues had been placed alongside the pears, and seizing one of these in each hand, he crushed them to a powder and stamped them into the carpet.

As he did this he came out with one or two short grunts. Then he suddenly launched into a little speech about there being no pleasure like the pleasure of fouling and no orgy to match the waste-in. 'We're all natural vandals!' he shouted at us, 'all yearning for the rampage! You limited cunt and prick introverts and fun-haters – you see! You haven't begun to live until you've begun to spoil ...' And with this, he proceeded to strip off his shirt and cram dollops of maple ice into his armpits.

You could feel the shock vibrate through the room. Even I was astonished, for this was the first time Eric had shown any serious inclination to use his own body as a means of fouling the food. Everyone had fallen silent for a minute and now stood gaping at him not knowing whether to laugh or scream. There was a rich, sweet smell in the air created by the crushed meringue and melting maple ice. But it was laced, so to speak, with sharper savoury tangs of garlic and shell-fish and the liver and brandy pâté. And above it all hung the heavy scent of Eric's Essence cologne. Eric, for his part, stood legs astride, staring at us, his mouth opening in as rude a smile as I had ever seen on his face. He was mocking us, daring us to join in.

For a second or two things could have gone either way. In fact, glancing at Mercutio, I could see that he was wondering whether we oughtn't to be calling for a straitjacket. Then Dan said something about it being a novel kind of deodorant, to which Lizzie responded that she herself would rather the lemon sorbet if no one else had any objections, and we all started giggling. This seemed to act as a cue for Eric to undress completely. He told us that in his office as high priest he had a number of libations and offerings to make. Then he took up a sauceboat of mayonnaise, tipped a couple of spoonfuls into the fruit salad, and started rubbing the remainder around the lower half of his body, inviting Mercutio, who was standing between him and myself to do the same. Mercutio, however, simply stood there smoking his cigar and watching Eric with a sly, amused grin on his face. Eric repeated the invitation, this time holding out the sauceboat to Mercutio, who again went on smoking and grinning at him for a moment. Then all of a sudden, he stubbed out his panatella in a nearby quiche, grabbed a fistful of mayonnaise, and before I knew what was happening I felt his hand reaching up the slit of my black velvet skirt and smearing it over my thighs. I leapt back from him, with a little cry of protest, but started giggling, lost my balance and fell sideways into a nearby gateau. This prompted Virginia to leap onto the table trampling several dishes as she made her way to the centre, where she stood laughing at us for a moment, drinking a glass of champagne, before stripping off all her clothes except for a black camisole, stockings and suspenders. She then lowered herself down on to the boar's back, which she told us was her little piggy which she was now going to ride into market, and taking up a grissini, she pretended to beat it into a canter, jogging up and down herself with such fury that the whole island of greenery on which it was mounted was more or less flattened into the surrounding sea of minced jelly.

Determined not to be outdone by Virginia, I too leapt on to the table at this point, and began to perform quite an exotic, foody striptease using the parsley, taramasalata, asparagus tips and other bits and pieces for special effects. When I got down to my bra and pants, Mercutio came up behind me, lifted me off the table and said he would see to the rest of the annointing. Meanwhile Don and Lizzie had started fooling around with Virginia, who had rolled off the boar's back and lay on her back while they plastered her with different sauces. Eric, on the other hand, who I noticed had hardly bothered to watch my striptease, had laid hands on another large perfume atomiser, and was systematically going round the tables of desert, spraying every dish he came to. Then he turned his attention to the game pies and pâtés, carefully drilling a number of little holes in each with a skewer before filling them up with scent.

Mercutio and I set to daubing each other fairly intimately, and this may have gone on for an hour or so, during which time I remember Dan coming round with more drinks for us all several times. After this, however, my memory grows a little hazy but I do know that after the session with Mercutio, several of us climbed back on the table together, and that eventually we were all at it together, rolling around and smearing food into every orifice. And I remember looking across at Eric once or twice. He seemed to be in an absolute frenzy, his eyes flashing, his whole face contorted with a quite terrible expression of greed or ravening hunger. This expression seemed to become more drawn and agonized as the evening wore on. It was as if the more we fouled ourselves and the food, the closer he came to some orgasm which nonetheless he could never quite reach. The other thing I noticed was that while the rest of us were treating the occasion as an excuse for a rather novel kind of sex orgy, Eric didn't seem interested in sex at all. The only thing which appeared to turn him on was messing up the food or watching us spoil it; so that while everyone else was really only using the food as a kind of supplement to the sex, Eric was interested in our sexual antics only insofar as they further polluted the food.

In the end, of course, it began to pall. Or for everyone except

Eric it did. He seemed quite indifferent to the chaos we had created, and kept insisting that he wouldn't let us out till dawn. It was at this point, that we discovered that he had locked not only the doors into the rouge-et-noir anteroom, but all the other exits from the dining room as well. This knowledge had a riveting effect: from then on no one apart from Eric could think of anything else except how they might escape to some place where they could clean up. It was as if a completely new light had been thrown on our situation. Suddenly the room itself seemed utterly sordid. So did our behaviour. Lizzie began to panic and started screaming, and Mercutio seized a bottle and said he was going to kill Eric. Fortunately, I managed to restrain him, but I'll never forget the shame and horror of the next half hour. I could hardly bear standing in the same room with anyone else, let alone touching them. And I think the others felt the same. It was as if we were all violently repelled by each other, but especially by Eric. He himself, however, seemed quite immune to any of these feelings, and had thrown himself across the table in a state of such manic ecstasy that we were all quite frightened of drawing near to him. For a while we tried coaxing the keys out of him by promising him all sorts of crazy things if he handed them over. But it soon became clear that this wasn't going to work. In fact it seemed doubtful that Eric had even heard us, he was so far gone. At this point, in desperation, we hit on a plan whereby we all came at him together, Dan to grab hold of his head, Virginia and I to pinion his arms, and Mercutio and Lizzie to do the same with his legs, and by these means we finally managed to extract the keys and escape upstairs to wash.

None of us spoke to each other again that evening, but I heard Dan and Lizzie drive off about half an hour later, followed by Mercutio shortly afterwards. Virginia, I watched from the window on the mezzanine trotting round the main lawn for a while on her white horse, before finally disappearing off. As for myself, I took a long bath and washed my hair and thought about returning to the dining room to check out Eric, but decided against it. My stomach, in fact, turned at the mere thought of it, and I realized that the morning would be quite soon enough for any visit of that kind.

The hangover I woke to was one of the worst. It was nearly midday before I felt well enough even to think of getting out of bed, and another hour before I plucked up the courage to look in on the dining-room. My head was beating violently as I opened the door, and I was overcome by a wave of nausea at the stench which met me as I did so. We had left Eric in a kind of swoon, splayed over the broken back of the glazed boar with his feet wedged in a truffle pâté and one of his hands lodged in the belly of the turbot. He had hardly shifted position at all, and all the chandeliers were still blazing. My first instinct – I suppose I thought it would somehow freshen up the atmosphere – was to move to the electronic panel, extinguish the lights and press the button to open the drapes. Outside the sky was grey. There were already large puddles on the verandah, and the rain was beating steadily against the plate glass.

I turned round to confront Eric, who – disturbed perhaps by the whirr of the curtains opening – groaned slightly and rolled over. As he did so, his hand fell out of the turbot and was left dabbling in the sea of jelly, which was now streaked with other foods and beginning to liquefy. On the panelled wall opposite, I saw that a globule of whipped cream with a glacé cherry attached had left a snail-like trail before coming to rest just above one of the sidetables. The carpet underfoot was thick with crushed cake and biscuit, quiche and mayonnaise. Some cigarette butts and one or two slices of mushroom and what looked like strips of smoked salmon were floating in the fruit salad. Someone's shoe – a man's shoe – had been left embedded in an enormous, otherwise undamaged, Sacher-Torte.

Looking on this scene, my disgust was such that I decided there and then that nothing would induce me to take part in any more of Eric's crazy waste-ins. In fact, I decided that there was no alternative but for me to quit. It was clear that what had started as a fairly innocent sort of pleasure and relaxation had got completely out of control. So I went upstairs, packed my bags and left almost immediately. Out of loyalty I have kept absolutely mum until now about what happened on that extraordinary evening, as have all the other guests who attended. But that was the end of my relationship with Eric, and I never saw him again. I have not had cause to regret this decision since, though I was sorry when the knighthood was announced that I would not be able to share in his honour.

Index

Index

Cold War 3, 28–32, 85, 89, 110–18 *passim*, 123n
Collins, M. 195n
Comecon 39
Communist Party (British) 91
Communist Party (East Germany) 5, 90
Communist Party (Polish) 90, 121n
Communist Party (of Soviet Union) 90
Conservative Party (British) 48
Cornell, Drusilla 198, 212, 215–17, 222n, 227n, 244n
Cottrell, Robert D. 193n
Creed, Barbara 243n
Critical Theory, *see* Frankfurt School
Cuba 123n
Czechoslovakia 5, 79, 90, 115

Daily Worker 91
Demeter 81, 271
Derrida, Jacques 150, 207, 216, 218, 227n, 235, 240–41
Descartes, René 146
Deutscher, Isaac 120n, 121n
Dews, Peter 160, 161n, 222n, 225n, 227n
Dickens, Charles 250
Dinnerstein, Dorothy 210, 212, 225n
Donne, John 249
Dubček, Alexander 104
Dunayevskaya, Raya 122n

Easlea, Brian 196n
Edgar, David 161n
Ekins, Paul 144n
Eliot, George 250
Ellmann, Richard 267n
Engels, Frederick 96, 102, 121n, 128, 130, 188
Enright, Tim 120n
Erasmus 83, 85n
Erysichthon 17, 81, 271
Europe 92, 114, 116
    Eastern 3–7, 24–9, 31–2, 38, 43n, 45, 47–9, 62, 70n, 111–15, 118, 123n
    Western 3–7, 24–5, 29, 31–3, 48, 62, 69n, 111–12, 115, 118, 120n, 122n, 123n, 161n
European Economic Community (EEC) 161n
European Nuclear Disarmament (END) 3, 19, 24, 69n, 111–13, 116, 123n, 124n
END Journal 5, 124

Fabianism 107

Falk, Richard 43n, 70n
Falklands 23, 43
Feuerbach, Ludwig 129
Flax, Jane 225n
Flynn, Thomas 145n
Forster, E.M. 139
    A Passage to India 139
Foucault, Michel 10, 74, 150, 160n, 161n, 198, 210–11, 218, 226n, 228, 237
France 51, 181
Frankel, Boris 144n
Frankfurt School 92, 119, 144n, 198–201, 218
Fraser, Nancy 201–3, 216–17, 224n
Freud, Sigmund; Freudianism 56, 101, 183, 213, 263
Fromm, Erich 92, 119n

Gaddafi, Colonel 36
Geras, Norman 19, 86n, 135, 144n, 145n
Germany 51
    Federal Republic of 3
    Christian Democratic Party of 4
    German Democratic Republic 3–4, 115
    united 4
Gilligan, Carol 208, 210, 223n, 225n
Glucksmann, André 85, 86n
Gollan, John 98, 120n
Gomulka, Władysław 109
Gorbachev, Mikhail 69n, 112, 116
Gorz, André 144n
Gould, C. 195n
Gramsci, Antonio 92
Graves, Robert 271
Greenham Common 79, 165–6
Griffiths, Morwenna 223n
The Guardian 167

Habermas, Jürgen 197, 204, 206, 210, 215, 218–19, 221–2, 222n, 223n, 224n, 225n, 227n, 237
Hall, Stuart 119
Hanen, Marsha P. 225n
Hanson, Harry 120n
Harding, Sandra 223n, 225n
Havel, Václav 5–6, 20n, 45
Hegedus, Andras 44n
Hegel, G.W.F. 92–4, 129, 185–6, 219, 225n
Heidegger, Martin 94, 228
Held, David 224n, 225n

291

Index

Herbert, George 249
Heriot-Watt University 25
Herodotus 158
Hewar, A. 225n
Hitler, Adolf 158
Hintikka, Merrill 223n, 225n
Hinton, James 124n
Hobbes, Thomas 131
Holden, Gerard 43n, 70n
Honecker, Erich 5
Hont, Istvan 85n
Hopper, Edward 86n
Houston, Barbara 225n, 226n
Hume, David 83–4, 85n
Hungary 90–91, 115
Husserl, Edmund 94
Huyssen, Andreas 128, 244n

Ignatieff, Michael 17, 71–86 *passim*, 271
   The Needs of Strangers 17, 71–86
      passim
India 241
Indonesia 122n
International Monetary Fund 39
Ireland 256–7, 267n
Irigaray, Luce 187, 189, 231–4, 237, 244n, 259
Islam 6, 160
Italy 43n

James, William 132, 144n
Jameson, Fredric 227n
Jardine, Alice 243n, 244n
Jonson, Ben 257, 259
Joyce, James 16–17, 86n, 232, 246–68
   passim
   A Portrait of the Artist as a Young Man 251, 255–6
   Dubliners 260–62
   Ulysses 16, 246–68 *passim*

Kaldor, Mary 43n, 70n
Kant, Immanuel; Kantianism 10, 137, 199, 222
Kaye, Harvey 120n
Keefe, Terry 193n
Keller, Evelyn Fox 223n
Kennedy, John F. 123n
Kettle, Arnold 98, 120n
Khrushchev, Nikita 103, 109, 123n
Kintz, Linda 241, 245n
Kohl, Helmut 4
Kohlberg, Lawrence 208, 225n

Kojève, Alexandre 119n
Kolakowski, Leszek 119n, 121n, 123n, 125n
Korsch, Karl 92
Kostov, T. 98
Kristeva, Julia 16, 187, 215, 226n, 227n, 228, 231–2, 237, 244n, 259, 268n
Kundera, Milan 86n

Labour Party (British) 48, 53, 104, 106, 115
Lacan, Jacques 199, 215, 217–18, 226n, 227n, 231–2
Lautréamont, Comte de (Isidore Ducasse) 232
Le Doeuff, Michèle 176, 194n
Legoeete, Franscina 37
Lenin, V.I. 129
Levine, C. 225n
Lévi-Strauss, Claude 218
Libya 23, 36, 40
Lindsay, Jack 120n, 124n
Live Aid 40, 117
Lloyd, Genevieve 195n, 196n
Lukács, G. 92–3
Lukes, Steven 126–45 *passim*, 150, 161
   Marxism and Morality 126–45
      passim, 151
Lyotard, François 218–19, 227n, 228–9, 237, 245n

McClelland, Keith 120n, 123n
Mackay, Louis 70n
MacKinnon, Catherine 209, 225n
Magri, Lucio 35, 44n, 124n
Mallarmé, Stéphane 232
Mangan, James Clarence 267n
Maoism 106
Marcuse, Herbert 108, 123n, 226n
Marvell, Andrew 249
Marx, Karl 51, 63–4, 72, 76, 80–81, 86n, 94–6, 100, 102, 105, 118, 121n, 122n, 124n, 126–45 *passim*, 197–206 *passim*, 223n, 229
   Capital 128
   Critique of the Gotha Programme 14, 134–7
   On the Jewish Question 130
   Paris Manuscripts 128
   The German Ideology 76, 103, 128–9
Marxism 9, 12–13, 49, 52–4, 58–9, 63, 67, 68, 70, 76, 86n, 92, 94, 99–100, 105, 107–8, 110, 120n, 121n, 122n, 126–45 *passim*, 149–50, 153, 179, 189, 191,

292

Index

Index

Printed in the United States
by Baker & Taylor Publisher Services